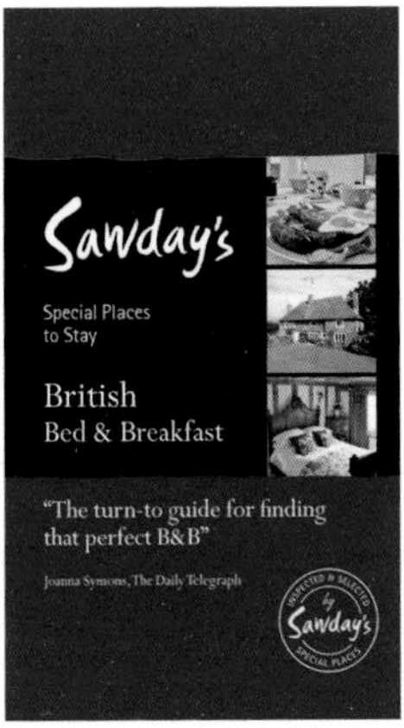

Sawday's

Special Places to Stay

Nineteenth edition

Published in September 2017
ISBN-13: 978-1-906136-84-0

Alastair Sawday Publishing Co. Ltd,
Merchants House, Wapping Road,
Bristol BS1 4RW, UK
Tel: +44 (0)117 204 7810
Email: info@sawdays.co.uk
Web: www.sawdays.co.uk

The Globe Pequot Press,
P. O. Box 480, Guilford,
Connecticut 06437, USA
Tel: +1 203 458 4500
Email: info@globepequot.com
Web: www.globepequot.com

Series Editor Alastair Sawday
Editor Tom Bell
Assistant to Editor Sarah Nuttall
Senior Picture Editor Alec Studerus
Coordinators Sarah Nuttall, Sarah Barratt
Writing Tom Bell
Inspections Tom Bell

Marketing & PR
0117 204 7801
marketing@sawdays.co.uk

We have made every effort to ensure the accuracy of the information in this book at the time of going to press. However, we cannot accept any responsibility for any loss, injury or inconvenience resulting from the use of information contained therein.

Production: Pagebypage Co Ltd
Maps: Maidenhead Cartographic Services
Printing: Pureprint, Uckfield
UK distribution: The Travel Alliance, Bath
info@pelotongrey.com

Cover photo credits.
Front 1. Combe Grove Hotel, entry 6 2. The St Mawes Hotel, entry 28 3. The Inn at Loch Tummel, entry 247
Back: 1. The Parisi Hotel, entry 202 2. Wright's Food Emporium, entry 257
3. Artist Residence Oxfordshire, entry 145
Spine: Six Brunton Place, entry 230

Sawday's

Special Places to Stay

British Hotels & Inns

Contents

Front	Page
A word from Alastair Sawday	**6**
How we choose our Special Places	**8**
Inspections	8
Feedback	8
Subscriptions	9
Disclaimer	9
Using this book	**11**
Finding the right place for you	11
Maps	11
Symbols	11
Hotel Awards	12
Practical matters	**13**
Types of places	13
Rooms	13
Meals	13
Prices and minimum stays	13
Booking and cancellation	14
Arrivals and departures	14
Closed	14
Hotel Awards 2018	**16–21**
Maps	**25–37**

Guide entries	Entry	Map
England		
Bath & N.E. Somerset	1-6	2
Berkshire	7-8	2
Brighton & Hove	9-11	3
Bristol	12-13	2
Cambridgeshire	14-15	3, 4,7
Cornwall	16-33	1
Cumbria	34-49	5, 6
Derbyshire	50-51	6
Devon	52-67	2
Dorset	68-80	2, 3
Durham	81-82	6
Essex	83-86	4
Gloucestershire	87-91	2,3
Hampshire	92-96	3
Herefordshire	97-101	2
Isle of Wight	102	3
Kent	103-109	4
Lancashire	110-111	5, 6
Lincolnshire	112-113	6, 7
London	114-125	3
Norfolk	126-136	7
Northumberland	137-138	9
Nottinghamshire	139-140	6
Oxfordshire	141-149	3
Rutland	150-151	6
Shropshire	152-157	5, 6
Somerset	158-167	2
Suffolk	168-178	4, 7
Sussex	179-190	3, 4
Warwickshire	193-199	3
Wiltshire	207-213	3
Worcestershire	200	3
Yorkshire	201-211	6

Guide entries	Entry	Map
Channel Islands		
Alderney	212	3
Guernsey	213-214	3
Jersey	215	3
Scotland		
Argyll & Bute	216-221	8, 10
Ayrshire	222	8
Dumfries & Galloway	223-225	5, 9
East Lothian	226	9
Edinburgh	227-231	9
Fife	232	9
Glasgow	233	8
Highland	234-238	8, 11
Isle of Skye	239-240	10,11
Moray	241	9
Perth & Kinross	242-250	8, 9
Scottish Borders	251-253	9
Western Isles	254	10
Wales		
Carmarthenshire	255-258	2
Ceredigion	259-260	2
Conwy	261-262	5
Denbighshire	263	5
Gwynedd	264-268	6, 7
Monmouthshire	269-270	2
Pembrokeshire	271-276	1
Powys	277-280	2

Back	Page
Quick reference indices	**328**
Wheelchair-accessible	328
Children of all ages welcome	328
Pets welcome	329
Swimming pool	330
Bikes to hire or borrow	330
Tennis court	331
Public transport	331
Special Places to Stay series	**335**
Index by property name	**337**
Index by town	**344**
What's in each entry?	**352**

Have you ever wondered why waiters in posh hotels, and even modest restaurants, hold their left hands behind their backs when serving you?

Some would say this is the very opposite of crossing your arms protectively in front of you. With a hand behind you, you are exposing the front of your body, and thus your vital organs. You are thus conveying an air of superiority, authority and power. Prince Charles does it, and so do other important people when inspecting troops or juniors. Senior hospital consultants do it. In which case, I wonder why waiters do the same. To me, it looks more like a contortion executed in order to make the diner uncomfortable.

Happily, much traditional hotel behaviour has changed, for which I give thanks; and much else has moved on too. Hotels are easier places to be now, many of them as informal as a pub. The few survivors of another age are curiosities, like the one I stayed at recently which was filled almost entirely with old couples (of my age) who appeared to have lost the will to speak to each other. Dinner was thus a hushed affair, and I felt animated, even entertaining, at my corner table.

Perhaps the best of recent changes has been the focus on paying living wages to hotel staff. The Gallivant on Camber Sands in East Sussex has agreed to pay all staff a living wage, rather than a minimum wage. They all share the profits, which must be fairer than just the waiters taking tips. This is becoming a trend.

Another, less welcome, trend is the move towards robotic 'solutions'. (I preferred the robotic behaviour of old-fashioned waiters with their hands behind their backs.) Some budget hotels give you a code to enable you to get in, then another to give you entry to your bedroom. Meals will one day be served by genial robots, perhaps programmed to sound like Manuel in *Fawlty Towers*.

But there is nothing to compare with real human beings. From the smiling welcome when you have arrived looking like a tramp, to the convivial meals and provocative conversations that the owners of small hotels often provide – the human wins every time for me. I cannot be the only digital disaster who longs for light relief.

Alastair Sawday

Photo above: Tom Germain
Photo right: Saracens Head, entry 135

17 GLORIOUS
YEARS = THANKS!!
Puddings £4.95
All with Cream, Ice Cream or Creme Fraiche
Treacle Tart
Orange Jus
Summer Pudding
Spicy Poached Pears
Creme Brulee + Marinated Red Fruits
Greek Yoghurt with honey or Marinated Red Fruits
Trio of Ice Cream or Sorbet
Cheese - Single £4.95 ~ Trio £6.95
Ad Lib Coffee or Various Teas £1.50
Don't forget:- Port, Brandy, etc etc Liquers, Whisky
STARTERS // SNACKS 5.75
Deep Fried Brie + Apricot Sauce
Crispy Fried Aubergine + Garlic Mayonnaise 5.75
Smoked Scottish Salmon "Off the Side" 6.95 / 11.75
Game + Cranberry Terrine 5.75
Grilled Smoked Mackerel + Toasted Almonds 5.95
Morston Mussels with Cider + Cream 6.25/12.50
Fiddly Shell on Prawns + Garlic Mayonnaise 5.75
Crispy Fried Meatballs + Mango Jus £5.75
Grilled Goats Cheese on a Croute £6.25 with Sun Blushed Tomatoes + Cream
On the Side - Olives £2.95
Roasted Head of Garlic + Pesto Mayonnaise £3.50
£39.50

It's simple. There are no rules, no boxes to tick. We choose places that we like and are fiercely subjective in our choices. We also recognise that one person's idea of special is not necessarily someone else's so there is a huge variety of places, and prices, in this book.

Those who are familiar with our Special Places series know that we look for comfort, originality, authenticity, and reject the anonymous and the banal. The way guests are treated comes as high on our list as the setting, the architecture, the atmosphere and the food.

Inspections

We visit every place in the guide to get a feel for how both hotel and owner tick. We don't take a clipboard and we don't have a list of what is acceptable and what is not. Instead, we chat for an hour or so with the owner or manager and look round. It's all very informal, but it gives us an excellent idea of who would enjoy staying there. If the visit happens to be the last of the day, we may stay the night. Once in the book, properties are re-inspected regularly, so that we can keep things fresh and accurate.

Feedback

In between inspections we rely on feedback from our army of readers, as well as from staff members who are encouraged to visit properties across the series. This feedback is invaluable to us and we always follow up on comments.

So do tell us whether your stay has been a joy or not, if the atmosphere was great or stuffy, the owners and staff cheery or bored. The accuracy of the book depends on what you, and our inspectors, tell us. A lot of the new entries in each edition are recommended by our readers, so keep telling us about new places you've discovered too. Please use the forms on our website at www.sawdays.co.uk.

However, please do not tell us if your starter was cold, or the bedside light broken. Tell the owner, immediately, and get them to do something about it. Most owners, or staff, are more than happy to correct problems and will bend over backwards to help. Far better than bottling it up and then writing to us a week later!

Photo: Backwell House, entry 13

Subscriptions

Owners pay to appear in this guide. Their fee goes towards the high costs of inspecting, of producing an illustrated book and of developing our website. We only include places that we find special: it is not possible for anyone to buy their way onto these pages. Nor is it possible for the owner to write their own description. We will say if the bedrooms are small, or if a main road is near. We do our best to avoid misleading people.

Disclaimer

We make no claims to pure objectivity in choosing these places. They are here simply because we like them. Our opinions and tastes are ours alone and this book is a statement of them; we hope you will share them. We have done our utmost to get our facts right but apologise unreservedly for any mistakes that may have crept in.

You should know that we don't check such things as fire alarms, swimming pool security or any other regulation with which owners of properties receiving paying guests should comply. This is the responsibility of the owners. At some of our smaller places – particularly our inns – you should request a contact number for emergencies if staff are not present overnight.

Do remember that the information in this book is a snapshot in time and may have changed since we published it; do call ahead to avoid being disappointed.

Photo: Scourie Hotel, entry 235

Finding the right place for you

All these places are special in one way or another. All have been visited and then written about honestly so that you can take what you want and leave the rest. Those of you who swear by Sawday's trust our write-ups precisely because we don't have a blanket standard; we include places simply because we like them. But we all have different priorities, so do read the descriptions carefully and pick out the places where you will be comfortable.

Maps

Each property is flagged with its entry number on the maps at the front. These maps are a great starting point for planning your trip, but please don't use them as anything other than a general guide – use a decent road map for real navigation. Most places will send you detailed instructions once you have booked your stay.

Symbols

These are explained at the very back of the book. They are based on the information given to us by the owners. However, things do change: bikes may be under repair or a new pool may have been put in. Please use the symbols as a guide rather than an absolute statement of fact and double-check anything that is important to you – owners occasionally bend their own rules, so it's worth asking if you may take your child or dog even if they don't have the symbol.

Wheelchair access ♿ – Some hotels are keen to accept wheelchair users into their hotels and have made provision for them. However, this does not mean that wheelchair users will always be met with a perfect landscape. You may encounter ramps, a shallow step, gravelled paths, alternative routes into some rooms, a bathroom (not a wet room), perhaps even a lift. In short, there may be the odd hindrance and we urge you to call and make sure you will get what you need.

Limited mobility – The limited mobility symbol shows those places where at least one bedroom and bathroom is accessible without using stairs. The symbol is designed to satisfy those who walk slowly, with difficulty, or with the aid of a stick. A wheelchair may be able to navigate some areas, but in our opinion these places are not fully wheelchair friendly. If you use a chair for longer distances, but are not too bad over shorter distances, you'll probably be OK; again, please ring and ask. There may be a step or two, a bath

Photo left: Another Place - The Lake, entry 37
Photo: Artist Residence Oxford, entry 145

or a shower with a tray in a cubicle, a good distance between the car park and your room, slippery flagstones or a tight turn.

Children – The symbol shows places which are happy to accept children of all ages. This does not mean that they will necessarily have cots, high chairs, etc. If an owner welcomes children but only those above a certain age, we have put these details at the end of their write-up. These houses do not have the child symbol, but even these folk may accept your younger child at quiet times. If you want to get out and about in the evenings, check when you book whether there are any babysitting services. Even very small places can sometimes organise this for you.

Pets – Our symbol shows places which are happy to accept pets. Do let the owners know when booking that you'd like to bring your pet – particularly if it is not the usual dog! Be realistic about your pet – if it is nervous or excitable or doesn't like the company of other dogs, people, chickens, children, then say so.

Owners' pets – The symbol is given when the owners have their own pet on the premises. It may not be a cat! But it is there to warn you that you may be greeted by a dog, serenaded by a parrot, or indeed sat upon by a cat.

Hotel Awards

We have picked those places that deserve a special mention. Our categories are:

Hotel of the Year
Favourite newcomer;
National Treasure;
Nicely priced;
Fabulous food.

More details are given on pages 16-21 and all the award winners have been stamped.

Photo: The Parisi Hotel, entry 202

Types of places

Hotels can vary from huge, humming and slick to those with only a few rooms that are run by owners at their own pace. In some you may not get room service or have your bags carried in and out. In smaller hotels there may be a fixed menu for dinner with very little choice, so if you have dishes that leave you cold, it's important to say so when you book your meal. If you decide to stay at an inn remember that they can be noisy, especially at weekends. If these things are important to you, then do check when you book.

Rooms

Bedrooms – These are described as double, twin, single, family or suite. A double may contain a bed which is anything from 135cm wide to 180cm wide. A twin will contain two single beds (usually 90cm wide). A suite will have a separate sitting area, but it may not be in a different room. Family rooms can vary in size, as can the number of beds they hold, so do ask. And do not assume that every bedroom has a TV.

Bathrooms – All bedrooms have their own bathrooms unless we say that they don't. If you have your own bathroom but you have to leave the room to get to it we describe it as 'separate'. There are very few places in the book that have shared bathrooms and they are usually reserved for members of the same party. Again, we state this clearly.

Photo: Letham House, entry 226

Meals

Breakfast is included in the room price unless otherwise stated. If only a continental breakfast is offered, we let you know.

Some places serve lunch, most do Sunday lunch (often very well-priced), the vast majority offer dinner. In some places you can content yourself with bar meals, in others you can feast on five courses. Most offer three courses for £25-£35, either table d'hôte or à la carte. Some have tasting menus, very occasionally you eat communally. Some large hotels (and some posh private houses) will bring dinner to your room if you prefer, or let you eat in the garden by candlelight. Always ask for what you want and sometimes, magically, it happens.

Prices and minimum stays

We quote the lowest price per night for two people in low season to the highest price in high season. Only a few places have designated single rooms; if no single

rooms are listed, the price we quote refers to single occupancy of a double room. In many places prices rise even higher when local events bring people flooding to the area, a point worth remembering when heading to Cheltenham for the racing or Glyndebourne for the opera.

The half-board price quoted is per person per night and includes dinner, usually three courses. Mostly you're offered a table d'hôte menu. Occasionally you eat à la carte and may find some dishes carry a small supplement. There are often great deals to be had, mostly mid-week in low season.

Most hotels do not accept one-night bookings at weekends. Small country hotels are rarely full during the week and the weekend trade keeps them going. If you ring in March for a Saturday night in July, you won't get it. If you ring at the last moment you may. Some places insist on three-night stays on bank holidays.

Photo above: Meeson Hall, entry 156
Photo right: Sands Hotel Margate, entry 108

Booking and cancellation

Most places ask for a deposit at the time of booking, either by cheque or card. If you cancel – depending on how much notice you give – you can lose all or part of this deposit unless your room is re-let.

It is reasonable for hotels to take a deposit to secure a booking; they have learnt that if they don't, the commitment of the guest wanes and they may fail to turn up.

Some cancellation policies are more stringent than others. It is also worth noting that some owners will take the money directly from your credit/debit card without contacting you to discuss it. So ask them to explain their cancellation policy clearly before booking so you understand exactly where you stand; it may well avoid a nasty surprise. And consider taking out travel insurance (with a cancellation clause) if you're concerned.

Arrivals and departures

Housekeeping is usually done by 2pm, and your room will usually be available by mid-afternoon. Normally you will have to wave goodbye to it between 10am and 11am. Sometimes one can pay to linger. Some inns are closed between 3pm and 6pm, so do try and agree an arrival time in advance or you may find nobody there.

Closed

When given in months this means for the whole of the month stated. So, 'Closed: November – March' means closed from 1 November to 31 March.

Sawday's British Hotel Awards

This is the time of year we throw a gong or two at some of our hotels, so here are 5 very special places that typify the Sawday's ethos.

Award categories:

Hotel of the Year

Favourite newcomer

National Treasure

Nicely priced

Fabulous food

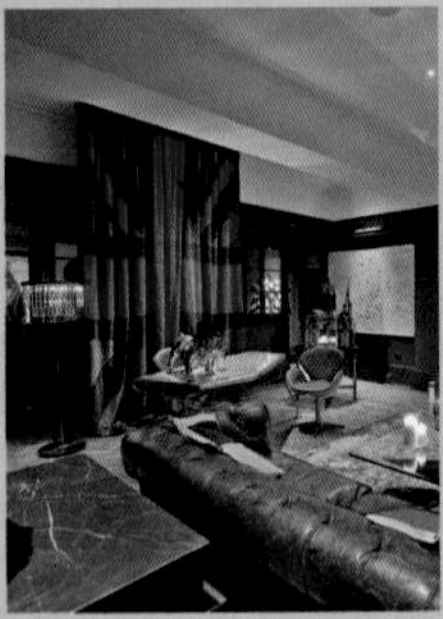

Hotel of the Year

We love small, intimate hotels and inns where the art of hospitality is practiced with flair – this wonder of our world has mastered that art in spades.

Glazebrook House Hotel, Devon
Entry 59

INSPECTED & SELECTED
Sawday's
BRITISH HOTEL AWARDS
2018

Favourite newcomer

New hotels are hard to find in tough economic times, but that hasn't stopped creative owners bursting onto the scene with beautiful new places that delight us.

Backwell House, Bristol
Entry 13

National Treasure

Like a good red wine, some hotels get better with age – this hotel has a clear instinct for hospitality and has been delighting guests for years.

Crug Glas, Pembrokeshire
Entry 274

Nicely priced

There's nothing like washing up at a lovely small hotel and finding it has a lovely small price too – this hotel does that with ease.

Scourie Hotel, Highland
Entry 235

INSPECTED & SELECTED
Sawday's
BRITISH HOTEL AWARDS
2018

Fabulous food

From hot kitchens come small miracles to delight your tastebuds and your pleasure receptors will delight in ambrosial food at this hotel.

The Punch Bowl Inn, Cumbria
Entry 46

INSPECTED & SELECTED
Sawday's
BRITISH HOTEL
AWARDS
2018

Photo: The Whitebrook, entry 269

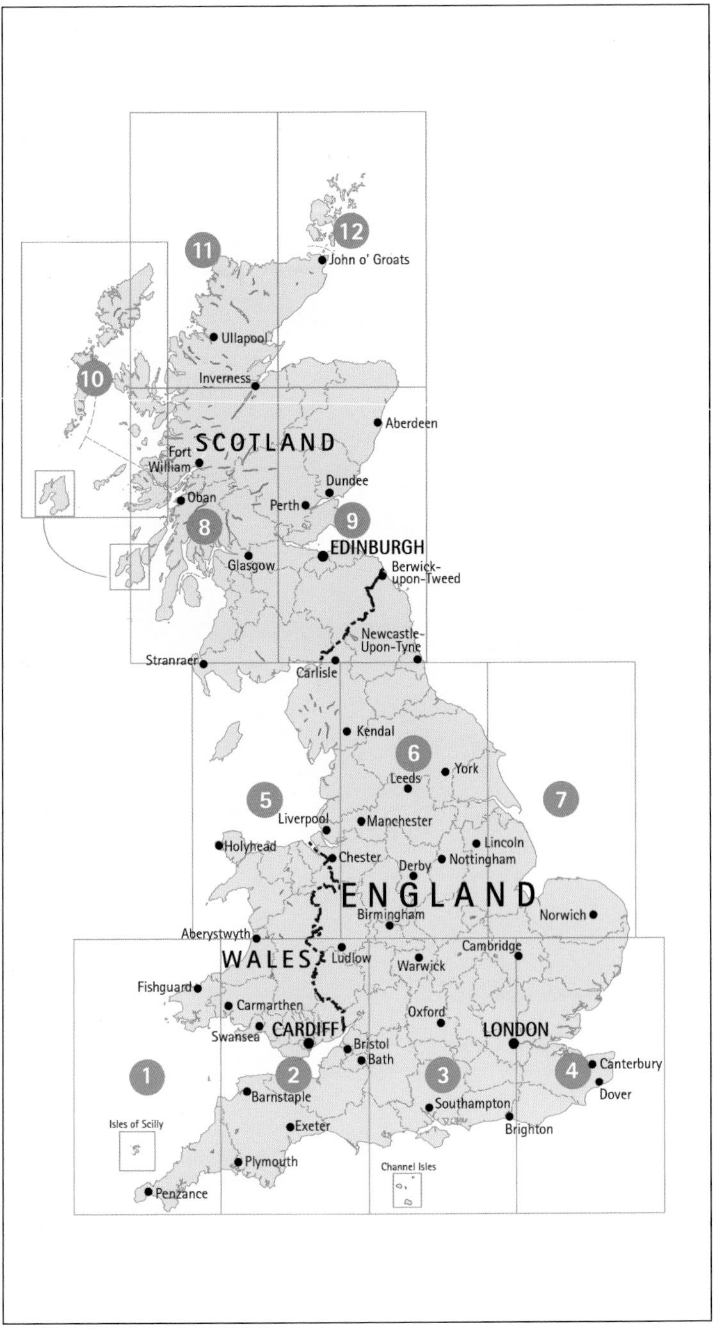
SCOTLAND
ENGLAND
WALES
John o' Groats
Ullapool
Inverness
Aberdeen
Fort William
Dundee
Oban
Perth
EDINBURGH
Glasgow
Berwick-upon-Tweed
Newcastle-Upon-Tyne
Stranraer
Carlisle
Kendal
York
Leeds
Liverpool
Manchester
Holyhead
Lincoln
Chester
Nottingham
Derby
Birmingham
Norwich
Aberystwyth
Cambridge
Ludlow
Warwick
Fishguard
Carmarthen
Oxford
Swansea
CARDIFF
LONDON
Bristol
Bath
Canterbury
Dover
Barnstaple
Southampton
Isles of Scilly
Exeter
Brighton
Plymouth
Channel Isles
Penzance
1
2
3
4
5
6
7
8
9
10
11
12

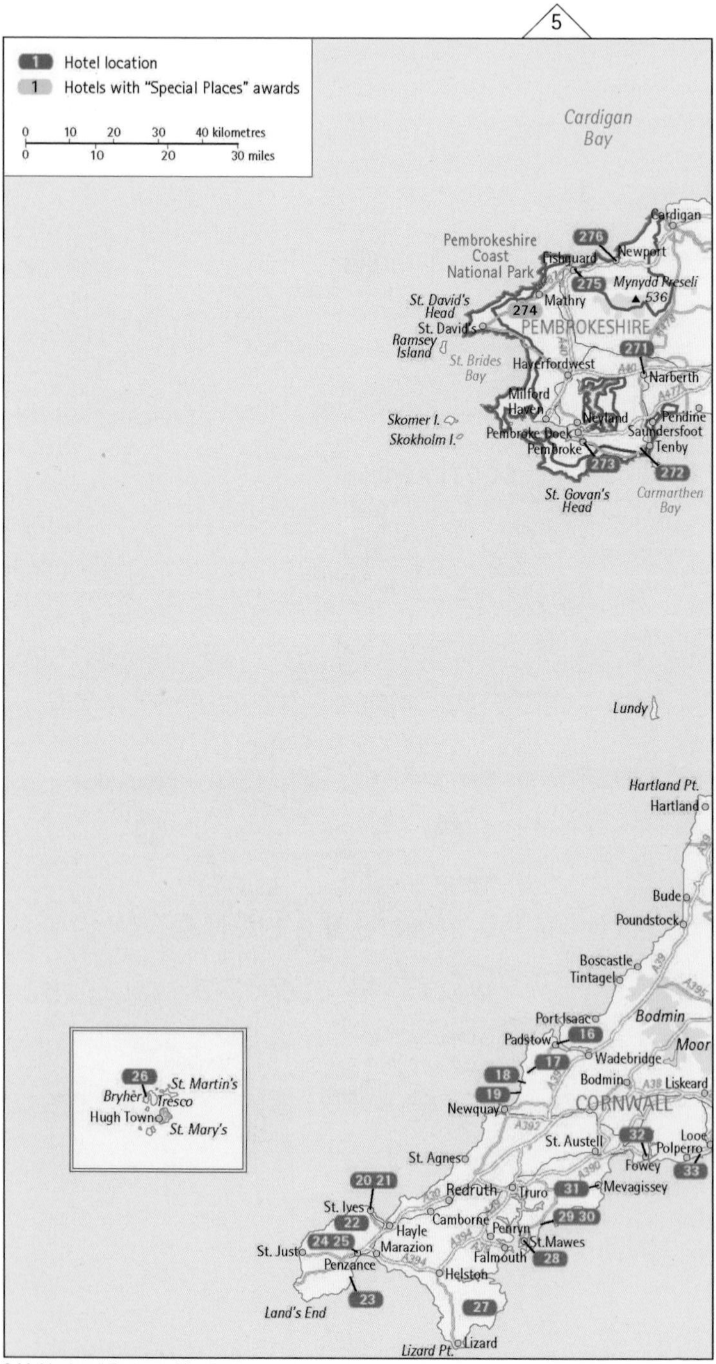

© Maidenhead Cartographic, 2017

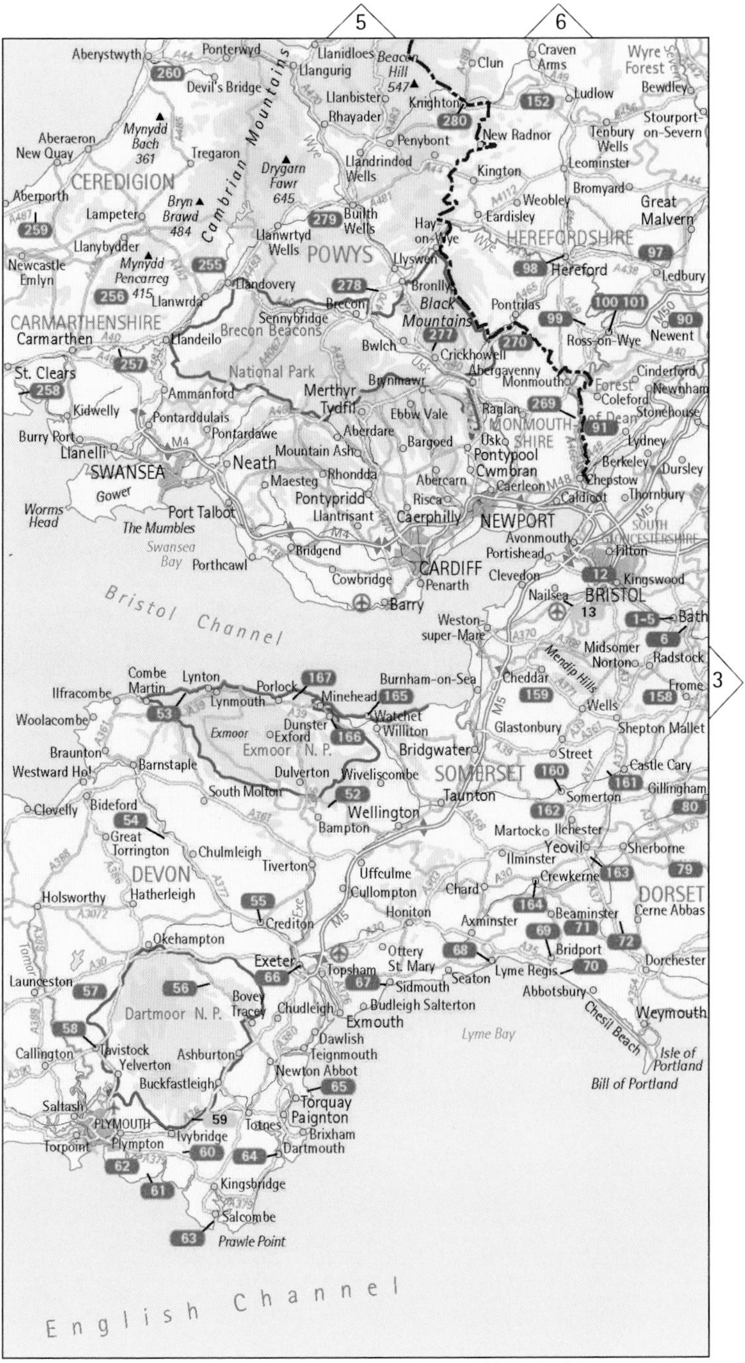
5
6
3
Aberystwyth
Ponterwyd
Devil's Bridge
Cambrian Mountains
Llanidloes
Llangurig
Beacon Hill 547
Clun
Craven Arms
Wyre Forest
Bewdley
Ludlow
Llanbister
Knighton
Rhayader
Stourport-on-Severn
Aberaeron
New Quay
Mynydd Bach 361
Tregaron
Penybont
New Radnor
Tenbury Wells
Drygarn Fawr 645
Llandrindod Wells
Leominster
Kington
CEREDIGION
Aberporth
Bryn Brawd 484
Bromyard
Weobley
Great Malvern
Lampeter
Eardisley
Builth Wells
Hay-on-Wye
Llanwrtyd Wells
HEREFORDSHIRE
Llanybydder
POWYS
Newcastle Emlyn
Mynydd Pencarreg 415
Llyswen
Hereford
Ledbury
Llandovery
Bronllys
Llanwrda
Black Mountains
Pontrilas
Brecon
CARMARTHENSHIRE
Sennybridge
Brecon Beacons
Ross-on-Wye
Newent
Carmarthen
Llandeilo
Bwlch
Crickhowell
National Park
Abergavenny
Monmouth
Cinderford
St. Clears
Brynmawr
Forest of Dean
Newnham
Ammanford
Merthyr Tydfil
Coleford
Kidwelly
Ebbw Vale
Raglan
Stonehouse
Pontarddulais
Aberdare
MONMOUTHSHIRE
Lydney
Burry Port
Pontardawe
Bargoed
Usk
Llanelli
Mountain Ash
Pontypool
Berkeley
Dursley
SWANSEA
Neath
Cwmbran
Chepstow
Maesteg
Rhondda
Abercarn
Caerleon
Gower
Pontypridd
Risca
Caldicot
Thornbury
Worms Head
Port Talbot
Llantrisant
Caerphilly
NEWPORT
The Mumbles
SOUTH GLOUCESTERSHIRE
Avonmouth
Swansea Bay
Bridgend
Portishead
Filton
Porthcawl
CARDIFF
Clevedon
Kingswood
Cowbridge
Penarth
Nailsea
BRISTOL
Bristol Channel
Barry
Bath
Weston-super-Mare
Mendip Hills
Midsomer Norton
Radstock
Combe Martin
Lynton
Porlock
Burnham-on-Sea
Cheddar
Frome
Ilfracombe
Lynmouth
Minehead
Watchet
Wells
Woolacombe
Dunster
Williton
Glastonbury
Shepton Mallet
Exmoor
Exford
Braunton
Exmoor N. P.
Bridgwater
Street
Westward Ho!
Barnstaple
Dulverton
Wiveliscombe
SOMERSET
Castle Cary
Gillingham
South Molton
Taunton
Somerton
Clovelly
Bideford
Wellington
Bampton
Martock
Ilchester
Great Torrington
Chulmleigh
Yeovil
Sherborne
Ilminster
DEVON
Tiverton
Uffculme
Crewkerne
Holsworthy
Hatherleigh
Cullompton
Chard
DORSET
Crediton
Honiton
Beaminster
Cerne Abbas
Axminster
Okehampton
Ottery St. Mary
Bridport
Exeter
Topsham
Lyme Regis
Dorchester
Launceston
Sidmouth
Seaton
Bovey Tracey
Abbotsbury
Dartmoor N. P.
Chudleigh
Budleigh Salterton
Weymouth
Exmouth
Chesil Beach
Dawlish
Lyme Bay
Callington
Tavistock
Ashburton
Teignmouth
Isle of Portland
Yelverton
Newton Abbot
Bill of Portland
Buckfastleigh
Saltash
Torquay
Paignton
PLYMOUTH
Totnes
Brixham
Torpoint
Plympton
Ivybridge
Dartmouth
Kingsbridge
Salcombe
Prawle Point
English Channel
260
280
152
259
279
255
97
98
256
278
100 101
99
90
277
270
257
258
269
91
12
13
1-5
6
167
165
159
158
53
166
160
161
52
162
80
54
163
79
55
164
69
71
72
68
70
66
67
56
57
58
65
59
60
64
62
61
63

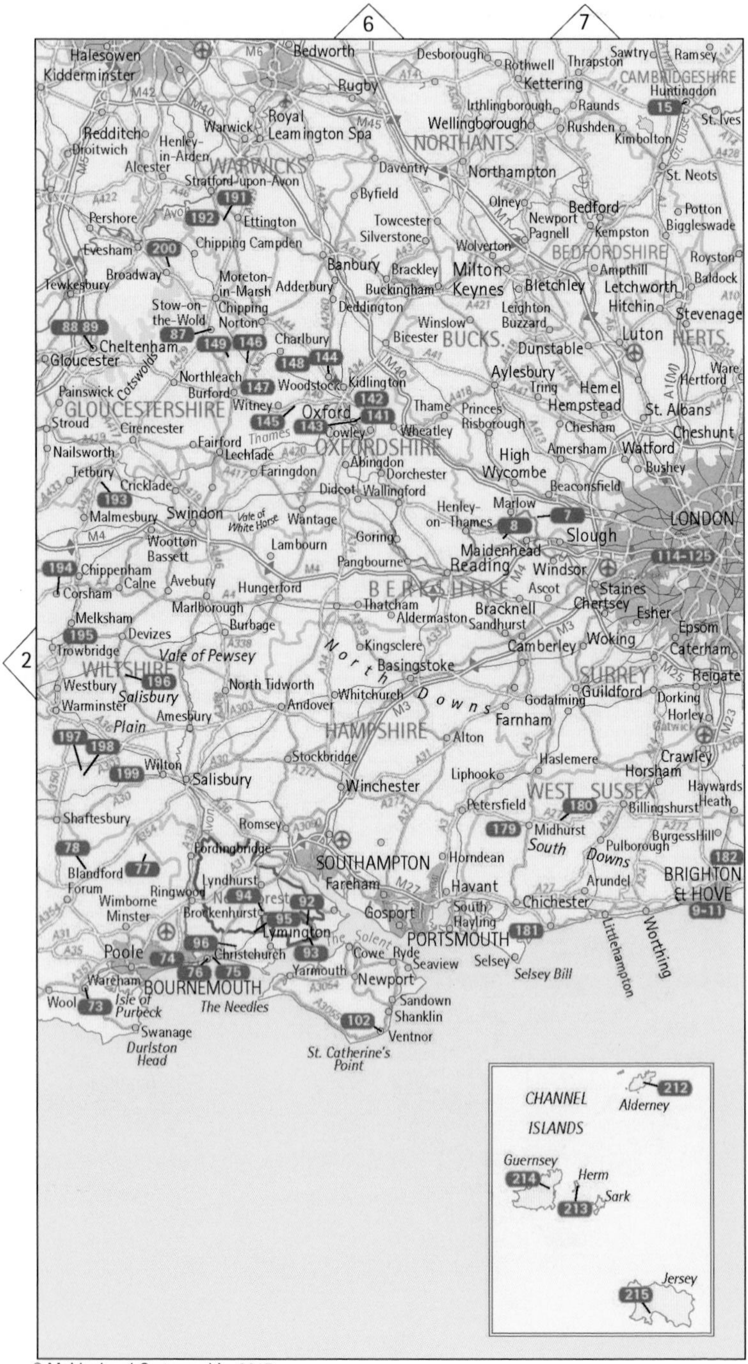
6
7
2
Halesowen
Kidderminster
Bedworth
Desborough
Rothwell
Thrapston
Sawtry
Ramsey
Kettering
CAMBRIDGESHIRE
Huntingdon
Rugby
Irthlingborough
Raunds
Redditch
Droitwich
Henley-in-Arden
Warwick
Royal Leamington Spa
Wellingborough
Rushden
Kimbolton
St. Ives
NORTHANTS.
Alcester
WARWICKS
Daventry
Northampton
St. Neots
Stratford-upon-Avon
Byfield
Olney
Bedford
Potton
Pershore
191
192
Ettington
Towcester
Newport Pagnell
Kempston
Biggleswade
Silverstone
Evesham
200
Chipping Campden
Wolverton
BEDFORDSHIRE
Royston
Broadway
Moreton-in-Marsh
Banbury
Brackley
Milton Keynes
Ampthill
Baldock
Tewkesbury
Adderbury
Buckingham
Bletchley
Letchworth
Stow-on-the-Wold
Chipping Norton
Deddington
Winslow
Leighton Buzzard
Hitchin
Stevenage
88 89
87
Bicester
BUCKS.
Luton
HERTS.
Cheltenham
149
146
Charlbury
Dunstable
Gloucester
Cotswolds
148
144
Aylesbury
Ware
Northleach
Kidlington
Tring
Hemel Hempstead
Hertford
Painswick
Burford
147
Woodstock
142
GLOUCESTERSHIRE
Witney
Oxford
Thame
Princes Risborough
St. Albans
Stroud
Cirencester
145
143
141
Cowley
Wheatley
Chesham
Cheshunt
Nailsworth
Fairford
Thames
OXFORDSHIRE
Amersham
Watford
Lechlade
Abingdon
High Wycombe
Bushey
Tetbury
Cricklade
Faringdon
Dorchester
193
Didcot
Wallingford
Beaconsfield
Malmesbury
Swindon
Vale of White Horse
Wantage
Henley-on-Thames
Marlow
7
LONDON
8
Wootton Bassett
Goring
Slough
Lambourn
Maidenhead
194
Chippenham
Pangbourne
Reading
Windsor
114-125
Corsham
Calne
Avebury
Hungerford
BERKSHIRE
Ascot
Staines
Marlborough
Thatcham
Bracknell
Chertsey
Melksham
Burbage
Aldermaston
Sandhurst
Esher
Epsom
195
Devizes
Kingsclere
Camberley
Woking
Caterham
Trowbridge
Vale of Pewsey
North Downs
Basingstoke
WILTSHIRE
196
SURREY
Reigate
Westbury
Salisbury Plain
North Tidworth
Whitchurch
Godalming
Guildford
Dorking
Warminster
Amesbury
Andover
Farnham
Horley
HAMPSHIRE
Alton
197
198
Crawley
Stockbridge
Haslemere
Horsham
Wilton
199
Salisbury
Winchester
Liphook
WEST SUSSEX
Haywards Heath
Petersfield
180
Billingshurst
Shaftesbury
Romsey
179
Midhurst
Burgess Hill
South Downs
Pulborough
78
Fordingbridge
SOUTHAMPTON
Horndean
182
Blandford Forum
77
Lyndhurst
Fareham
Havant
Arundel
BRIGHTON & HOVE
Ringwood
94
New Forest
92
Wimborne Minster
Brockenhurst
95
Gosport
South Hayling
Chichester
9-11
Lymington
PORTSMOUTH
181
Littlehampton
Worthing
96
The Solent
Poole
74
Christchurch
93
Cowes
Ryde
Selsey
76
75
Yarmouth
Seaview
Selsey Bill
Wareham
BOURNEMOUTH
Newport
Wool
73
Isle of Purbeck
The Needles
Sandown
Shanklin
102
Ventnor
Swanage
Durlston Head
St. Catherine's Point
CHANNEL ISLANDS
212
Alderney
Guernsey
214
Herm
Sark
213
Jersey
215

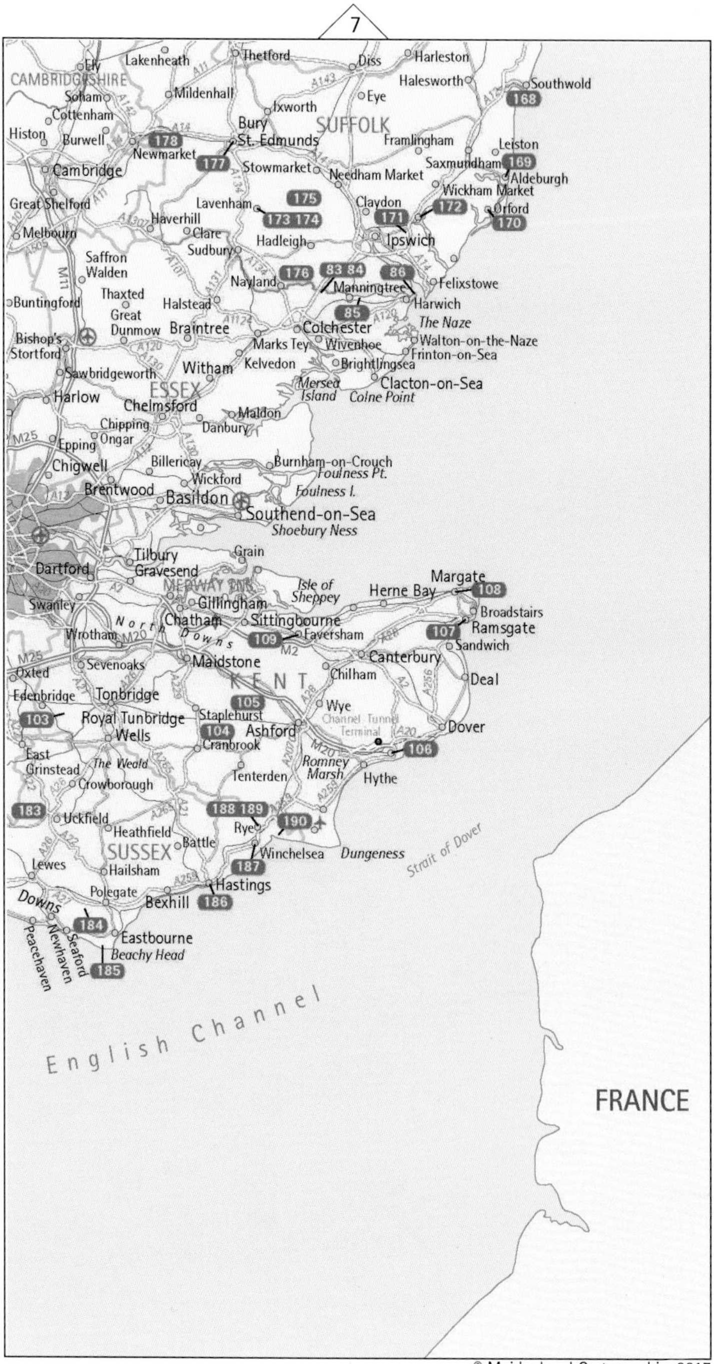

7

CAMBRIDGESHIRE

Ely Lakenheath Thetford Diss Harleston
Soham Mildenhall Ixworth Eye Halesworth Southwold
Cottenham 168
Histon Burwell Bury SUFFOLK Framlingham Leiston
Newmarket St. Edmunds 169
Cambridge 178 177 Stowmarket Saxmundham Aldeburgh
Great Shelford Lavenham 175 Needham Market Wickham Market 172 Orford
Melbourn Haverhill 173 174 Claydon 171 170
Saffron Clare Sudbury Hadleigh Ipswich
Walden Nayland 176 83 84 86
Buntingford Thaxted Halstead Manningtree Felixstowe
Bishop's Great Dunmow Braintree Marks Tey 85 Harwich
Stortford Sawbridgeworth Witham Kelvedon Colchester The Naze
Harlow Chelmsford Wivenhoe Walton-on-the-Naze
ESSEX Brightlingsea Frinton-on-Sea
Chipping Maldon Mersea Clacton-on-Sea
Epping Ongar Danbury Island Colne Point
Chigwell Billericay Burnham-on-Crouch
Brentwood Wickford Foulness Pt.
Basildon Foulness I.
Southend-on-Sea
Shoebury Ness
Tilbury Grain
Dartford Gravesend Isle of Margate
Swanley Sheppey Herne Bay 108
North Gillingham Broadstairs
Wrotham Chatham Sittingbourne 107 Ramsgate
Oxted Downs 109 Faversham Sandwich
Sevenoaks Maidstone Canterbury
Edenbridge Tonbridge KENT Chilham Deal
103 Staplehurst 105 Wye
Royal Tunbridge 104 Ashford Channel Tunnel Dover
East Wells Cranbrook Terminal 106
Grinstead The Weald Romney
Crowborough Tenterden Marsh Hythe
183 Uckfield 188 189
Heathfield Battle Rye 190
Lewes SUSSEX Winchelsea Dungeness
Hailsham 187
Polegate Hastings
Downs 184 Bexhill 186
Newhaven Seaford Eastbourne
Peacehaven 185 Beachy Head

English Channel

FRANCE

Strait of Dover

© Maidenhead Cartographic, 2017

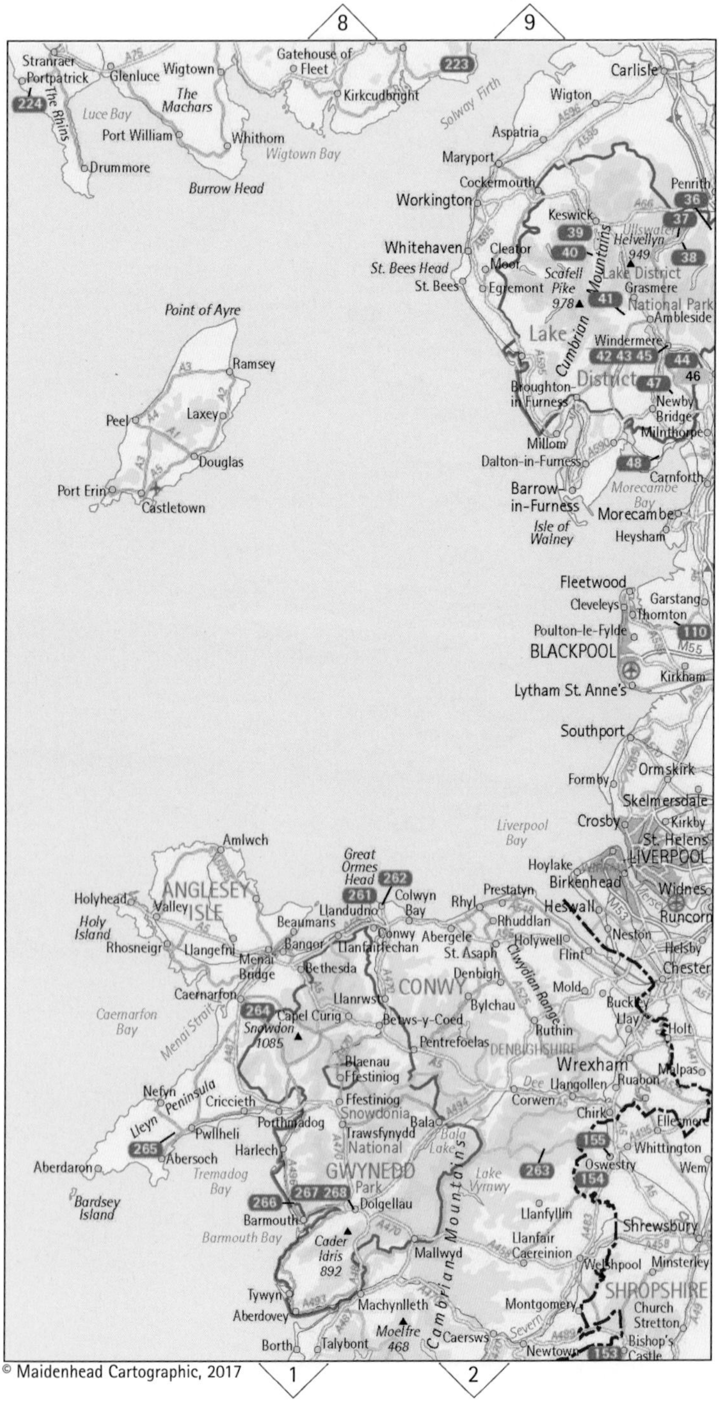
8
9
Stranraer
Portpatrick
224
The Rhins
Glenluce
Wigtown
The Machars
Luce Bay
Port William
Whithorn
Wigtown Bay
Drummore
Burrow Head
Gatehouse of Fleet
Kirkcudbright
223
Solway Firth
Carlisle
Wigton
Aspatria
Maryport
Cockermouth
Workington
Penrith
36
37
Keswick
39
40
Ullswater
Helvellyn
949
38
Whitehaven
Cleator Moor
St. Bees Head
St. Bees
Egremont
Scafell Pike
978
Cumbrian Mountains
Lake District National Park
Grasmere
41
Ambleside
Lake District
Windermere
42 43 45
44
46
47
Broughton-in-Furness
Newby Bridge
Milnthorpe
Millom
Dalton-in-Furness
48
Carnforth
Barrow-in-Furness
Morecambe Bay
Morecambe
Isle of Walney
Heysham
Point of Ayre
Ramsey
Laxey
Peel
Douglas
Port Erin
Castletown
Fleetwood
Garstang
Cleveleys
Thornton
Poulton-le-Fylde
110
M55
BLACKPOOL
Kirkham
Lytham St. Anne's
Southport
Ormskirk
Formby
Skelmersdale
Liverpool Bay
Crosby
Kirkby
St. Helens
LIVERPOOL
Hoylake
Birkenhead
Widnes
Heswall
Runcorn
M53
Neston
Helsby
Chester
Amlwch
ANGLESEY ISLE
Holyhead
Valley
Holy Island
Rhosneigr
Llangefni
Great Ormes Head
262
261
Llandudno
Colwyn Bay
Rhyl
Prestatyn
Rhuddlan
Holywell
Flint
Beaumaris
Conwy
Abergele
Menai Bridge
Bangor
Llanfairfechan
St. Asaph
Bethesda
Denbigh
Clwydian Range
Mold
Caernarfon
CONWY
Llanrwst
Buckley
Bylchau
Llay
Holt
Caernarfon Bay
264
Capel Curig
Betws-y-Coed
Snowdon
1085
Ruthin
Menai Strait
Pentrefoelas
DENBIGHSHIRE
Wrexham
Blaenau Ffestiniog
Malpas
Dee
Llangollen
Ruabon
Nefyn
Lleyn Peninsula
Criccieth
Ffestiniog
Corwen
Chirk
Ellesmere
Snowdonia National Park
Bala
Porthmadog
Pwllheli
Trawsfynydd
Bala Lake
265
Abersoch
Harlech
155
Whittington
Oswestry
Wem
Aberdaron
Tremadog Bay
GWYNEDD
263
154
Lake Vyrnwy
Bardsey Island
267 268
266
Dolgellau
Llanfyllin
Barmouth
Shrewsbury
Barmouth Bay
Cader Idris
892
Llanfair Caereinion
Mallwyd
Cambrian Mountains
Welshpool
Minsterley
SHROPSHIRE
Tywyn
Aberdovey
Machynlleth
Montgomery
Church Stretton
Moelfre
468
Severn
Borth
Talybont
Caersws
Newtown
153
Bishop's Castle
1
2

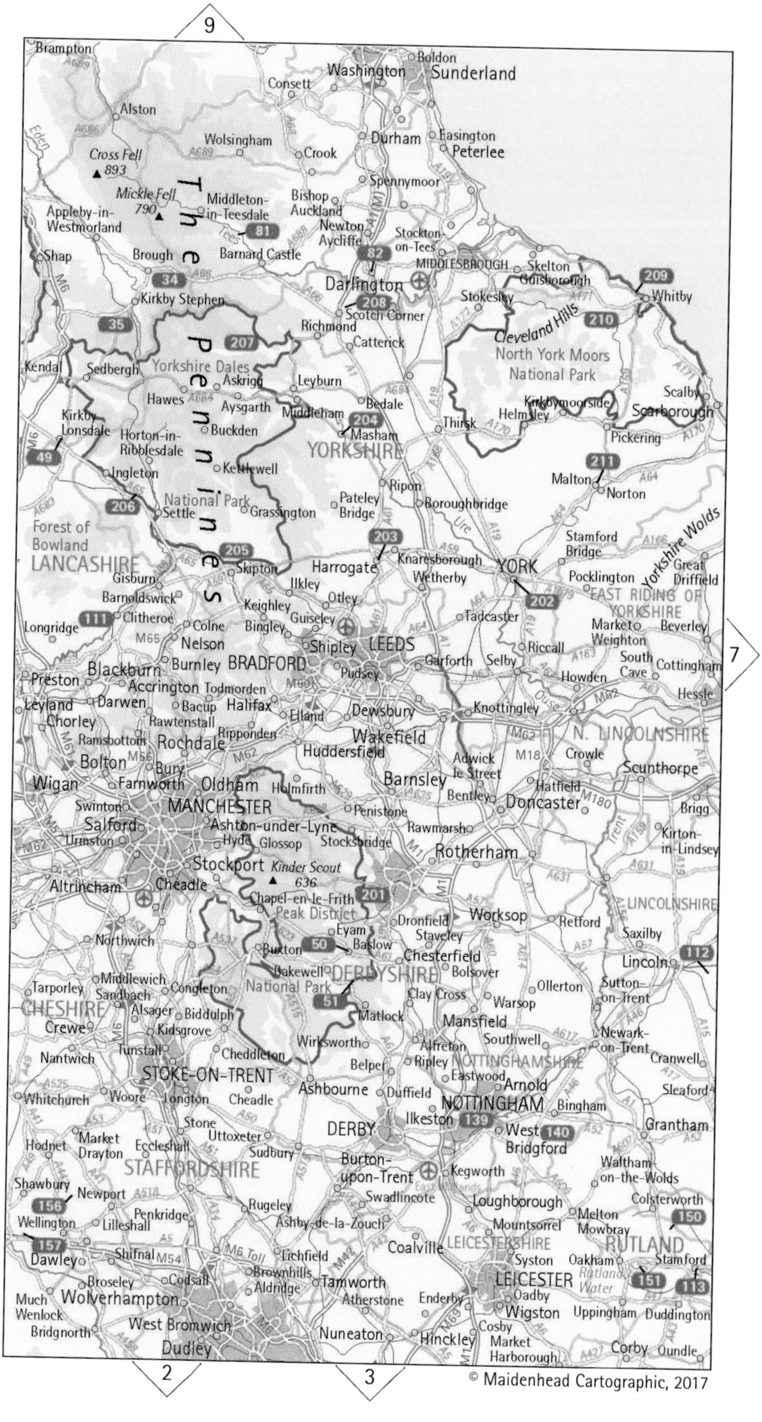
9
Brampton
Boldon
Washington
Sunderland
Consett
Alston
Eden
Wolsingham
Durham
Easington
Peterlee
Crook
Cross Fell
893
Spennymoor
Mickle Fell
790
The Pennines
Middleton-in-Teesdale
Bishop Auckland
Appleby-in-Westmorland
Newton Aycliffe
Stockton-on-Tees
Tees
81
Shap
Brough
Barnard Castle
82
MIDDLESBROUGH
Skelton
Guisborough
209
Whitby
34
M6
Darlington
Stokesley
Kirkby Stephen
208
Scotch Corner
Cleveland Hills
210
Richmond
35
Catterick
North York Moors
National Park
207
Yorkshire Dales
Kendal
Sedbergh
Askrigg
Leyburn
Scalby
Hawes
Bedale
Aysgarth
Kirkbymoorside
Kirkby Lonsdale
Middleham
204
Thirsk
Helmsley
Scarborough
Buckden
Masham
Pickering
Horton-in-Ribblesdale
YORKSHIRE
49
211
Ingleton
Kettlewell
Malton
Norton
Ripon
206
National Park
Pateley Bridge
Boroughbridge
Settle
Grassington
Ure
Forest of Bowland
203
Stamford Bridge
Yorkshire Wolds
LANCASHIRE
205
Knaresborough
YORK
Skipton
Harrogate
Great Driffield
Gisburn
Wetherby
Pocklington
Ilkley
EAST RIDING OF YORKSHIRE
Barnoldswick
202
Otley
Keighley
Guiseley
Tadcaster
111
Clitheroe
Market Weighton
Beverley
Longridge
Colne
Bingley
M65
Nelson
Shipley
LEEDS
Riccall
7
South Cave
Cottingham
Blackburn
Burnley
BRADFORD
Garforth
Selby
Preston
Pudsey
Accrington
Todmorden
Howden
Hessle
Leyland
Darwen
Bacup
Halifax
Ouse
M62
Elland
Dewsbury
Knottingley
Chorley
Rawtenstall
Ripponden
Wakefield
N. LINCOLNSHIRE
M61
Ramsbottom
Rochdale
M62
Huddersfield
M18
Crowle
Bolton
Adwick le Street
Bury
Scunthorpe
Wigan
Farnworth
Oldham
Holmfirth
Barnsley
Hatfield
Bentley
M180
Swinton
MANCHESTER
Penistone
Doncaster
Brigg
Salford
Ashton-under-Lyne
Rawmarsh
Kirton-in-Lindsey
M62
Urmston
Hyde
Glossop
Stocksbridge
Trent
Rotherham
Stockport
Kinder Scout
636
Altrincham
Cheadle
M1
Chapel-en-le-Frith
201
LINCOLNSHIRE
Peak District
Dronfield
Worksop
Retford
Eyam
Staveley
Saxilby
Northwich
50
Baslow
Buxton
Chesterfield
112
Lincoln
Bolsover
Middlewich
Bakewell
DERBYSHIRE
Tarporley
Sandbach
Congleton
National Park
Clay Cross
Ollerton
Sutton-on-Trent
51
Warsop
CHESHIRE
Alsager
Biddulph
Matlock
Mansfield
Crewe
Kidsgrove
Newark-on-Trent
Southwell
M6
Wirksworth
Alfreton
Nantwich
Tunstall
Cheddleton
Ripley
NOTTINGHAMSHIRE
Cranwell
Belper
STOKE-ON-TRENT
Eastwood
Arnold
Ashbourne
Whitchurch
Woore
Longton
Cheadle
Duffield
Sleaford
NOTTINGHAM
Bingham
Stone
Ilkeston
139
Market Drayton
Uttoxeter
DERBY
West Bridgford
140
Grantham
Hodnet
Eccleshall
Sudbury
STAFFORDSHIRE
Burton-upon-Trent
Kegworth
Waltham-on-the-Wolds
Shawbury
Newport
Swadlincote
156
Loughborough
Colsterworth
Rugeley
Wellington
Lilleshall
Penkridge
Ashby-de-la-Zouch
Melton Mowbray
150
157
Mountsorrel
LEICESTERSHIRE
RUTLAND
Coalville
Dawley
Shifnal
M54
M6 Toll
Lichfield
Syston
Oakham
Stamford
Broseley
Codsall
Brownhills
Rutland Water
151
113
Aldridge
Tamworth
LEICESTER
Much Wenlock
Wolverhampton
Atherstone
Enderby
Oadby
West Bromwich
Wigston
Uppingham
Duddington
Bridgnorth
M69
Cosby
Nuneaton
Hinckley
Market Harborough
Corby
Oundle
Dudley
M1
2
3

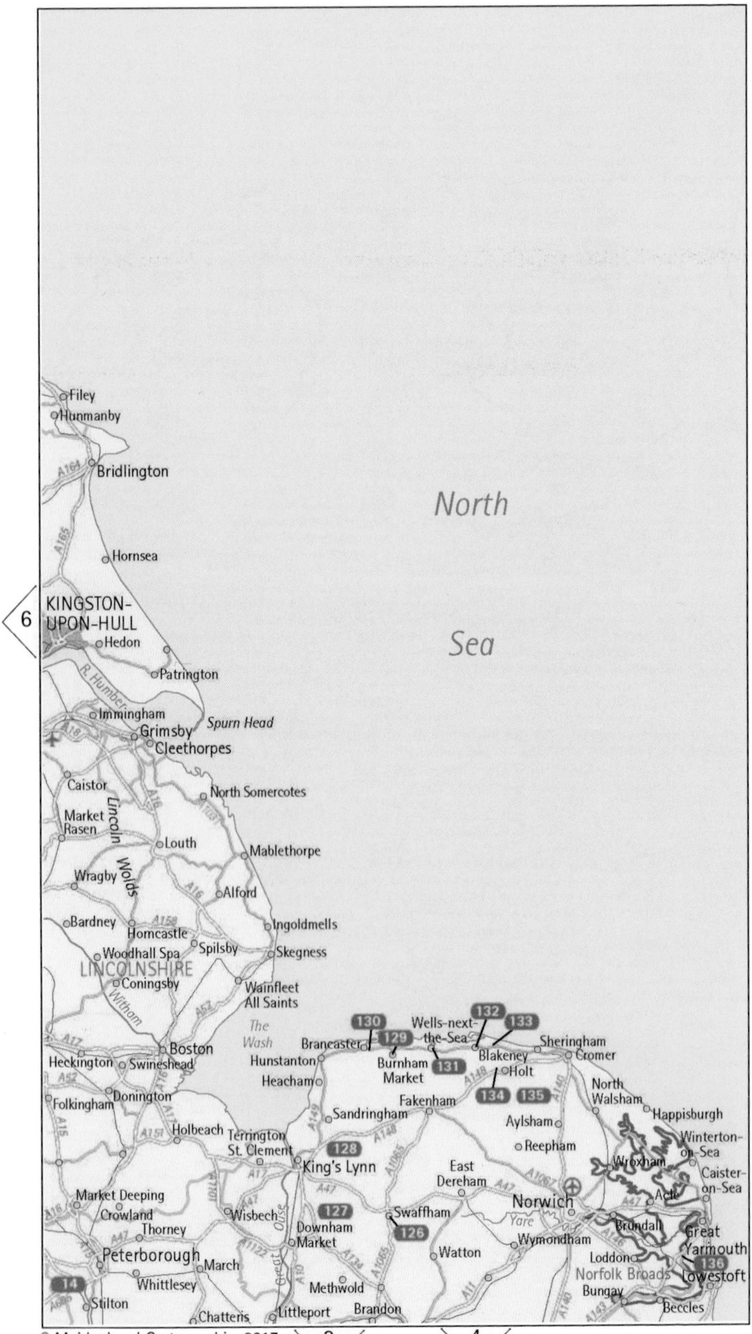
North
Sea
Filey
Hunmanby
Bridlington
Hornsea
KINGSTON-
UPON-HULL
Hedon
Patrington
R. Humber
Spurn Head
Immingham
Grimsby
Cleethorpes
Caistor
North Somercotes
Market
Rasen
Lincoln
Wolds
Louth
Mablethorpe
Wragby
Alford
Bardney
Horncastle
Ingoldmells
Woodhall Spa
Spilsby
Skegness
LINCOLNSHIRE
Coningsby
Wainfleet
All Saints
Witham
The
Wash
Boston
Heckington
Swineshead
Folkingham
Donington
Holbeach
Terrington
St. Clement
Market Deeping
Crowland
Thorney
Peterborough
Whittlesey
March
Wisbech
Stilton
Chatteris
Littleport
Brandon
Methwold
Downham
Market
Great
Ouse
King's Lynn
Sandringham
Heacham
Hunstanton
Brancaster
Burnham
Market
Wells-next-
the-Sea
Blakeney
Holt
Sheringham
Cromer
Fakenham
Swaffham
Watton
East
Dereham
Aylsham
Reepham
North
Walsham
Happisburgh
Winterton-
on-Sea
Wroxham
Caister-
on-Sea
Acle
Norwich
Yare
Wymondham
Brundall
Great
Yarmouth
Loddon
Norfolk Broads
Lowestoft
Bungay
Beccles
126
127
128
129
130
131
132
133
134
135
136
14
6
3
4
A164
A165
A18
A16
A1031
A158
A52
A17
A15
A151
A1101
A47
A149
A148
A1065
A134
A10
A1122
A140
A1067
A146
A11
A143

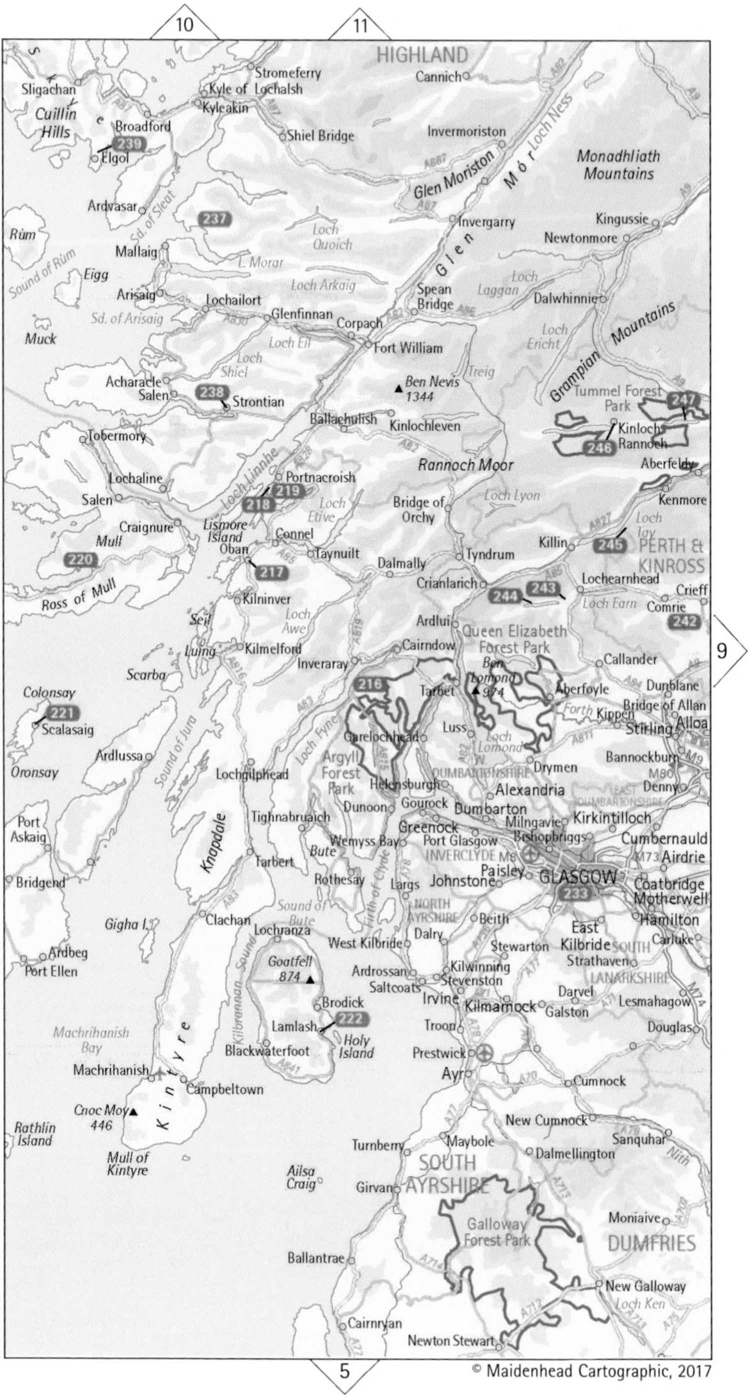
10
11
9
5
HIGHLAND
Sligachan
Cuillin Hills
Stromeferry
Kyle of Lochalsh
Kyleakin
Broadford
239
Elgol
Cannich
Shiel Bridge
Invermoriston
Glen Moriston
Loch Ness
Glen Mór
Monadhliath Mountains
Ardvasar
Sd. of Sleat
237
Rùm
Mallaig
Loch Quoich
Invergarry
Kingussie
Newtonmore
Sound of Rùm
Eigg
L. Morar
Loch Arkaig
Spean Bridge
Loch Laggan
Dalwhinnie
Arisaig
Lochailort
Glenfinnan
Sd. of Arisaig
Corpach
Muck
Loch Eil
Fort William
Loch Ericht
Grampian Mountains
Loch Shiel
Treig
Acharacle
Salen
238
Strontian
Ben Nevis 1344
Tummel Forest Park
247
Ballachulish
Kinlochleven
Tobermory
Kinloch Rannoch
246
Loch Linnhe
Rannoch Moor
Aberfeldy
Lochaline
Portnacroish
219
218
Salen
Loch Etive
Bridge of Orchy
Loch Lyon
Kenmore
Craignure
Lismore Island
Connel
Loch Tay
Mull
Oban
Taynuilt
Killin
245
PERTH & KINROSS
220
217
Dalmally
Tyndrum
Ross of Mull
Kilninver
Crianlarich
244
243
Lochearnhead
Crieff
Loch Earn
Comrie
242
Seil
Loch Awe
Ardlui
Queen Elizabeth Forest Park
Luing
Kilmelford
Cairndow
Inveraray
Ben Lomond 974
Callander
Scarba
216
Tarbet
Aberfoyle
Dunblane
Colonsay
221
Scalasaig
Loch Fyne
Forth
Kippen
Bridge of Allan
Stirling
Alloa
Garelochhead
Luss
Loch Lomond
Ardlussa
Sound of Jura
Bannockburn
Oronsay
Lochgilphead
Argyll Forest Park
Drymen
DUMBARTONSHIRE
Helensburgh
Alexandria
EAST DUNBARTONSHIRE
Denny
Dunoon
Gourock
Bumbarton
Knapdale
Tighnabruaich
Port Askaig
Greenock
Milngavie
Kirkintilloch
Wemyss Bay
Port Glasgow
Bishopbriggs
Cumbernauld
Bute
INVERCLYDE
Airdrie
Tarbert
Bridgend
Rothesay
Firth of Clyde
Largs
Johnstone
Paisley
GLASGOW
233
Coatbridge
Motherwell
Gigha I.
Clachan
Sound of Bute
NORTH AYRSHIRE
Beith
Hamilton
Lochranza
East Kilbride
Dalry
West Kilbride
Carluke
Ardbeg
Port Ellen
Goatfell 874
Stewarton
SOUTH LANARKSHIRE
Ardrossan
Kilwinning
Strathaven
Saltcoats
Stevenston
Kilbrannan Sound
Irvine
Darvel
Kilmarnock
Galston
Lesmahagow
Brodick
Lamlash
222
Troon
Douglas
Machrihanish Bay
Holy Island
Blackwaterfoot
Prestwick
Kintyre
Machrihanish
Ayr
Campbeltown
Cumnock
Cnoc Moy 446
Rathlin Island
New Cumnock
Sanquhar
Nith
Turnberry
Maybole
Dalmellington
Mull of Kintyre
SOUTH AYRSHIRE
Ailsa Craig
Girvan
Moniaive
Galloway Forest Park
DUMFRIES
Ballantrae
New Galloway
Loch Ken
Cairnryan
Newton Stewart
Lothians
A87
A887
A82
A9
A86
A830
A828
A85
A827
A819
A816
A83
A815
A84
A811
M9
M80
M8
M73
M74
A78
A71
A77
A76
A70
A713
A702
A714
A712
A75
A841

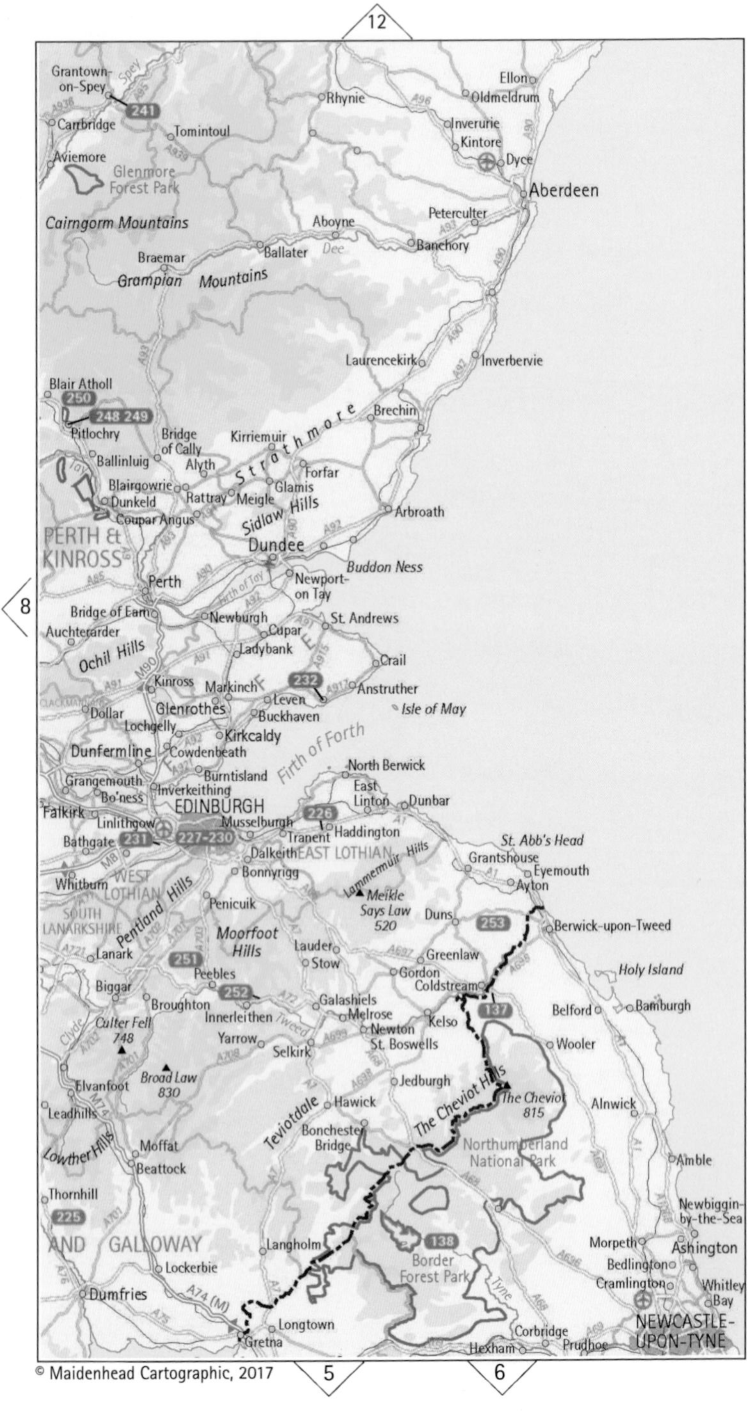
12
8
5
6
Grantown-on-Spey
Carrbridge
Tomintoul
Aviemore
Glenmore Forest Park
Cairngorm Mountains
Braemar
Grampian Mountains
Rhynie
Ellon
Oldmeldrum
Inverurie
Kintore
Dyce
Aberdeen
Peterculter
Aboyne
Ballater
Dee
Banchory
Laurencekirk
Inverbervie
Blair Atholl
Pitlochry
Ballinluig
Bridge of Cally
Kirriemuir
Brechin
Strathmore
Alyth
Forfar
Glamis
Blairgowrie
Dunkeld
Rattray
Meigle
Coupar Angus
Sidlaw Hills
Arbroath
PERTH & KINROSS
Dundee
Buddon Ness
Perth
Newport-on Tay
Firth of Tay
Bridge of Earn
Newburgh
Cupar
St. Andrews
Auchterarder
Ladybank
Crail
Ochil Hills
Kinross
Markinch
Anstruther
Leven
Dollar
Glenrothes
Buckhaven
Isle of May
Lochgelly
Kirkcaldy
Dunfermline
Cowdenbeath
Firth of Forth
Burntisland
North Berwick
Grangemouth
Inverkeithing
East Linton
Dunbar
Bo'ness
Falkirk
EDINBURGH
Linlithgow
Musselburgh
Tranent
Haddington
Bathgate
Dalkeith
EAST LOTHIAN
St. Abb's Head
Lammermuir Hills
Grantshouse
Eyemouth
Bonnyrigg
Ayton
Whitburn
WEST LOTHIAN
Meikle Says Law 520
Penicuik
Duns
Berwick-upon-Tweed
SOUTH LANARKSHIRE
Pentland Hills
Moorfoot Hills
Lauder
Greenlaw
Lanark
Stow
Gordon
Holy Island
Peebles
Coldstream
Biggar
Broughton
Galashiels
Belford
Bamburgh
Melrose
Innerleithen
Tweed
Kelso
Culter Fell 748
Yarrow
Newton St. Boswells
Wooler
Selkirk
Clyde
Broad Law 830
Jedburgh
Elvanfoot
The Cheviot Hills
The Cheviot 815
Teviotdale
Hawick
Alnwick
Leadhills
Bonchester Bridge
Moffat
Lowther Hills
Northumberland National Park
Beattock
Amble
Thornhill
Newbiggin-by-the-Sea
AND GALLOWAY
Langholm
Border Forest Park
Morpeth
Ashington
Lockerbie
Bedlington
Dumfries
Cramlington
Whitley Bay
Tyne
Longtown
Corbridge
NEWCASTLE-UPON-TYNE
Gretna
Hexham
Prudhoe
241
250
248 249
232
226
231
227-230
253
251
252
137
138
225
A74 (M)

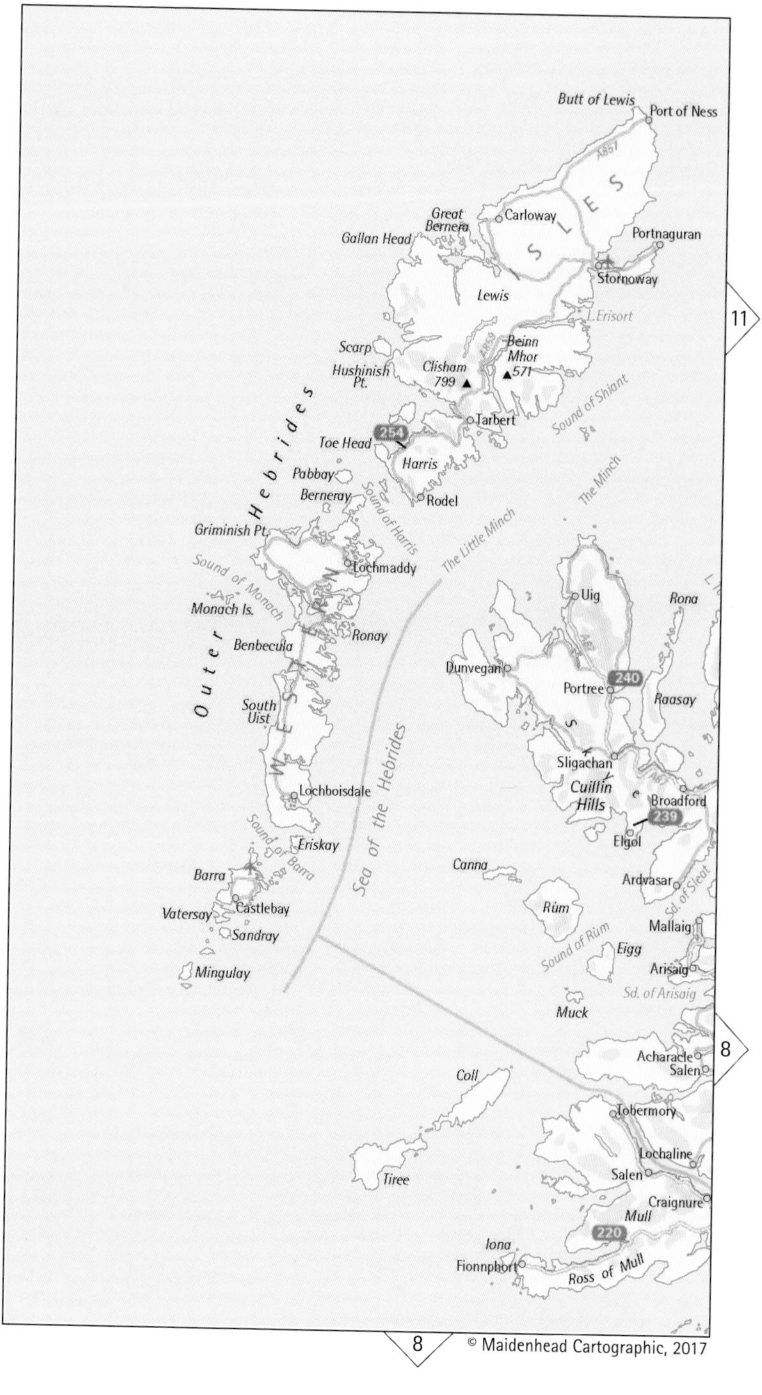
Butt of Lewis
Port of Ness
A857
I S L E S
Carloway
Great Bernera
Gallan Head
Portnaguran
Stornoway
Lewis
L. Erisort
11
Scarp
Hushinish Pt.
Clisham 799
Beinn Mhor 571
A859
Tarbert
Sound of Shiant
254
Toe Head
Harris
Pabbay
Berneray
Rodel
Sound of Harris
The Minch
Outer Hebrides
Griminish Pt.
Sound of Monach
Lochmaddy
The Little Minch
Monach Is.
W E S T E R N
Ronay
Benbecula
Uig
Rona
A87
Dunvegan
240
Portree
Raasay
South Uist
S K Y E
Sligachan
Cuillin Hills
Broadford
Lochboisdale
Sea of the Hebrides
239
Elgol
Sound of Barra
Eriskay
Canna
Barra
Ardvasar
Sd. of Sleat
Rùm
Castlebay
Vatersay
Mallaig
Sandray
Sound of Rùm
Eigg
Mingulay
Arisaig
Sd. of Arisaig
Muck
Acharacle
8
Salen
Coll
Tobermory
Lochaline
Tiree
Salen
Craignure
Mull
220
Iona
Fionnphort
Ross of Mull
8

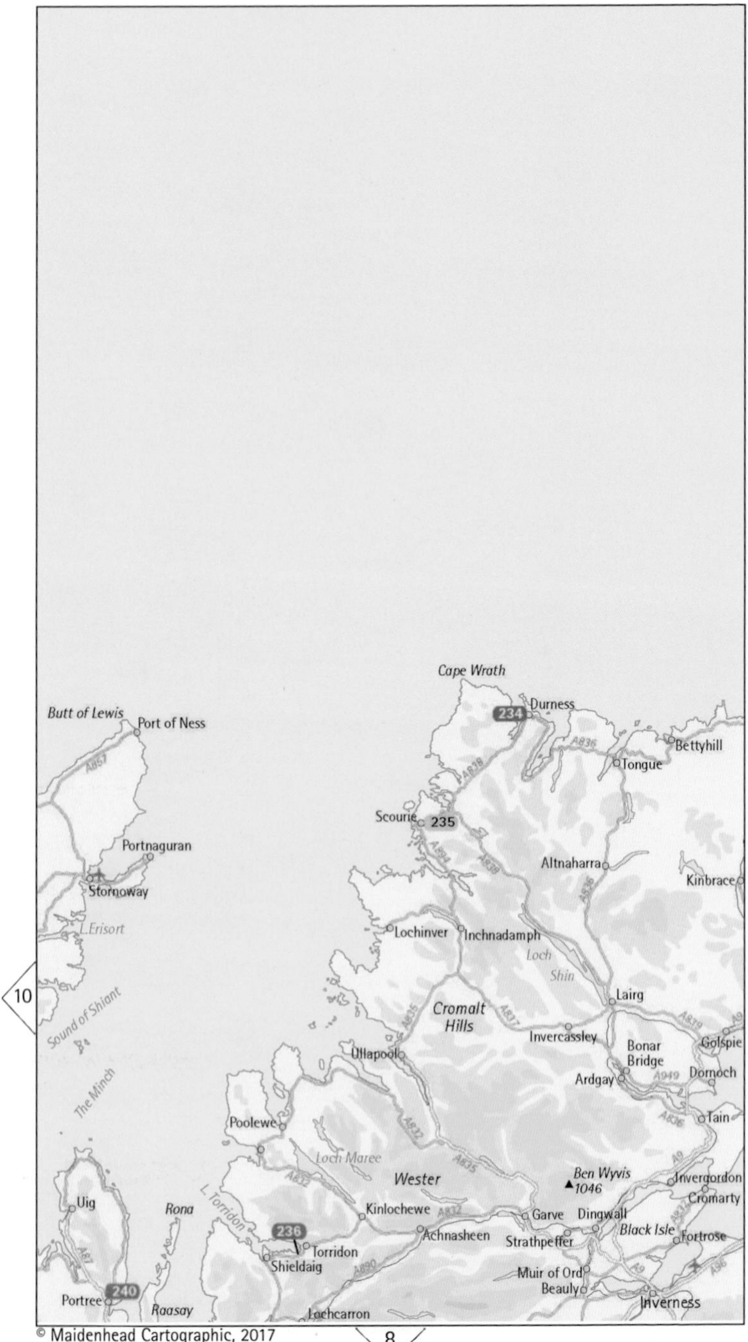
Cape Wrath
Durness
234
Butt of Lewis
Port of Ness
Bettyhill
Tongue
Scourie
235
Portnaguran
Stornoway
Altnaharra
Kinbrace
L.Erisort
Lochinver
Inchnadamph
Loch Shin
Lairg
10
Sound of Shiant
Cromalt Hills
Invercassley
Bonar Bridge
Golspie
Ullapool
Ardgay
Dornoch
The Minch
Poolewe
Tain
Loch Maree
Wester
Ben Wyvis 1046
Invergordon
Cromarty
Uig
Rona
L. Torridon
Kinlochewe
Garve
Dingwall
Black Isle
Fortrose
236
Achnasheen
Strathpeffer
Torridon
Shieldaig
Muir of Ord
Beauly
Portree
240
Raasay
Lochcarron
Inverness
8

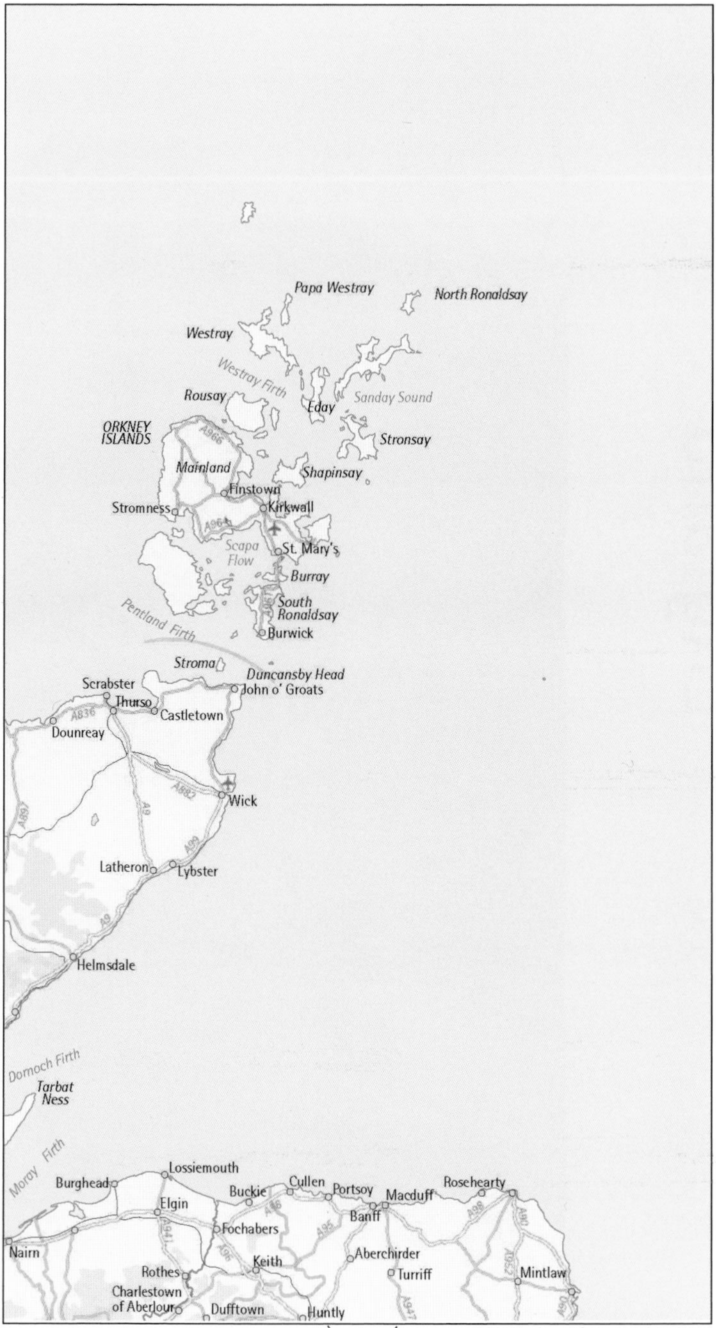
Papa Westray
North Ronaldsay
Westray
Westray Firth
Sanday Sound
Rousay
Eday
ORKNEY ISLANDS
A966
Stronsay
Mainland
Shapinsay
Finstown
Stromness
Kirkwall
A964
Scapa Flow
St. Mary's
Burray
South Ronaldsay
Pentland Firth
Burwick
Stroma
Duncansby Head
Scrabster
John o' Groats
Thurso
Castletown
A836
Dounreay
A882
Wick
A9
A897
A99
Latheron
Lybster
A9
Helmsdale
Dornoch Firth
Tarbat Ness
Moray Firth
Lossiemouth
Burghead
Cullen
Rosehearty
Buckie
Portsoy
Macduff
Elgin
Banff
A98
Fochabers
A95
A941
Nairn
Keith
Aberchirder
Rothes
Turriff
Mintlaw
Charlestown of Aberlour
Dufftown
Huntly

9

England

Photo: Borrowdale Gates, entry 40

Abbey Hotel

You're in the epicentre of Bath, just behind the abbey, in one of the prettiest quarters in town. Parade Gardens waits across the road, the river Avon pours over the weir at Pulteney Bridge, Bath rugby club stands on the far bank. As for the hotel, in summer you take to the terrace café for coffee and watch the world go by; in winter it turns into an après-ski bar for mince pies and mulled wine. Inside, the sitting room doubles as a contemporary art gallery, while wine glasses hang from the ceiling in the bar. There's lovely food in the restaurant, perhaps flame-grilled mackerel, slow-roasted venison, vanilla panna cotta with rhubarb sorbet; a pre-theatre menu is available from 5.30pm. Smart rooms upstairs have comfy beds, woollen throws and colourful headboards. Some are small, others big, all have iPads for room service, while most have stylish new bathrooms (ask for a room with one of these). Bath waits on your doorstep: rugby at the Rec, the Christmas market, the Roman Baths, Victoria Art gallery, all things thespian and plenty of Jane Austen. You're close to the station, too, so leave your car at home. *Pets by arrangement.*

Rooms	46 doubles, 10 twin/doubles: £105-£330. 6 family rooms for 4: £140-£295.
Meals	Lunch from £7.50. Dinner, 3 courses, £35-£45; pre-theatre menu £21.50-£27.50 (5.30pm-7pm). Sunday lunch £24-£28.
Closed	Never.
Directions	In central Bath, 100m south of the abbey, 100m west of the river. Parking in Southgate car park £13 a day.

Andrew Foulkes
Abbey Hotel
North Parade, Bath, BA1 1LF

Tel	+44 (0)1225 461603
Email	reception@abbeyhotelbath.co.uk
Web	www.abbeyhotelbath.co.uk

No. 15 Great Pulteney

You're on one of the grandest streets in Bath, once home to Jane Austen; the Holburne Museum of Art stands at one end, Robert Adam's famous Pulteney Bridge at the other. As for No.15, this is a quirky boutique hotel that doubles as a contemporary art gallery. You'll find a 'lost-earring' chandelier in reception, collections of curios all over the place, coffee machines hidden away in dolls' houses in bigger rooms. Bedrooms are sumptuous, some smaller, others enormous, each with an original piece of art on the walls. Several have exposed plaster walls, all have Hypnos mattresses and beautiful bathrooms, perhaps a copper basin, a walk-in shower or a claw-foot bath. Vast suites flood with light courtesy of high windows, while a help-yourself larder waits on the landing for popcorn, soft drinks and ice cream. There's a sitting-room bar for coffee and cocktails, then the stylish Café 15 for prosecco 'on the house' at breakfast and a feisty fish pie at lunch. The hotel is a work in progress: treatment rooms, a small garden and a car park are on the way. Good restaurants are a short stroll. Hard to beat.

Rooms	14 doubles: £140-£280. 8 suites for 2: £180-£400.
Meals	Lunch from £7.50. Afternoon tea £28. Restaurants within 500m.
Closed	Never.
Directions	M4, junc. 18; A46 south; A4 into Bath. Left with main flow for A36. Right at park, then 2nd right. Hotel on right.

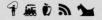

Jonathan Walker
No. 15 Great Pulteney
15 Great Pulteney Street, Bath, BA2 4BS
Tel +44 (0)1225 807015
Email enquiries@no15greatpulteney.co.uk
Web www.no15greatpulteney.co.uk

Villa at Henrietta Park

The Villa is one of those lovely boutique hotels that scores top marks across the board. You're pretty much in the middle of town, but hidden away on a quiet side street opposite a pretty park. Then, there's a batch of smart bedrooms, which have style and comfort in equal measure. Add to this lovely staff on hand to book restaurants, balloon flights or day trips to Stonehenge and you have a perfect base. You're a five-minute stroll from magnificent Pulteney Bridge; the station isn't much further, so leave your car at home. You can hire bikes in town, then follow the towpath along the canal out into the country. Back home, there's tea and cake on arrival, buck's fizz for breakfast, even bats and balls for children who want to go to the park. Breakfast – served in an airy dining room – is excellent: smoked salmon and free-range scrambled eggs, buttermilk pancakes, the full cooked works. Rooms vary in size, but all have excellent beds, pretty wallpaper and sparkling bathrooms. Good restaurants wait close by. Don't miss the Roman Baths or the Fashion Museum. There's off-street parking, too, a real boon. *Minimum stay: 2 nights at weekends.*

Rooms	9 doubles, 11 twin/doubles: £99–£325. 1 family room for 4: £175–£475. Singles from £89. Extra bed/sofabed £45 p.p.p.n.
Meals	Restaurant within 500m.
Closed	Christmas.
Directions	West into Bath on A4. Left into Cleveland Place (signed 'Through Traffic & University'). Over bridge, 2nd right and on right opposite park.

Caroline Browning
Villa at Henrietta Park
Henrietta Street, Bath, BA2 6LX

Tel	+44 (0)1225 466329
Email	enquiries@villahenriettapark.co.uk
Web	www.villahenriettapark.co.uk

The Queensberry Hotel & Olive Tree Restaurant

"No stilts, pogo sticks, space hoppers, flaming torches or whips in the bar." Such are the rules of the house, a nod in deference to the ninth Marquis of Queensberry, whose family built this street, and who wrote the rules of boxing in 1865. As for the hotel, it occupies four gleaming Georgian townhouses on a grand old street around the corner from the Royal Crescent. It's an extremely comfortable base, with an elegant sitting room, a snazzy bar, a beautiful courtyard garden and some of the best food in town. Potter about and find fresh flowers, contemporary art, the daily papers, kind staff on hand to help. Bedrooms come in different sizes, but all are full of their own delights: Vi Spring mattresses, stylish fabrics, bold colours, flat-screen TVs. Smaller rooms overlooking the garden are lovely – size doesn't matter here – though one of the suites does come with a chaise longue in its super-stylish bathroom. Chris Cleghorn's delicious food waits below, perhaps langoustine tails with cheddar gnocchi and basil or Anjou pigeon with celeriac, shallots and hazelnuts. Finish with a delicious chocolate and mandarin mousse served with stem ginger granita.

Rooms	16 doubles, 10 twin/doubles: £100-£300. 3 suites for 2: £260-£460. Extra bed/sofabed £25 p.p.p.n.
Meals	Bar meals from £6.95. Lunch, set menu (Fri-Sun), £26-£32.50. Dinner, 3 courses, £49.50. Tasting menu available, 5-7 courses, £58-£80.
Closed	Never.
Directions	Into Bath on A4 London Road to Paragon, then 1st right into Lansdown, 2nd left into Bennett Street & 1st right into Russel Street.

Laurence & Helen Beere
The Queensberry Hotel & Olive Tree Restaurant
Russel Street, Bath, BA1 2QF
Tel +44 (0)1225 447928
Email reservations@thequeensberry.co.uk
Web www.thequeensberry.co.uk

Bath Paradise House Hotel

The view here is sublime, a wide sweep across the city that's best observed on a sunny afternoon while tucking into afternoon tea in the garden. Not that you will spend your time looking out of the windows, even if most of the rooms do have the view: what you find inside is just as special. This is a hugely welcoming house with owners and staff who go out of their way to help you make the most of Bath. Downstairs, a smart sitting room has three arched windows framing the city and an airy breakfast room with Lloyd Loom furniture. Bedrooms are lovely, even the smallest, coveted by returning guests for its doors onto the terrace. Others are more substantial, especially those with bay windows that look the right way. You'll find four-posters, beautiful fabrics, warm colours, no clutter at all. Some have vast bedheads, others travertine bathrooms; bigger rooms have sitting areas, perhaps a claw-foot bath. Menu Gordon Jones, a very short stroll, is a top spot for dinner, while the occasional peal of bells comes from a nearby church. The Thermae Spa with its rooftop pool is a must. *Minimum stay: 2 nights at weekends.*

Rooms	3 doubles, 3 twins, 4 four-posters: £120-£175. 1 family room for 3: £130-£185. Singles £75-£120.
Meals	Restaurants in Bath 0.5 miles.
Closed	24-25 December.
Directions	From train station one-way system to Churchill Bridge. A367 exit from r'bout up hill; 0.75 miles, left at Andrews estate agents. Left down hill into cul-de-sac; on left.

David & Annie Lanz
Bath Paradise House Hotel
86-88 Holloway, Bath, BA2 4PX

Tel	+44 (0)1225 317723
Email	info@paradise-house.co.uk
Web	www.paradise-house.co.uk

Combe Grove Hotel

This fine old house sits above Bath in 70 acres of woodland and gardens with views that stretch south for miles over unblemished country. It was recently bought by the Elmhurst Foundation and plans are afoot to expand the spa into a centre for health and wellbeing, with retreats, talks and meditation. As for Combe Grove, it's not your average hotel, but a place to wind down and nourish the soul; you can have a massage, swim in two pools, join fitness classes from yoga to spin, book a personal trainer. There's a stylish bar serving fresh juices and homemade cakes, then an outside dining terrace, where you can play boules while waiting for your dinner. Big bedrooms in the main house have padded headboards and beautiful fabrics; garden rooms – most with terraces or balconies – have cool colours and fine walk-in showers. There's a spa with a sauna, a steam room and an indoor pool. Delicious food awaits in the muralled dining room, perhaps roasted courgettes and red quinoa, a 28-day, dry-aged ribeye, lavender meringues with Jersey cream. Bath waits for Christmas fairs and all things Jane Austen. *Minimum stay: 2 nights at weekends in summer.*

Rooms	28 doubles, 9 twin/doubles: £100-£280. 3 suites for 2: £250-£370. Singles from £90.
Meals	Lunch from £6. Dinner, 3 courses, about £35. Afternoon tea from £15.
Closed	Never.
Directions	South from Bath on A36. Right after 4 miles at Limply Stoke traffic lights. Up hill and on left after 0.5 miles.

Sharon Love
Combe Grove Hotel
Brassknocker Hill, Monkton Combe,
Bath, BA2 7HU

Tel +44 (0)1225 834644
Email hello@combegrove.com
Web www.combegrove.com

Cliveden House

Cliveden has no match in Britain, a country house of epic proportions that dates to 1605. It has been home to earls, dukes and one Prince of Wales, but it's best known for the Profumo affair, which almost sank a government; its famous pool is at your disposal. It sits in 376 acres of National Trust land with sublime gardens, marble fountains, sculptures by the dozen. You'll think you've arrived at Versailles and not without reason – the Astors bought Madame de Pompadour's drawing room and had it installed here! The Great Hall, a panelled masterpiece with vast portraits on its walls, is a fine spot for cocktails before dinner. Elsewhere, Corinthian columns, muralled ceilings and a dining room for ambrosial food, perhaps Orkney scallops, Anjou squab pigeon, rice pudding soufflé with Balvenie ice cream; there's a bistro in the old stables, too. Bedrooms, some in the main house, others in the wings, have huge beds, period art, white marble bathrooms. Some have hot tubs on private terraces, stately suites are vast, the riverside cottage is divine. Don't miss the pop-up cinema in the spa garden.

Rooms	18 doubles, 10 twin/doubles: £445-£800. 19 suites for 2: £865-£1,585. 1 cottage for 6: £2,055-£2,650. Extra bed £30 (no charge during school holidays).
Meals	Lunch from £8. Dinner, 3 courses, £55-£75. Tasting menu, 7 courses, £97.50. Sunday lunch £60. Afternoon tea, £37.
Closed	Never.
Directions	M4, junc. 7, north for Taplow. Left at 1st r'bout, right at 2nd (by Sainsbury's). Straight for 2.5 miles, right onto Cliveden Rd. Left at junction; drive on left.

Kevin Brooke
Cliveden House
Taplow, SL6 0JF

Tel +44 (0)1628 668561
Email reservations@clivedenhouse.co.uk
Web www.clivedenhouse.co.uk

Hurley House Hotel

For 250 years an inn has stood on this land. The current version is newly built and its delights are hard to miss: a cool bar with Chesterfield sofas in front of a wood burner; a panelled restaurant with intimate booths for two; bedrooms laden with comfort that stand peacefully away from the bar. You'll find excellent service, an informal feel, delicious food, an easy style that runs throughout. Gardens at the back look onto fields, the terrace comes with a barbecue that's busy in summer. The food is good, the kitchen headed by Michael Chapman, who had a Michelin star at his last restaurant and is keen to have one again. You might find blow-torched Brixham mackerel, Berkshire hogget with braised shoulder cannelloni, Yorkshire rhubarb mousse with stem ginger ice cream. Bedrooms have crisp fabrics, silky white cotton, half panelled walls, engineered wood floors. You get coffee machines, super-fast WiFi, then sparkling bathrooms with robes and power showers, perhaps a claw-foot bath; one room opens onto a terrace. Henley and Windsor are close. The road passes quietly at night.

Rooms	9 doubles, 1 twin/double: £170-£295.
Meals	Lunch from £7. Dinner, 3 courses, £35-£45.
Closed	Never.
Directions	A404(M) north from M4, junc. 8/9 or south from M40, junc. 4. Exit for Hurley, north at roundabout, on left after 500m.

Justin Ellis
Hurley House Hotel
Henley Road, Hurley, SL6 5LH
Tel +44 (0)1628 568500
Email hello@hurleyhouse.co.uk
Web www.hurleyhouse.co.uk

Artist Residence Brighton

At the top of a square, looking down to the sea, a cute hotel with an arty vibe. You're bang in the middle of Brighton with all the stuff you'd want on your doorstep: galleries, bars, the pier and the Brighton Pavilion. As for the hotel, good food, great staff, relaxed informality and a playful style are the hallmarks here. You get stripped boards, exposed brick walls, then an old garage door that slides back to reveal a chic restaurant with an open kitchen on display. In typical AR style, it's now one of the best places to eat in Brighton – delicious tasting menus that get you talking as well as eating. You'll find cool art, the odd wall clad in corrugated iron, even an ornamental drainpipe! Bedrooms come in different styles. Some have Pop Art murals, others come in Regency colours, a new batch are super-cool with baths in the room. Most have small, stylish shower rooms, one has a decked terrace. There's a quirky bar for cocktails, a ping pong table that doubles as a boardroom, then lunch in the front restaurant with views through big windows down to the sea. The beach waits below. *Minimum stay: 2 nights at weekends.*

Rooms	12 doubles, 5 twins: £95-£310. 1 suite for 6: £300-£360. 5 triples: £150-£250.
Meals	Breakfast £2.50-£8. Lunch from £7. Dinner, 4 courses, about £30. Restaurants within 500m.
Closed	Never.
Directions	A23 south into Brighton. Right at pier along seafront. Right after 1 mile into Regency Square. Hotel in northeast corner. Car park below square.

Charlie & Justin Salisbury
Artist Residence Brighton
33 Regency Square,
Brighton, BN1 2GG

Tel +44 (0)1273 324302
Email brighton@artistresidence.co.uk
Web www.artistresidencebrighton.co.uk

brightonwave

A small, friendly, boutique B&B hotel in the epicentre of trendy Brighton. The beach and the pier are a two-minute walk, the bars and restaurants of St James Street are around the corner. An open-plan sitting room/dining room comes in cool colours with big suede sofas, fairy lights in the fireplace and ever-changing art on the walls. Bedrooms at the front are big and fancy, with huge padded headboards that fill the wall and deluge showers in sandstone bathrooms. Those at the back may be smaller, but so is their price and they come with spotless compact showers; if you're out more than in, why worry? All rooms have fat duvets, white linen, flat-screen TVs and DVD/CD players; the lower-ground king-size has its own whirlpool bath and garden. Richard and Simon are easy-going and happy for guests to chill drinks in the kitchen (there are corkscrews in all the rooms). Breakfast, served late at weekends, offers pancakes, the full English or sautéed tarragon mushrooms on toast. Good food waits on your doorstep: Riddle and Finns, The Salt Rooms, an Italian restaurant up the road. Fabulous Brighton waits. *Children over 14 welcome.*

Rooms	3 doubles, 4 twin/doubles, 1 four-poster: £90-£190. Singles £74-£79.
Meals	Restaurants nearby.
Closed	1 week over Christmas & 2 weeks in January.
Directions	A23 to Brighton Pier roundabout at seafront; left towards Marina; 5th street on left. On-street parking vouchers £9 for 24 hours.

Richard Adams & Simon Throp
brightonwave
10 Madeira Place,
Brighton, BN2 1TN

Tel +44 (0)1273 676794
Email info@brightonwave.co.uk
Web www.brightonwave.co.uk

Drakes

Drakes has the lot: cool rooms, sea views and one of the best restaurants in town. It stands across the road from the beach, with the famous pier a three-minute walk. Inside, a cocktail bar doubles as reception, while a chic style has conquered all corners. Bedrooms are exemplary. Eleven have free-standing baths in the room, all have waffle bathrobes and White Company lotions, but what impresses most is the detail and workmanship. Handmade beds rest on carpets that are changed every year, contemporary plaster mouldings curl around ceilings like mountain terraces, and Vi-Spring mattresses, wrapped in the crispest linen, are piled high with pillows. Don't worry if you can't afford the best rooms; others may be smaller and those at the back have city views, but all are fantastic and the attic rooms are as cute as could be (one has a balcony). As for the food, it's some of the best in Brighton, perhaps seafood chowder with razor clams, marinated wild boar with a quince purée, pineapple soufflé with lime and tequila ice cream. The Lanes are close and packed with hip shops. Don't miss the Royal Pavilion.

Rooms	16 doubles, 1 twin/double: £120-£290. 1 suite for 2: £300-£360. 2 singles: £120-£160. Dinner, B&B from £92.50 p.p. Extra bed/sofabed £25 p.p.p.n.
Meals	Breakfast £7.50-£15. Lunch, 2-3 courses, £20-£25. Dinner, 2-3 courses, £34-£45. Chef's Taster menu £60.
Closed	Never.
Directions	M23 & A23 into Brighton. At seafront, with pier in front, turn left up the hill. Drakes on left after 300 yds.

Richard Hayes
Drakes
43-44 Marine Parade,
Brighton, BN2 1PE

Tel +44 (0)1273 696934
Email info@drakesofbrighton.com
Web www.drakesofbrighton.com

Bristol Harbour Hotel

You're in the heart of old Bristol, opposite St Nicholas' market, with Broad Quay at the bottom of the hill. As for this chic new hotel, it was once the home of two grand banks. The exterior stone work was modelled on the façade of St Mark's Library in Venice, but the interiors are just as good: a cool restaurant with high windows in one of the tiller's halls; a spectacular event space with 50 Corinthian columns in the other. There's a spa in the vaults which you enter through the door of an old safe, then a funky bar – once the bank manager's office – with gilded domes, ornate ceilings and flock wallpaper. Bedrooms come fully loaded: smart colours, fat mattresses, leather armchairs, decanters of sherry and gin. Bathrooms are a delight: walk-in showers, robes and White Company oils, perhaps a bath in the room. As for the Jetty Restaurant, expect fish and seafood in abundance, maybe fruits de mer and South Coast lobster; alternatively, try a twice-baked cheese soufflé, a rib-eye steak, a warm chocolate fondant with cherry ice cream. Bristol – often voted the coolest city in Britain – waits around you. *Minimum stay: 2 nights at weekends.*

Rooms	9 doubles: £155-£205. 10 twin/doubles: £155-£265. 3 suites for 2: £265-£655. Extra bed £20.
Meals	Lunch from £12.75. Dinner, 3 courses, £30-£40. Afternoon tea £15.95. Sunday lunch £19.95.
Closed	Never.
Directions	North over Bristol Bridge, up hill, then right onto Corn St (pedestrian access only); on right in 50m. Nearest car park on Fairfax St, Bristol BS1 3BB.

Grant Callaghan
Bristol Harbour Hotel
55 Corn St,
Bristol, BS1 1HT

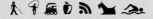

Tel +44 (0)117 203 4445
Email bristol@harbourhotels.co.uk
Web www.bristol-harbour-hotel.co.uk

Backwell House

Deep copper baths, fibre optic chandeliers, a snug cinema for Sunday afternoons, a chic up-cycled bar for cocktails – that's what you find at this gorgeous country-house hotel. It's all the result of a remarkable renovation that blends old and new to great effect, and wherever you go something beautiful catches the eye: a curved mahogany door, polished wood floors, classical and contemporary art. Views from the front door stretch out over rolling hills. At the back, a large kitchen garden climbs up to fields, beyond which woodland walks wait. Back inside, you find high ceilings, vast windows, period colours and hungry wood-burners. Lamps hang in the restaurant, where you dig into local or home-grown food, perhaps game terrine, spicy cod, sticky toffee pudding. Fabulous rooms wait above. Four at the back are smaller and come with planked bedheads and garden views. Those at the front are bigger, with king-size beds, copper baths, perhaps a walk-in shower; all have robes and smart TVs. An outdoor pool is coming soon; beehives, a biomass boiler, and a whisky bar all wait, as does vibrant Bristol. Don't miss it.

Rooms	8 doubles, 1 twin/double: £95-£245. Extra beds £40.
Meals	Lunch from £6.50 (Wed-Sat). Dinner, 3 courses, £22.50-£28. Sunday lunch from £17.50.
Closed	Never.
Directions	West from Bristol on A370 for 5 miles. Through Flax Burton and signed left after 500m.

Sawday's British Hotel Awards 2018

Favourite newcomer

Guy Williams
Backwell House
Farleigh Road,
Bristol, BS48 3QA

Tel	+44 (0)117 325 1110
Email	enquiries@backwellhouse.co.uk
Web	www.backwellhouse.co.uk

The Crown Inn

A thatched inn built of mellow stone that stands on the green in this pretty village. Paths lead out into open country and you can follow the river up to Fotheringhay, where Mary Queen of Scots lost her head. Back at the pub, warm interiors mix style and tradition to great effect. The bar has stone walls, ancient beams, flagstone floors and a roaring fire; in summer you decant onto the terrace and sip a pint of Black Sheep while watching village life pass by. Back inside, a beautiful new restaurant has recently appeared with golden stone walls, pale olive panelling and some very good food, anything from glazed ham and local eggs to oxtail lasagne, saddle of venison, sticky toffee tart with toffee sauce. You can also eat in the sitting-room bar on smart armchairs in front of another fire. Stylish bedrooms – some in the main house, others off the courtyard – are all different. You'll find smart colours, chic wallpapers, excellent bathrooms and good art. The bar hosts quiz nights, live music and the odd game of rugby on the telly, while on May Day there's a hog roast for the village fête.

Rooms	6 doubles, 2 twin/doubles: £73-£210. Singles from £55. Sofabed £30 per child per night.
Meals	Lunch & dinner £5-£25. Not Sun eve. Restaurant closed first week January.
Closed	Never.
Directions	A1(M), junc. 17, then A605 west for 3 miles. Right on B671 for Elton. In village left, signed Nassington.

Marcus Lamb
The Crown Inn
8 Duck Street, Elton,
Peterborough, PE8 6RQ
Tel +44 (0)1832 280232
Email inncrown@googlemail.com
Web www.thecrowninn.org

The Old Bridge Hotel

The Old Bridge is one of those places that mixes old-fashioned hospitality with contemporary flair, a template of excellence for others to follow. It's a big hit with the locals, who come for delicious food and exceptional wines, and it inspired the founders of Hotel du Vin, who were amazed how busy it was. Ladies lunch, businessmen chatter, kind staff weave through the throng. You can eat wherever you want: in the beautifully refurbished restaurant; on a sofa in the lounge; or sitting in a winged armchair in front of the fire in the bar. You feast on anything from homemade soup to rack of lamb (starters are available all day), while breakfast is served in a panelled morning room with Buddha in the fireplace. It's all the work of owners John and Julia Hoskins. Julia's interiors are dreamy, with style and comfort going hand in hand. Beautiful bedrooms have fresh colours, chic fabrics, crisp linen, padded bedheads. All have posh TVs and robes in excellent bathrooms, some of which overlook the river Ouse. John, a Master of Wine, has a wine shop in reception; you can taste before you buy (and you will).

Rooms	18 doubles, 1 twin, 3 four-posters: £125-£230. 2 singles: £99. Dinner, B&B £90-£130 p.p.
Meals	Lunch & dinner £5-£35.
Closed	Never.
Directions	A1, then A14 into Huntingdon. Hotel on southwest flank of one-way system that circles town.

John & Julia Hoskins
The Old Bridge Hotel
1 High Street, Huntingdon, PE29 3TQ
Tel +44 (0)1480 424300
Email oldbridge@huntsbridge.co.uk
Web www.huntsbridge.com

The Seafood Restaurant

In 1975 a young chef called Rick Stein opened a restaurant in Padstow. These days he has four more as well as a deli, a pâtisserie, a seafood cookery school and 40 beautiful bedrooms. Despite this success, his homespun philosophy has never wavered: buy the freshest seafood from fisherman on the quay, then cook it simply and eat it with friends. It is a viewpoint half the country seems to share – the Seafood Restaurant is now a place of pilgrimage – so come to discover the Cornish coast, walk on the cliffs, paddle in the estuary, then drop into this lively restaurant for a fabulous meal, perhaps black risotto with Cornish cuttlefish, grilled Padstow lobster with fine herbs, hot chocolate fondant with toasted marshmallow ice cream. Book in for the night and a table in the restaurant is yours, though flawless bedrooms are hard to leave. They are scattered about town, some above the restaurant, others at the bistro or just around the corner at St Petroc's House. All are immaculate. Expect the best fabrics, Vi-Spring mattresses, stunning bathrooms, the odd terrace with estuary views. *Minimum stay: 2 nights at weekends.*

Rooms	32 doubles, 8 twin/doubles: £120-£315.
Meals	Lunch £38.50. Dinner £58.50.
Closed	25-26 December.
Directions	A39, then A389 to Padstow. Follow signs to centre; restaurant on left opposite harbour car park.

Jill & Rick Stein
The Seafood Restaurant
Riverside, Padstow, PL28 8BY
Tel +44 (0)1841 532700
Email reservations@rickstein.com
Web www.rickstein.com/stay

Bedruthan Hotel & Spa

Bedruthan has the lot – stunning sea views, a couple of swimming pools, a spa with treatment rooms, then sitting rooms and restaurants galore. The most recent addition is a sensory spa garden offering seven steps to heaven: a salt scrub; a sauna; a cold bucket shower; a dip in the hot tub; a wet scrub; a visit to the sky garden; a second bite at the hot tub. Adults get the run of the place in school time, then children come in the holidays and slide down zip wires or sign up to surf school. Qualified staff look after younger children, who can paint, play, or jump into a cage of coloured balls while their parents snooze on sunbeds by the pool. There's a wood burner in the quiet sitting room, a cocktail bar that opens onto a terrace, then stylish bedrooms with retro colours and sparkling bathrooms. Some have separate rooms for children, others have terraces or sea views, a few overlook the car park. Younger children have early suppers, adults return later for a slap-up meal, perhaps guinea fowl, whole lemon sole, chilled strawberry soup with prosecco sorbet. The beach is a short stroll.

Rooms	38 twin/doubles: £135-£270. 27 suites for 4: £205-£490. 30 family rooms for 4: £175-£305. 6 singles: £75-£125. Dinner, B&B from £95 p.p.
Meals	Lunch from £6. Dinner £27.50-£32.50. Sunday lunch from £13-£24.50.
Closed	3 weeks in January.
Directions	On B3276 in Mawgan Porth.

Janie White
Bedruthan Hotel & Spa
Mawgan Porth,
Newquay, TR8 4BU

Tel +44 (0)1637 860860
Email stay@bedruthan.com
Web www.bedruthan.com

The Scarlet

The Scarlet does what few others can – this may be a super-cool design hotel with one of the loveliest spas in the land, but the service here is fantastic: friendly, attentive, ready to help. As for the hotel, it sits above the sea with a vast wall of glass in reception to frame the view. Outside, you'll find a hot tub in the garden from which you can stargaze at night; inside, there's a stylish restaurant that opens onto a decked terrace, where you scoff delicious Cornish food while gazing out to sea. Elsewhere, an open fire in the sitting room, a pool table in the library, then a cool bar for Cornish wines and ales. Exceptional bedrooms all have sea views, then balconies or terraces, private gardens or viewing pods. Expect organic cotton, oak floors from sustainable forests, perhaps a free-standing bath or a huge walk-in shower. As for the spa, you get tented treatment rooms, chill-out pods that hang from the ceiling, and then a couple of swimming pools flanked by sunbeds. Finally, the hotel is green to its core, with a biomass boiler, solar panels and state-of-the-art insulation. *Minimum stay: 2 nights at weekends.*

Rooms	21 doubles, 8 twin/doubles: £195-£405. 8 suites for 2: £270-£460. Dinner, B&B £140-£280 p.p.
Meals	Lunch, 3 courses, £24.50. Dinner, 3 courses, £45.50.
Closed	Rarely.
Directions	North from Newquay on B3276 to Mawgan Porth. Signed left in village halfway up hill.

Meeche Hudd
The Scarlet
Tredragon Road,
Mawgan Porth, TR8 4DQ

Tel	+44 (0)1637 861800
Email	stay@scarlethotel.co.uk
Web	www.scarlethotel.co.uk

Watergate Bay Hotel

Watergate Bay is one of those lovely Cornish landscapes where nature rules the roost, a world of sand, sea, sky and nothing but. The hotel sits directly above one of the best beaches in Cornwall – two miles long! They've really made the most of the views, with walls of glass in the café/bar – 'The Living Space' – a super swimming pool that gazes over the ocean and a smart terrace strewn with sun loungers. Outside, the hotel's surf school will kit you out to ride the waves; you can kite surf and paddle board, too, while beach polo and music festivals come in summer. Coastal light floods through the windows, there's a very comfortable sitting room with an open fire, then treatment rooms and a hot tub in the spa. Airy bedrooms – some with sea views, others with balconies – have jaunty seaside colours and spotless bathrooms. As for the food, you can eat in The Living Space or Zacry's – the grill, or walk 50 paces to the Beach Hut for a burger, or try Jamie Oliver's Fifteen. A great family hotel.

Rooms	47 twin/doubles: £160-£345. 2 suites for 2, 22 suites for 4: £255-£495. Singles £120-£268. Dinner, B&B £160-£335 p.p.
Meals	Lunch from £7. Dinner, 3 courses, £25-£38.
Closed	Never.
Directions	Leave A30 at Indian Queens & follow signs past Newquay Airport. Left at the T-junction; hotel in village.

Mark Williams
Watergate Bay Hotel
On the Beach,
Watergate Bay, TR8 4AA

Tel	+44 (0)1637 860543
Email	reservations@watergatebay.co.uk
Web	www.watergatebay.co.uk

Blue Hayes Private Hotel

The view from the terrace is magical, a clean sweep across the bay to St Ives. You breakfast here in good weather in the shade of a Monterey pine, as if transported back to the French Riviera circa 1950. As for the hotel, it's an unadulterated treat, mostly due to Malcolm, whose limitless generosity is stamped over every square inch. Few hotels close for four months to redecorate every winter, but that's the way things are done here – this may explain why so many guests book for the following year when checking out. The house shines in ivory white with the occasional dash of colour from carpets and curtains. A wall of glass in the bar weatherproofs the view. Big rooms are gorgeous, two with balconies, one with a terrace, all with sparkling bathrooms. Light suppers are on hand, though a short stroll into town leads to dozens of restaurants; Alfresco on the harbour is excellent and torches are provided for the journey back. Penzance, Zennor, Tate St Ives and a host of beaches are all close. There's folk and jazz for the September festival, a great time to visit. A true one-off. *Children over 10 welcome.*

Rooms	4 doubles: £200-£280. 1 suite for 2: £260-£280. 1 triple: £210-£240. Singles £130-£150.
Meals	Packed lunch by arrangement. Light suppers from £12. Restaurants within walking distance.
Closed	1 November to 28 February.
Directions	A30, A3074 to St Ives. Through Lelant & Carbis Bay, over mini-r'bout (Tesco on left) & down hill. On right immediately after garage on right.

Malcolm Herring
Blue Hayes Private Hotel
Trelyon Avenue,
St Ives, TR26 2AD

Tel	+44 (0)1736 797129
Email	info@bluehayes.co.uk
Web	www.bluehayes.co.uk

Trevose Harbour House

This super-chic B&B started life in the 1850s as a fisherman's cottage. These days it's a small-scale version of a design hotel, pristine from top to toe. It's all the result of an 18-month renovation and it sits in the old town, a two-minute stroll from the beach. Inside, form and function rule the roost: everything is beautiful, nothing superfluous. Interiors come in blue and white with fresh flowers, local art, beautiful ceramics, and umbrellas in case it rains. Downstairs is open-plan – a small sitting room with an honesty bar concealed in a '50s dresser on one side, on the other a dining room where you sit at Ercol tables and tuck into an excellent breakfast under hanging lamps. Rooms have Hypnos beds, crisp linen, beautiful fabrics and impeccably upholstered armchairs. Three have sea views, all have smart TVs, coffee machines and hot-water bottles. Bathrooms are flawless: underfloor heating, walk-in showers, white robes and Neal's Yard oils, perhaps a claw-foot bath. Outside, labyrinthine lanes lead to the harbour, sandy beaches, art galleries and lots of delicious restaurants. Dreamy. *Minimum stay: 2 nights. Children over 12 welcome.*

Rooms	5 doubles: £155-£245. 1 suite for 2: £235-£275. Singles from £145.
Meals	Restaurants 500m.
Closed	Mid-November to mid-March
Directions	A30 west, then A3074 for St Ives. Park in station car park above beach (£7.50 for 24 hours). At car park entrance take steps down to the Warren. House on left after 300m.

Angela & Olivier Noverraz
Trevose Harbour House
22 The Warren, St Ives, TR26 2EA

Tel	+44 (0)1736 793267
Email	hi@trevosehouse.co.uk
Web	trevosehouse.co.uk

The Gurnard's Head

This quirky inn is one of the best, the sort of place you'd hope to find at the end of the road. Outside, the wild west coast weaves up to St Ives; secret beaches appear at low tide, cliffs tumble down to the water, wild flowers streak the land pink in summer. Inside, it's earthy, warm, stylish and friendly, with rustic interiors, colour-washed walls, stripped wooden floors and fires at both ends of the bar. Logs are piled high in an alcove, maps and art hang on the walls, books fill every shelf; if you pick one up and don't finish it, take it home and post it back. Cosy rooms have warm colours and the odd antique, then Vi-Spring mattresses, crisp white linen, colourful throws and Roberts radios. Downstairs, you can scoff delicious food in the bar, the restaurant or out in the garden in good weather. Tasty snacks wait – pork pies, crab claws, half a pint of Atlantic prawns – as does more substantial fare, maybe grilled sardines, Cornish lamb with root vegetables, roasted apples and pears. Picnics can be arranged, there's bluegrass folk music in the bar most weeks. Dogs are very welcome.

Rooms	3 doubles: £120-£135. 4 twin/doubles: £120-£185. Dinner, B&B £170-£235 (based on double occupancy). Camp bed available for children, £25 per night for children 5+ years, free for under 5's.
Meals	Lunch from £12. Dinner, 3 courses, £25-£35. Sunday lunch from £13.
Closed	Christmas.
Directions	On B3306 between St Ives & St Just, 2 miles west of Zennor, at head of Treen village.

Charles & Edmund Inkin
The Gurnard's Head
Zennor, St Ives, TR26 3DE

Tel +44 (0)1736 796928
Email enquiries@gurnardshead.co.uk
Web www.gurnardshead.co.uk

The Old Coastguard

The Old Coastguard stands on the water in one of Cornwall's loveliest coastal villages. It's a super spot and rather peaceful – very little has happened here since the Spanish sacked the place in 1595. It's owned by Edmund and Charles Inkin, brothers who are past masters at running lovely small hotels; warm colours, attractive prices, great food and kind staff are their hallmarks. Downstairs, the airy bar and the dining room come together as one, the open plan informality creating a great space to hang out. You get smart rustic tables, earthy colours, local ales and local art, then wooden floors and a crackling fire. Drop down a few steps to find a bank of sofas and a wall of glass framing sea views; in summer, doors open onto a decked terrace, a lush lawn, then the coastal path weaving down to the small harbour. Bedrooms hit the spot: warm colours, excellent beds, robes in fine bathrooms, books everywhere. Most have the view, eight have balconies. Don't miss dinner: salt and pepper monkfish, fish stew with mussels, chocolate mousse with tonka bean ice cream. Dogs are very welcome.

Rooms	10 doubles: £140-£225. 3 twin/doubles: £140-£225. 2 suites for 2: £180-£225. 1 family room for 4: £180-£195. Dinner, B&B £192.50-£277.50 (based on double occupancy).
Meals	Lunch from £6. Dinner, 3 courses, about £30. Sunday lunch from £12.50.
Closed	1 week in early January.
Directions	Take coastal road west from Penzance, through Newlyn and on to Mousehole. Hotel on left after car park.

Charles & Edmund Inkin
The Old Coastguard
The Parade, Mousehole,
Penzance, TR19 6PR

Tel +44 (0)1736 731222
Email bookings@oldcoastguardhotel.co.uk
Web www.oldcoastguardhotel.co.uk

Chapel House

Everything here is beautiful – a stunning Georgian house; views over town that stretch out to sea; bedrooms and bathrooms to rival those in the best designer hotels. All of which would be blossom in the wind without Susan, whose instinct to go the extra mile knows no restraint – this is not just a gorgeous house, but a friendly one, too. Outside, smart red bricks give some idea of the grandeur within, but step inside and find a contemporary wonderland that took two years to refurbish. The hall is home to works from the Newlyn School of Art, the double sitting room has high ceilings, an open fire and a baby grand piano, doors lead onto a balcony and down to a courtyard garden, a peaceful retreat in summer. Bedrooms are hard to fault: white walls soak up the light; handmade beds give a fine night's sleep; super-chic wet rooms have fabulous showers. One has a wood-burner in the room, another a bath under a glass roof that slides open. There's much more: delicious kitchen suppers at weekends; cooking demonstrations with local chefs; great restaurants along the road. The magical west coast waits.

Rooms	6 doubles: £150-£200. Singles from £100. Extra beds available for children under 12 free; 12+ £10.
Meals	Kitchen suppers on Friday/Saturday £22-£25 (or on request during the week). Sunday lunch from £14.50.
Closed	Rarely.
Directions	Along harbourside with sea on left. Opp. docks, right into Quay St. Up hill; on right opp. St Mary's Church. Parking can be tricky.

Susan Stuart
Chapel House
Chapel Street,
Penzance, TR18 4AQ

Tel +44 (0)1736 362024
Email hello@chapelhousepz.co.uk
Web chapelhousepz.co.uk

Artist Residence Penzance

This groovy little bolthole is hard to beat – distinctly hip, deliciously quirky and overflowing with colour and style. The house dates to 1600 and stands on the ley line that connects St Michael's Mount to Stonehenge. You're in the old town, a stone's throw from the harbour. It's a very friendly place, open all day, with staff who stop to chat. Interiors overflow with originality: the restaurant has pop art on walls of wood, there's a wood-burner in the playful sitting-room bar, then ping pong and table football in the garden, where you'll find a beach bar, a smokehouse and the odd barbecue. Bedrooms come in different shapes and sizes. Some have brightly colourful murals, others have wood-clad walls and up-cycled furniture. All have super-comfy beds, Roberts radios, white linen and toppers to assure a good night's sleep. Gorgeous new rooms have sliding doors to flawless bathrooms, one has a copper bath and a balcony. You get American pancakes, local eggs and homemade granola at breakfast, perhaps home-smoked ribs or roasted sea bass for dinner. Don't miss St Michael's Mount or the wild west coast. *Minimum stay: 2 nights at weekends in summer.*

Rooms	8 doubles, 2 twin/doubles: £75-£180. 1 family room for 5: £110-£235. 2 triples: £125-£200. 1 cottage for 6: £125-£440. 1 suite for 2-3, with extra sofabed, kitchenette & sitting room: £200-£350. Singles £75-£125.
Meals	Lunch & dinner from £6; 3 courses £20-£25.
Closed	Never.
Directions	A30 into Penzance. Follow signs to town centre; up main street; left at top; keep left and on right after 200m.

Charlie & Justin Salisbury
Artist Residence Penzance
20 Chapel Street,
Penzance, TR18 4AW

Tel	+44 (0)1736 365664
Email	penzance@artistresidence.co.uk
Web	artistresidencecornwall.co.uk

Hell Bay

Ship-wrecked sailors would refuse rescue from this chic island bolthole. It's a castaway's dream with sandy beaches, pretty coves and this wonderfully spoiling hotel. It's a friendly place with lovely staff who look after you with great warmth. As for the unremitting luxuries, you'll find a convivial bar for games and island ales, a sun-trapping terrace for afternoon tea and a smart restaurant for the best food on the Scillies: perhaps tandoori scallops, wild sea bass, prune and Armagnac soufflé with Earl Grey ice cream. Airy bedrooms have a beach-house feel with seaside colours, wicker sofas, robes in sparkling bathrooms, then a terrace or balcony with big sea views. There's a swimming pool with sun loungers and a treatment room, and the impossibly popular Crab Shack for seafood delights in summer. The hotel is very family friendly, children can gather eggs from the coop and have them cooked for breakfast, there's a mini-golf course, a games room, babysitters are on hand. Elsewhere: other islands to explore, kayaks to hire, gardens to visit. Dogs are very welcome. A honeymooner's heaven.

Rooms	25 suites for 2: £250-£640. Price includes dinner for 2. Singles from £160. Under 2's free.
Meals	Lunch from £6.95. Dinner included; non-residents £45.
Closed	November to mid-March.
Directions	Ship from Penzance, or fly to St Mary's from Exeter, Newquay or Land's End; boat transfer to Bryher.

Philip Callan
Hell Bay
Bryher,
Isles of Scilly, TR23 0PR

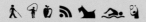

Tel +44 (0)1720 422947
Email contactus@hellbay.co.uk
Web www.hellbay.co.uk

Bay Hotel

The Bay Hotel sits under a vast Cornish sky with views to the front of nothing but sea – unless you count the beach at low tide, where buckets and spades are mandatory. Outside, the lawn rolls down to the water. In summer it's sprinkled with deckchairs and loungers, so grab a book or snooze in the sun and listen to the sounds of the seaside. Airy interiors are just the ticket: stylish and homely with lots of comfort. The view follows you around, keeping your eyes glued to the horizon. There are flowers everywhere, cavernous sofas, a small bar for pre-dinner drinks. Bedrooms vary in size, one has its own balcony, all have sea views (some from the side). Expect tongue-and-groove panelling, coastal colours, super bathrooms and smart TVs. As for the food, lobsters come courtesy of the next door neighbour, while the steak and kidney pie never leaves the menu. Try moules marinières, sea bass with samphire, lemon and caper butter, Grand Marnier crème brûlée. Harbour cruises often bump into dolphins, seals, even basking sharks. You're on the coastal path, so bring your boots, but don't miss afternoon tea. *Children over 4 welcome. Pets by arrangement.*

Rooms	6 doubles, 5 twin/doubles: £140-£280. 3 suites for 2: £250-£330. Price includes dinner for 2. Singles from £105.
Meals	Lunch from £6. Dinner included; non-residents £34.95.
Closed	November – February.
Directions	A3083 south from Helston, then left onto B3293 for St Keverne. Right for Coverack after 8 miles. Down hill, right at sea, second on right.

Ric, Gina & Zoe House
Bay Hotel
North Corner, Coverack,
Helston, TR12 6TF

Tel	+44 (0)1326 280464
Email	enquiries@thebayhotel.co.uk
Web	www.thebayhotel.co.uk

The St Mawes Hotel

Seaside chic, a relaxed feel and some lovely rooms are the hallmarks of this small hotel that stands on the water with big views out to sea. Outside, pavement tables are popular with people watchers, though those in the know head upstairs to the balcony, an unbeatable spot on a good day. Inside, you'll find sofas in front of the fire in the bar, then rugs on stripped boards in the colourful first-floor dining room. The food is delicious, the best local produce cooked simply, perhaps calamari with lemon mayonnaise, a crispy goat's cheese pizza, peanut butter brownie with vanilla ice cream. Beautiful bedrooms are scattered about, some with beautiful timber frames. Those at the front have watery views, all have chic fabrics, colourful art, the best beds, then robes and walk-in showers; a couple have baths, too. You'll find driftwood art scattered about, well-kept ales waiting at the bar and a small cinema for films if it rains. The harbour stands directly outside, so hire kayaks and explore the bay. Don't miss the castle or cricket on the beach. The coastal path starts at the front door. *Minimum stay: 2 nights at weekends.*

Rooms	7 twin/doubles: £140-£290. Cots/children in parents' room from £25.
Meals	Continental breakfast included; full English £8. Lunch from £6.50. Dinner, 3 courses, £25-£30.
Closed	Never.
Directions	Hotel on the seafront in town. Parking available in public car park (£6 a day in high season, free in low season).

Ben Bass
The St Mawes Hotel
Harbourside,
St Mawes, TR2 5DW

Tel +44 (0)1326 270170
Email stay@stmaweshotel.com
Web www.stmaweshotel.com

Driftwood Hotel

The position here is hard to beat. Views head out to sea, the coastal path sweeps you away, six acres of beautiful gardens drop down to a private beach. As for Driftwood, Cape Cod meets Cape Cornwall, with chic, airy interiors at every turn. The sitting room is stuffed with beautiful things – fat armchairs, deep sofas, driftwood lamps, a smouldering fire – while big windows pull in the view. In summer, doors open onto a decked terrace for breakfast and lunch in the sun. Bedrooms are gorgeous (all but one have sea views), some big, others smaller, one in a cabin halfway down the cliff with its own terrace. All have the same clipped elegance: warm colours, big beds, white linen, wicker chairs. There are Roberts radios on bedside tables, cotton robes in excellent bathrooms. Drop down to the dining room for a Michelin-starred dinner, perhaps lemon sole with crystallised ginger, local lamb with candied pine nuts, spiced pineapple with lemongrass and lime. There are high teas for children, hampers for beach picnics and rucksacks for walkers. On clear nights the sky is full of stars. Brilliant. *Minimum stay: 2 nights at weekends.*

Rooms	13 doubles, 1 twin: £185-£290. 1 cabin for 4: £235-£275. Dinner, B&B £125-£155 p.p.
Meals	Dinner, 3 courses, £65, Vegetarian tasting menu £75. Tasting menu, 8 courses, £85; 10 courses, £105.
Closed	Early December to early February.
Directions	From St Austell, A390 west. Left on B3287 for St Mawes; left at Tregony on A3078 for approx. 7 miles. Signed left down lane.

Paul & Fiona Robinson
Driftwood Hotel
Rosevine, Portscatho,
Truro, TR2 5EW

Tel	+44 (0)1872 580644
Email	info@driftwoodhotel.co.uk
Web	www.driftwoodhotel.co.uk

The Rosevine

This is a chic, family-friendly hotel on the Roseland Peninsula, where views shoot over the semi-tropical garden, then splash into the sea. Children are welcomed with open arms, but guests of all ages have fun here. There's a playroom for kids (Xbox, plasma screen, DVDs and toys), then an elegant sitting room for adults, with sofas in front of a wood-burner. You'll find an indoor pool, a beach at the bottom of the lane, then nearby ferries to whisk you across to Falmouth for the day. Come back to a good dinner. Little ones eat at a children's tea party at 5pm; parents come in later for some tasty food, perhaps crispy squid, Cornish lamb, chocolate brownie with vanilla ice cream; babysitters can be arranged. Suites and apartments have small kitchenettes (fridge, sink, dishwasher, microwave/oven), so you can cook for yourself, too. Some rooms are open-plan, others have separate bedrooms with bunk beds for children, those on the ground floor open onto terraces. Expect stylish interiors, flat-screen TVs, crisp linen and robes in good bathrooms. St Mawes is close. *Pets by arrangement.*

Rooms	6 suites for 5 with kitchenette: £189-£379. 2 apartments for 5 with kitchenette: £169-£369. 7 studios for 2 with kitchenette: £139-£229.
Meals	Lunch from £8. Dinner £29-£36. Afternoon tea £4-£15.
Closed	January.
Directions	From A390 south for St Mawes on A3078. Signed left after 8 miles. Right at bottom of road; just above beach.

Martin Nicholas
The Rosevine
Rosevine, Portscatho,
Truro, TR2 5EW

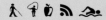

Tel +44 (0)1872 580206
Email info@rosevine.co.uk
Web www.rosevine.co.uk

Trevalsa Court Hotel

Trevalsa stands at the top of a cliff with sea views stretching far and wide. In summer life spills into the garden, where you can loll about in deck chairs and fall asleep in the sun. Explorations wait, too. You can nip down to a sandy beach or pick up the coastal path, which passes at the end of the garden; turn left for cliff walks or right for Mevagissey, an old fishing village of mazy lanes. Don't stray too far. Trevalsa is a treat: friendly, stylish, gently spoiling. Inside, the view is weatherproofed by an enormous mullioned window in the sitting room, a great place to watch a storm spin past. You'll find a small bar with colourful art, then a panelled dining room for tasty food, perhaps mussels steamed in Cornish cider, a bavette steak with a peppercorn sauce, treacle tart with brown bread ice cream. Bedrooms have warm colours, crisp linen, padded headboards, the odd wall of paper. Most have sea views, bigger rooms have sofas, all have excellent bathrooms, the suite has a private deck. Breakfast is served on the terrace in summer. The Lost Gardens of Heligan and St Mawes are close.

Rooms	7 doubles, 5 twin/doubles: £125-£275. 1 suite for 2: £205-£295. 2 singles: £70-£120. Dinner, B&B from £85 p.p. Extra bed/sofabed £20-£60 p.p.p.n.
Meals	Dinner £31-£38.
Closed	20 November to 10 February.
Directions	B3273 from St Austell signed Mevagissey, through Pentewan to top of the hill, left at the x-roads, over mini r'bout. Hotel on left, signed.

Susan & John Gladwin
Trevalsa Court Hotel
School Hill, Mevagissey,
St Austell, PL26 6TH

Tel +44 (0)1726 842468
Email stay@trevalsa-hotel.co.uk
Web www.trevalsa-hotel.co.uk

The Old Quay House Hotel

You drop down the hill, weave through narrow lanes, then pull up at this boutique hotel which started life as a seaman's mission. It's a lovely spot, with the estuary lapping behind the house and a waterside terrace for summer dining; at breakfast you can watch local boats zipping past. Inside, stylish bedrooms have goose down duvets, colourful fabrics and smart wicker furniture, then lovely bathrooms with white robes, the odd claw-foot tub, perhaps a walk-in shower. Most rooms look the right way, eight have balconies (some tiny), the view from the penthouse suite is hard to beat. Downstairs, good food waits in the restaurant, so slink onto the terrace for a cocktail, then dig into some excellent local fare, perhaps oysters with red wine shallots, lobster thermidor with salad and fries, espresso crème brûlée with cinnamon beignets. Fowey is enchanting, bustles with life and fills with sailors for the August Regatta. If you want to escape, you can take the ferry across to Polruan where Daphne du Maurier lived, then walk over to spectacular Lantic Bay for a picnic lunch on the beach. *Minimum stay: 2 nights in high season.*

Rooms	5 doubles, 5 twin/doubles: £145-£285. 1 suite for 2: £335. Singles from £105.
Meals	Lunch (Easter-October) about £15. Dinner £30-£37.50.
Closed	Rarely.
Directions	Entering Fowey, follow one-way system past church. Hotel on right where road at narrowest point, next to Lloyds Bank. Nearest car park 500m.

Martin Nicholas
The Old Quay House Hotel
28 Fore Street,
Fowey, PL23 1AQ

Tel	+44 (0)1726 833302
Email	info@theoldquayhouse.com
Web	www.theoldquayhouse.com

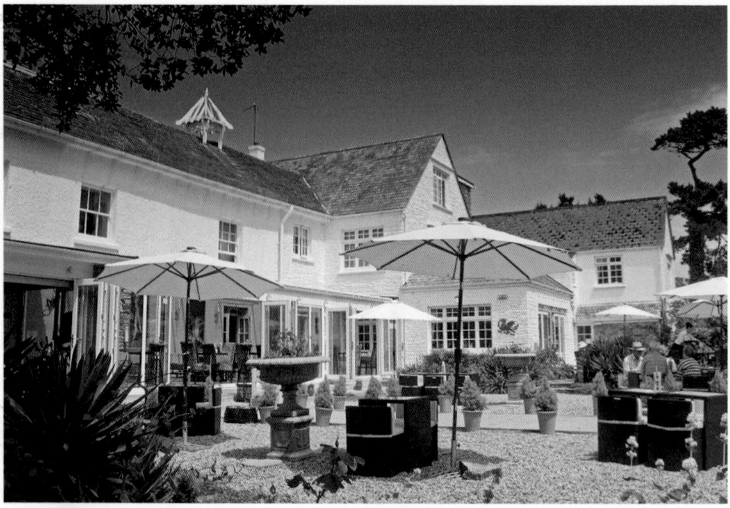

Talland Bay Hotel

The position here is magical. First you plunge down rollercoaster lanes leaving the world behind, then you arrive at this lovely hotel and find a rather good view – a vast carpet of sea that shoots off to the horizon. Pine trees stand guard on one side, an old church crowns a hill on the other, then two acres of lawns roll down to a ha-ha before the land tumbles down to the bay. In summer, loungers and croquet hoops appear on the lawn, and you can nip down to a beach café for lunch by the water. Back at the hotel there's a conservatory brasserie, a sitting room bar and a roaring fire in the half-panelled dining room. You'll find art on the walls, polished flagstones, a terrace for afternoon tea. Follow the coastal path over the hill, then return for a good dinner, perhaps roasted scallops with caramelised orange, loin of venison with chestnut purée, lemongrass panna cotta with peach sorbet. Bedrooms have warm colours, vast beds, beautiful linen, the odd panelled wall. One has a balcony, a couple open onto terraces, all have lovely bathrooms. Gardens, beaches and the coastal path wait. *Pets by arrangement.*

Rooms	15 twin/doubles: £120-£240. 4 suites for 2: £200-£280. 3 cottages for 2: £160-£240. Dinner, B&B £95-£180 p.p.
Meals	Lunch from £5.50. Sunday lunch £21.50-£25. Afternoon tea from £6. Dinner: brasserie from £12.95; restaurant £36-£42.
Closed	Never.
Directions	From Looe A387 for Polperro. Ignore 1st sign to Talland. After 2 miles, left at x-roads; follow signs.

Stephen Waite
Talland Bay Hotel
Porthallow,
Looe, PL13 2JB

Tel +44 (0)1503 272667
Email info@tallandbayhotel.com
Web www.tallandbayhotel.co.uk

Augill Castle

Augill is a one-off, a folly castle in beautiful country. It may look grand, but it's anything but – Simon and Wendy run their home with a rod of pure sponge. It's wonderfully informal and children love it. There are no uniforms, no rules, you just come to kick off your shoes and relax. You can do this in various places: on sofas in front of the fire in the hall; by a grand piano in the music room; in the honesty bar that opens onto a terrace; or in the cinema in the old potting shed. Breakfast is served communally in a vast dining room under a fine, ornate ceiling – local bacon, eggs from resident hens, homemade breads and jams. Elsewhere, panelled walls, roaring fires, books, art and antiques. Colourful bedrooms are all different. Some are enormous, one has a wardrobe in the turret, you'll find big bathrooms, bold colours and vintage luggage. Cottages are good for families and there's lots for children to do – dressing up boxes, five acres of gardens, a treehouse and playground, too. The Dales and the Lakes are close, but sybarites may just want to stay put. You can come to get married, too. *Minimum stay: 2 nights at weekends.*

Rooms	8 doubles, 2 four-posters: £160-£220. 1 suite for 2: £200-£240. 6 cottages for 4: £220-£300. Singles from £100.
Meals	Dinner £25-£30. Supper platters £15. Afternoon tea £18. Children's high tea £10.
Closed	Never.
Directions	M6 junc. 38; A685 thro' Kirkby Stephen. Before Brough right for South Stainmore; signed on left in 1 mile. Kirkby Stephen station 3 miles.

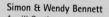

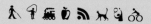

Simon & Wendy Bennett
Augill Castle
South Stainmore,
Kirkby Stephen, CA17 4DE
Tel +44 (0)17683 41937
Email enquiries@stayinacastle.com
Web www.stayinacastle.com

The Black Swan

A lovely small hotel in the middle of a pretty village that's surrounded by blistering country. It's all things to all men – a smart restaurant, a lively bar, pretty rooms – and very dog-friendly. A stream runs through the big garden, where you can eat in good weather; free-range hens live in one corner. Inside, chic country interiors fit the mood perfectly. You get fresh flowers, tartan carpets, games and books galore. There's a bar for local ales, a sitting-room bar with an open fire, but the hub of the hotel is the bar in the middle, where village life gathers. You can eat wherever you want – there's an airy restaurant, too – so dig into delicious country fare, with meat from the hills around you, perhaps a tasty home-made soup, Galloway beef and root vegetable stew, sticky toffee pudding with vanilla ice cream. Pretty bedrooms are fantastic for the money. Expect warm colours, beautiful linen, smart furniture, super bathrooms; one suite has a wood-burner. Stunning walking waits, the Lakes and Dales are close, children and dogs are welcome. A very happy place.

Rooms	5 doubles, 1 twin/double: £85-£115. 4 suites for 2: £120-£145. 6 annexes for 2: £105-£150. Singles £75-£140. 3 double bell tents available.
Meals	Lunch from £4.50. Dinner, 3 courses, £25-£30.
Closed	Never.
Directions	Off A685 between M6 junc. 38 & A66 at Brough.

Louise Dinnes
The Black Swan
Ravenstonedale,
Kirkby Stephen, CA17 4NG

Tel +44 (0)15396 23204
Email enquiries@blackswanhotel.com
Web www.blackswanhotel.com

Askham Hall

Askham is a dream, one of the loveliest houses in the Lakes. It's a Grade I-listed manor house with a 12th-century peel tower, but grand as it is, Charlie grew up here and it retains the feel of home, making it a delightfully informal base. Expect contemporary art and open fires, a beautiful drawing room with an honesty bar, a small spa with an outdoor pool, then a café for lunch and gardens that open to the public. The hall sits in 40 acres of prime Cumbrian grazing land with paths that follow a river into glorious parkland. It's all part of the Lowther estate, where Charlie rears his own meat for Richard Swale's kitchen. As for the food, it's out of this world, ambrosial stuff that makes you want to move in permanently. You might find Askham pork cheek and barbecued hock, rough fell lamb with wild garlic risotto, Yorkshire rhubarb tart with brown butter ice cream; a kitchen garden and two polytunnels provide much for the table. Chic bedrooms have a cool country-house style (Prince Philip loved his). Some are vast, one has a tented bathroom, others have views to Knipe Scar. One of the best.

Rooms	11 twin/doubles: £150-£260. 4 suites for 2: £250-£320. Extra bed/sofabed £35 p.p.p.n.
Meals	Lunch from £9. Dinner, 3 courses, £50. Tasting menu, 5 courses, £65.
Closed	Sundays & Mondays. January to early February.
Directions	M6, junc. 39, then A6 north. Askham signed left after 7 miles. In village.

Charlie Lowther
Askham Hall
Askham, CA10 2PF

Tel +44 (0)1931 712350
Email enquiries@askhamhall.co.uk
Web www.askhamhall.co.uk

Another Place – The Lake

This is a fantastic renovation of a fine old Lakeland hotel. It sits on Ullswater in 18 acres of beautiful grounds that roll down to the lake. Both house and water offer lots to do. You can swim in the lake, jump into a sailing boat, or hire a paddle board and set off to explore. If that sounds too energetic, then hang out at the hotel, where you'll find sofas to sink into and a swimming pool, where walls of glass frame the view. The main house dates to 1714 and comes with ornate ceilings, marble fireplaces, the odd panelled wall. Potter about and find an airy restaurant for lovely food, a library with books and games, then sofas and banquettes in the 'living space,' where you can chill out by the fire, stop for lunch or spin onto the terrace for drinks in the sun. There's a gym, a hot tub, a sauna and treatment rooms, then forest school for kids. Rooms, some coolly traditional, others warmly contemporary, have fine beds, bold colours, the best linen, robes in smart bathrooms. Most have the view, some have baths that look the right way. There's a kitchen garden and a croquet lawn, too. *Minimum stay: 2 nights at weekends.*

Rooms	28 twin/doubles: £160-£205. 12 suites for 2: £207-£305. Singles from £120. Extra bed from £40.
Meals	Lunch from £7. Dinner, 3 courses, £40.
Closed	Never.
Directions	M6, junc. 40, west 1 mile on A66, then south on A592 for Watermillock. Signed on left after 5 miles.

Alison Mathewson
Another Place – The Lake
Watermillock,
Penrith, CA11 0LP

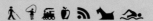

Tel +44 (0)1768 486442
Email life@another.place
Web www.another.place/the-lake

Howtown Hotel

Welcome to Howtown, a world lost in time on a lane that goes nowhere on the quiet side of Ullswater. The position here is heavenly – water, mountain, field and sky – one of the best in the Lakes. The house sits in its own hamlet, dates to 1640, and has been welcoming guests for 117 years, a licensed farmhouse that has passed though five generations of the same family, who still run sheep and cattle on 400 acres of Lakeland fell. Inside, the past lives on: a panelled bar, William Morris wallpaper, smouldering coal fires, wall clocks and lots of brass. Homely bedrooms upstairs have simple pleasures: good beds, sheets and blankets, toile throws, fabulous views. Most are en suite, three have bathrooms one step across the landing. Dinner is old-school – you're summoned by a gong – then served at oak tables with a beautiful dresser at one end of the dining room. The food is a joy, perhaps Stilton soufflé, loin of venison, steamed marmalade pudding; there's a walkers' café and a locals' bar, too. David has an amphibious car for the odd lake cruise. Walks start from the front door. Matchless. *No email – phone enquiries only.*

Rooms	8 doubles; 3 twin/doubles each with separate bathroom: £208. 1 single sharing shower room: £104. 2 cottages for 5, 2 cottages for 7: £420-£800 per week. Price includes dinner for 2.
Meals	Lunch from £4.50. Packed lunches £8.50. Dinner included in room price; non-residents £33. Sunday lunch £20.
Closed	10 November to mid March.
Directions	South from Pooley Bridge with Ullswater on right. Hotel on left after 4 miles.

Jacquie & David Baldry
Howtown Hotel
Ullswater,
Penrith, CA10 2ND

Tel +44 (0)17684 86514
Web www.howtown-hotel.co.uk

The Cottage in the Wood

This lovely restaurant with rooms is a great base for the northern Lakes. You're on the side of Whinlatter Pass with views that shoot off to a chain of Lakeland peaks – pre-dinner drinks on the terrace are hard to beat. Inside, chic interiors are just the ticket: the sitting room has a fire that burns on both sides, there are books and games to keep you amused, then windows galore in the restaurant. Rooms – some bigger, others smaller – have excellent beds, crisp linen and sparkling bathrooms. One in the eaves has a claw-foot bath, four have mountain views, the garden room has its own terrace. There's lots to do – lakes to visit, hills to climb, cycle trails to follow. Whatever you do, come back to Liam's fantastic food. His six-course tasting menu is a big draw; highlights include seaweed broth, langoustine with grapefruit, sweetbreads with wild garlic, fennel with olive oil jam. There's a drying room for walkers, secure storage for bikes, a burn that tumbles down the hill. Night skies amaze, red squirrels and woodpeckers visit the gardens. Two-night, midweek breaks are a steal and include dinner. *Minimum stay: 2 nights at weekends.*

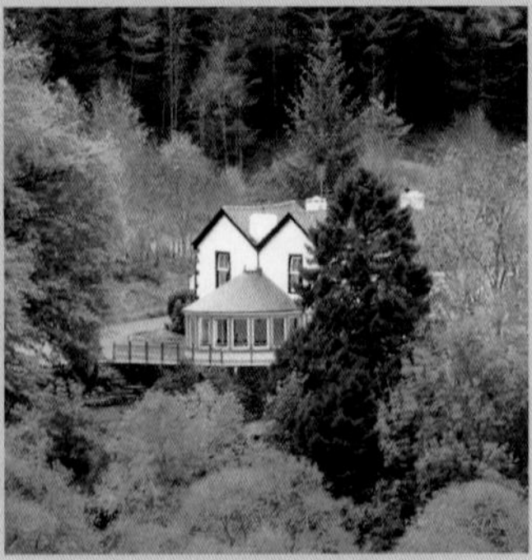

Rooms	5 doubles, 3 twin/doubles: £110-£175. 1 suite for 2: £190-£205. Dinner, B&B from £100 p.p.
Meals	Lunch £35 (Thur-Sat). Dinner, 3 courses, £45; 6-course tasting menu £65. Not Sunday night.
Closed	January. Mondays.
Directions	M6 junc. 40, A66 west to Braithwaite, then B5292 for Lorton. On right after 2.5 miles (before visitor centre).

Kath & Liam Berney
The Cottage in the Wood
Braithwaite,
Keswick, CA12 5TW

Tel +44 (0)17687 78409
Email relax@thecottageinthewood.co.uk
Web www.thecottageinthewood.co.uk

Borrowdale Gates

If you want deep peace, spectacular landscapes and a slice of luxury in a stylish hotel, you'll find it here. This is Borrowdale, an unchanged corner of the rural idyll, "the loveliest square mile in Lakeland" to quote Alfred Wainwright. High peaks encircle you, sheep graze the fields, the river Derwent meanders past. The view from the top of High Seat is one of the best in the Lakes, with Derwentwater sparkling under a vast sky. Lowland walking is equally impressive: long or short, high or low, Borrowdale delivers. At the end of the day roll back to this lovely hotel. Big windows downstairs frame majestic views. You get binoculars, the daily papers, afternoon tea in front of roaring fires or out on the terrace in summer. Bedrooms are great value for money, with warm colours, super beds, smart bathrooms, a sofa if there's room. Some open onto terraces, several have small balconies, all have the view. As for the restaurant, a wall of glass looks out over the village and beyond, a fine spot for a good meal, perhaps hand-dived scallops, fell-bred lamb, lemon tart with cassis sorbet.

Rooms	18 twin/doubles: £214-£256. 3 suites for 2: £246-£276. 4 singles: £97-£113. Price includes dinner.
Meals	Light lunches from £8. Dinner included; non-residents £34.50-£43. Afternoon tea from £15. Sunday lunch £25.
Closed	3-19 January.
Directions	M6 to Penrith, A66 to Keswick, then B5289 south for 4 miles. Right at humpback bridge, through Grange, hotel on right.

Ross Harper
Borrowdale Gates
Grange-in-Borrowdale,
Keswick, CA12 5UQ

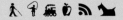

Tel +44 (0)1768 777204
Email hotel@borrowdale-gates.com
Web www.borrowdale-gates.com

The Eltermere Inn

This gorgeous Lakeland inn, once a Georgian farmhouse, seems lost to the world, yet it's only a couple of miles from Grasmere. In summer you sit in the peaceful garden with local sheep for company and dig into afternoon tea; in winter you order a pint at the bar, then roast away in front of the fire. You're in an unblemished village that stands back from the water in the shade of forested hills. Inside, beautiful interiors are part country house, part village inn. There's a grand piano in the dining room, ancient slate floors in the bar, then big sofas and lovely art in the airy sitting room. Upstairs, stylish rooms have warm colours, local wool carpets, big beds and Mulberry fabrics. Some have padded window seats, others are open to the eaves, all have excellent bathrooms; those at the front have views of lake and mountain. Downstairs, you find the sort of food you hanker for after a day in the hills, perhaps bouillabaisse, steak and kidney pie, banana gingerbread with toffee sauce. Walks start from the front door, there's croquet on the lawn, they even grow their own vegetables. *Minimum stay: 2 nights at weekends.*

Rooms	12 twin/doubles: £149-£295. Singles £134-£280.
Meals	Lunch from £5.50. Dinner, set menu £18.50-£28.50; 3 courses à la carte £30-£35. Afternoon tea from £13.25.
Closed	Christmas.
Directions	West from Ambleside for 3 miles on A593, then right for Eltermere. On right in village.

Mark & Ruth Jones
The Eltermere Inn
Elterwater,
Ambleside, LA22 9HY

Tel	+44 (0)15394 37207
Email	info@eltermere.co.uk
Web	www.eltermere.co.uk

Cedar Manor Hotel

A small country house on the edge of Windermere with good prices, pretty interiors and delicious food. Jonathan and Caroline love their world and can't stop spending money on it. They recently added a smart terrace at the front, turned the office into another sitting room, and put in a couple of fancy bathrooms. This 17th-century house was once home to a retired vicar, hence the ecclesiastic windows. Outside, an ancient cedar of Lebanon shades the lawn. Inside, cool colours and an easy style flow throughout. The big sitting room doubles as the bar and comes in browns and creams with sofas and local art. Bedrooms – some warmly traditional, others nicely contemporary – have Zoffany fabrics, Lloyd Loom wicker and flat-screen TVs; most have fancy bathrooms, some have big views, the bathroom in the coach house suite is out of this world. You eat in a pretty dining room with views to the front or on the terrace in good weather, perhaps goat's cheese with a red pepper mousse, local lamb with tarragon gnocchi, warm chocolate fudge cake with real-ale ice cream. All things Windermere are on your doorstep. *Minimum stay: 2 nights at weekends.*

Rooms	7 doubles, 1 twin: £145-£225. 2 suites for 2: £245-£425. Singles from £105.
Meals	Dinner £32.95-£39.95.
Closed	Rarely.
Directions	From Windermere A591 east out of town for Kendal; hotel on right, next to church, before railway station.

Jonathan & Caroline Kaye
Cedar Manor Hotel
Ambleside Road,
Windermere, LA23 1AX

Tel +44 (0)15394 43192
Email info@cedarmanor.co.uk
Web www.cedarmanor.co.uk

Gilpin Hotel

Gilpin is one of the loveliest places to stay in the country, simple as that. It's a family affair and delivers at every turn, its staff delightful, its Michelin-starred food divine, its interiors a treasure trove of beautiful things. It is one of those rare places that never stands still and recent additions include five stunning spa lodges above a small lake and a second restaurant serving pan-Asian food. Despite all this, it remains an English country-house hotel. A cool elegance flows throughout with smouldering fires, Zoffany wallpapers, gilded mirrors, flowers everywhere. An elegant sitting room runs into a chic bar, where doors open onto a terrace for Pimm's in the sun; magnolia trees, cherry blossom and a copper beech wait in the 20-acre garden. Bedrooms are divine: crisp linen, smart fabrics, robes in beautiful bathrooms. The garden suites have hot tubs, the spa suites have saunas, too. As for the food, it's all whisked up by Hrishikesh Desai (who won Chefs On Trial to land his job), perhaps chilli-glazed lobster, spring lamb with masala sauce, Yorkshire rhubarb with Bergamot panna cotta. *Minimum stay: 2 nights at weekends*

Rooms	8 doubles, 12 twin/doubles: £335-£385. 6 suites for 2: £385-£535. 5 suites for 2 (spa lodges on the lake): £635. Price includes dinner for 2. Special rates for three or more nights.
Meals	Dinner included; non-residents £65. Lunch from £6.50. Sunday lunch £35. Afternoon tea from £22.50.
Closed	Never.
Directions	M6 junc 36, A591 north, then B5284 west for Bowness. On right after 5 miles.

John, Christine, Barnaby & Zoe Cunliffe
Gilpin Hotel
Crook Road,
Windermere, LA23 3NE

Tel	+44 (0)15394 88818
Email	hotel@thegilpin.co.uk
Web	www.thegilpin.co.uk

Gilpin Lake House & Spa

Every now and then you bump into a hotel that knocks your socks off, and Gilpin Lake House does just that. This is an extraordinary little place – a tiny spa hotel with only six rooms, luxury and intimacy entwined. It sits away from the crowds, lost in the hills, surrounded by acres of peaceful woodland. A swimming pool in the house opens onto a terrace, where you can flop on sun loungers and gaze down on the lake. Elsewhere, beautiful gardens, a rowing boat, and a second hot tub overlooking fells. There's a treatment room in a cabin that sits above the lake, then a snug boathouse with a deck on the water. As for the house, you'll find sofas in front of a wood-burner in the sitting room, then lake views, books galore and beautiful art. Spoiling rooms have fabulous beds, sofas and armchairs, beautiful fabrics, bathrooms that don't hold back. Breakfast is served wherever you want: in your room, on the terrace, in the conservatory. There's a chauffeur to whizz you up to their sister hotel for dinner (included in the price). Come with friends and take the whole place. Out of this world. *Minimum stay: 2 nights at weekends; 3 at bank holidays & Easter. Children over 7 welcome.*

Rooms	6 twin/doubles: £495-£605. Price includes dinner for 2 at Gilpin Hotel, chauffeur included!
Meals	Dinner included; non-residents £65. Lunch from £6.50. Sunday lunch £35. Afternoon tea from £22.50.
Closed	Never.
Directions	B5284 west for Bowness. Left at Wild Boar pub, right through village and straight ahead for 2 miles. Keep right at fork and on left.

John, Christine, Barnaby & Zoe Cunliffe
Gilpin Lake House & Spa
Crook,
Windermere, LA8 8LN

Tel +44 (0)15394 88818
Email hotel@thegilpin.co.uk
Web www.thegilpin.co.uk/lake-house

Linthwaite House

It's not just the view that makes Linthwaite so special, though Windermere sparkling half a mile below with a chain of peaks rising beyond does grab your attention. There's loads to enjoy here – 14 acres of gardens and grounds, a fantastic terrace for sunny days and interiors that go out of their way to pamper your pleasure receptors. The house itself is beautiful, one of those grand Lakeland Arts & Crafts wonders, with original woodwork and windows in all the right places. Logs are piled high by the front door, fires smoulder, sofas wait in the conservatory sitting room, where big views loom. Country-house bedrooms are coolly uncluttered with warm colours, chic fabrics, hi-tech gadgetry, fabulous bathrooms. Those at the front have lake views, a couple have hot tubs, you can stargaze from one of the suites. Downstairs, ambrosial food waits in the dining rooms (one is decorated with nothing but mirrors), perhaps seared tuna with pickled ginger, chargrilled pigeon with beetroot purée, caramelised banana tart with peanut butter ice cream. Sunbeds wait on the terrace. Fabulous. *Minimum stay: 2 nights at weekends.*

Rooms	21 doubles, 5 twin/doubles: £306-£454. 4 suites for 2: £492-£684. Price includes dinner for 2.
Meals	Lunch, 3 courses, from £24.95. Dinner included; £58 for non-residents.
Closed	Rarely.
Directions	M6 junc. 36. A590 north, then A591 for Windermere. Left at roundabout onto B5284. Past golf course and hotel signed left after 1 mile.

Nic Crow
Linthwaite House
Crook Road, Bowness-on-Windermere,
Windermere, LA23 3JA

Tel	+44 (0)15394 88600
Email	stay@linthwaitehouse.com
Web	www.linthwaitehouse.com

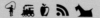

The Punch Bowl Inn

This gorgeous inn is hard to beat. You're in the hills above Windermere in a pretty village encircled by lanes that defeat most tourists. It's deeply rural with ten-mile views down the valley and a church next door; there's a bench to drink in the view, bell ringers practise on Friday mornings, the occasional bride glides out in summer. As for the Punch Bowl, it was rescued from neglect, renovated beautifully, and now sparkles, a stylish mix of old and new. Outside, honeysuckle and roses ramble on stone walls. Inside, rustic elegance runs throughout: Farrow & Ball colours, rugs on wood floors, sofas in front of the wood-burner. Arthur Bridgeman Quin's ambrosial food is a big draw, perhaps Lancashire cheese soufflé, Cumbrian venison with smoked beetroot, banana soufflé with vanilla ice cream. Chic bedrooms hit the spot, with beautiful linen, pretty fabrics and Roberts radios. Excellent bathrooms have double-ended baths, separate showers and white robes. Four have the view, the suite is enormous, smaller rooms are nicely priced. There's a terrace for lunch in the sun, too.

Rooms	5 doubles, 2 twin/doubles, 1 four-poster: £105-£235. 1 suite for 2: £235-£305. Singles from £85.
Meals	Lunch from £5. Dinner, 3 courses, £30-£35.
Closed	Never.
Directions	M6 junc. 36, A590 for Newby Bridge. Right onto A5074, right for Crosthwaite after 3 miles. Pub on southern flank of village, next to church.

Richard Rose
The Punch Bowl Inn
Crosthwaite,
Kendal, LA8 8HR

Tel +44 (0)15395 68237
Email info@the-punchbowl.co.uk
Web www.the-punchbowl.co.uk

Inspected & Selected Sawday's British Hotel Awards 2018

Fabulous food

The Masons Arms

The Masons is a Lakeland institution, an ancient inn lost in blissful country. You're on the side of a hill with 15-mile views across a quilt of fields to Scout Scar; in summer, pub life decants onto a beautiful terrace – a sitting room in the sun – where window boxes and flowerbeds tumble with colour. The inn dates to the 16th century and is impossibly pretty. The bar is gorgeous, with low ceilings, wavy beams, flagged floors and roaring fires, then splendid local ales to quench your thirst. Rustic elegance upstairs comes courtesy of stripped floors, country rugs and red walls in the first-floor dining room, so grab a window seat for fabulous views and dig into local fare, perhaps cheese soufflé, haunch of venison, toffee and banana sundae. Rooms (in the main house) and cottages (off the courtyard, great for families) are a steal. All have comfort and style in spades. You'll find lovely beds, pretty fabrics and super bathrooms; several have private terraces, too. As befitting a community local, events are often on the menu: live music, a food market, even the odd busker. Cartmel Priory is close. *Minimum stay: 2 nights at weekends.*

Rooms	5 apartments for 2: £85-£140. 1 cottage for 4, 1 cottage for 6: £110-£175. Travel cots/extra beds from £10.
Meals	Breakfast & lunch from £4.95. Bar meals from £9.95. Dinner, 3 courses, £25-£30. Sunday lunch from £12.95.
Closed	Never.
Directions	M6 junc. 36; A590 west, then A592 north. 1st right after Fell Foot Park. Straight ahead for 2.5 miles. On left after sharp right-hand turn.

John & Diane Taylor
The Masons Arms
Strawberry Bank, Cartmell Fell,
Grange-over-Sands, LA11 6NW

Tel +44 (0)15395 68486
Email info@masonsarmsstrawberrybank.co.uk
Web www.masonsarmsstrawberrybank.co.uk

Aynsome Manor Hotel

A small country house with a big heart. It may not be the grandest place in the book but the welcome is genuine, the peace is intoxicating and the value unmistakable. From the front, a long sweep across open meadows leads south to Cartmel and its priory, a view that has changed little in 800 years. The house, a mere pup by comparison, dates to 1512. Step in to find red armchairs, a grandfather clock and a coal fire in the hall. There's a small bar for a dram at the front and a cantilever staircase with cupola dome that sweeps you up to a first-floor drawing room, where panelled windows frame the view. Downstairs, you eat under a wildly ornate ceiling with Georgian colours and old portraits on the walls. You get lovely country cooking, too: French onion soup, roast leg of Cumbrian lamb, rich chocolate mousse served with white chocolate sauce. Bedrooms are simple, spotless, cosy and colourful. Some have views over the fields, one may be haunted, all have good bathrooms. Staff are lovely, nothing is too much trouble, kippers with lemon at breakfast are a treat. Windermere and Coniston are close.

Rooms	5 doubles, 4 twins, 1 four-poster: £90-£125. 2 family rooms for 4: £90-£150. Dinner, B&B from £75 p.p.
Meals	Packed lunches by arrangement £9.50. Dinner, 4 courses, £33.
Closed	Christmas.
Directions	From M6 junc. 36 take A590 for Barrow. At top of Lindale Hill follow signs left to Cartmel. Hotel on right 3 miles from A590.

Christopher & Andrea Varley
Aynsome Manor Hotel
Aynsome Lane, Cartmel,
Grange-over-Sands, LA11 6HH

Tel +44 (0)15395 36653
Email aynsomemanor@btconnect.com
Web www.aynsomemanorhotel.co.uk

The Sun Inn

This fine old inn sits between the Dales and the Lakes in an ancient market town, one of the prettiest in the north. It backs onto St Mary's churchyard, where wild flowers flourish, and on the far side you'll find "the fairest view in England" to quote John Ruskin. Herons fish the river, lambs graze the fells beyond, a vast sky hangs above. Turner came to paint it in 1825 and benches wait for those who want to linger. As for the Sun, it does what all good inns do, it looks after you in style. It dates to 1670 and started life as a butcher's. Inside, there's lots of pretty old stuff – stone walls, rosewood panelling, wood-burners working overtime – then warm colours, fresh flowers and the daily papers. You'll find leather banquettes, local art and dining-room chairs from Cunard's Mauretania, so eat in style, perhaps goats cheese with honey, hogget with onion jam, banana parfait with chocolate sorbet. Rooms have good beds, smart fabrics, robes in spotless bathrooms. Parking permits come with your room and can be used far and wide. Market day is Thursday, dogs are welcome, don't miss Sunday lunch. *Minimum stay: 2 nights at weekends.*

Rooms	9 doubles, 2 twin/doubles: £135-£189. Dinner, B&B from £90 p.p. Singles from £85. Extra beds £20.
Meals	Lunch from £6 (not Mon). Dinner, £21-£34. Sunday lunch from £14.50.
Closed	Never.
Directions	M6 junc. 36, then A65 for 5 miles following signs for Kirkby Lonsdale. In town centre.

Iain & Jenny Black
The Sun Inn
6 Market Street, Kirkby Lonsdale,
Carnforth, LA6 2AU

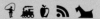

Tel +44 (0)15242 71965
Email email@sun-inn.info
Web www.sun-inn.info

Cavendish Hotel

The Cavendish has impeccable credentials. It stands on the Chatsworth Estate, is owned by the Duke and Duchess of Devonshire, and Chatsworth House itself stands a mile or two across the fields from this smart hotel. All of which means you can rise leisurely, have a good breakfast, then follow paths across to one of Britain's loveliest houses; fine gardens and a jaw-dropping art collection wait. As for the hotel, it has a warm country-house feel: sofas in front of the fire in the sitting room; art from the 'big house' on the walls; afternoon tea served on the lawn in summer. Bedrooms mix pretty florals with period colours and smart fabrics. None are small, all but one have country views, some are rather swanky. You get robes in excellent bathrooms, a sofa if there's room, crisp linen on comfy beds. Downstairs you can eat in the Garden Room or out on its terrace (more informal, lovely views) or in the elegant restaurant, perhaps hand-dived scallops, haunch of venison, Granny Smith apple crumble. Outside, the Peak District waits for walkers, while fishing can be arranged.

Rooms	20 doubles, 2 twins: £189-£219. 1 suite for 2: £300. 1 family room for 4: £169-£219. Singles from £133.
Meals	Continental breakfast £9.70; full English £18.90. Lunch from £6. Dinner £30-£45.
Closed	Never.
Directions	M1 junc. 29, A617 to Chesterfield, A619 to Baslow. On left in village.

Philip Joseph
Cavendish Hotel
Church Lane, Baslow,
Bakewell, DE45 1SP

Tel +44 (0)1246 582311
Email info@cavendish-hotel.net
Web www.cavendish-hotel.net

The Peacock at Rowsley

The Peacock sits between two fine houses, Haddon Hall and Chatsworth House. You can follow rivers up to each – the Derwent to Chatsworth, the Wye to the hall – both a stroll through beautiful parkland. As for the hotel, it was built in 1652 and was home to the steward of Haddon. Inside, old and new mix gracefully: mullioned windows, hessian rugs, aristocratic art, then striking colours that give a contemporary feel. You'll find Mouseman tables and chairs in the restaurant, where French windows open onto the terrace. Elsewhere, a fire smoulders in the bar every day, the daily papers wait in the sitting room, the garden lawn runs down to the river. Stylish bedrooms have crisp linen, good beds, Farrow & Ball colours, the odd antique; one has a bed from Belvoir Castle. Good food waits in the restaurant, with meat and game from the estate, perhaps venison terrine, roast partridge, Bakewell tart with buttermilk ice cream. There's afternoon tea in the garden in summer and you can fish both rivers, with day tickets available from reception. Guests also receive a discount on entry to Haddon Hall. *Minimum stay: 2 nights at weekends.*

Rooms	10 doubles, 2 four-posters: £205-£310. 1 suite for 2: £250-£310. 2 singles: £130-£145.
Meals	Lunch from £4.50. Dinner £60. Sunday lunch £22.50-£29.50.
Closed	Rarely.
Directions	A6 north through Matlock, then to Rowsley. On right in village.

Laura Ball
The Peacock at Rowsley
Bakewell Road, Rowsley,
Matlock, DE4 2EB

Tel	+44 (0)1629 733518
Email	reception@thepeacockatrowsley.com
Web	www.thepeacockatrowsley.com

Loyton Lodge

You get the impression the tiny lanes that wrap around this small estate act as a sort of fortification, one designed to confuse invaders and protect this patch of heaven. And heaven it is – 280 acres of rolling hills and ancient woodland, with wild flowers, pristine rivers, strutting pheasants and the odd red deer commuting across the fields. It's England circa 1964 with nothing but birdsong to break the peace and glorious walks that start at the front door. As for Loyton, it's a great little base for a night or two deep in the hills. It mixes contemporary interiors with an old-school feel – roaring fires, comfy sofas, wonderful art, even a snooker room. Bedrooms have warm colours and smart fabrics, perhaps a sleigh bed or a claw-foot bath, then books and robes and crisp white linen. Breakfast is a treat – bacon and sausages from home-reared pigs, eggs from estate hens – and there's dinner by arrangement, perhaps local asparagus, lemon sole, walnut and fruit crumble. Take the whole house and bring the family or come for the odd night of live jazz. Exmoor waits, as do good local restaurants.

Rooms	7 doubles, 2 twin/doubles, 1 twin: £95-£130. Singles from £80. Extra beds £20 (under 12s free).
Meals	Dinner, 3 courses, about £30, by arrangement.
Closed	Rarely.
Directions	A396 north from Tiverton to Bampton, then right onto B3227. After 1 mile, left for Loyton. Over x-roads, left at hill. Lodge on right after 0.5 mile.

Isobel, Sally & Angus Barnes
Loyton Lodge
Morebath, Tiverton, EX16 9AS

Tel	+44 (0)1398 331051
Email	thelodge@loyton.com
Web	www.loyton.com

The Old Rectory Hotel Exmoor

A gorgeous small hotel in the hills above the Exmoor coast. The road from Lynton is a great way in, through woods that cling to a hill with the sea below. As for the Old Rectory, it's a mini Gidleigh Park, charming from top to toe. Three acres of spectacular gardens wrap around you, only birdsong disturbs you, though Exmoor deer occasionally come to drink from the pond. Inside, Huw and Sam continue to lavish love and money in all the right places. Their most recent addition is a beautiful orangery with smart sofas, warm colours and doors onto the garden for afternoon tea in the sun. Interiors are lovely: Farrow & Ball colours, the odd stone wall, a cute little sitting room, fresh flowers and books everywhere. Bedrooms are just as good with big beds, crisp linen, cool colours and beautiful bathrooms. You'll find digital radios, flat-screen TVs and the odd leather sofa, too. Spin into the restaurant for an excellent meal, perhaps Ilfracombe crab, Exmoor duck, strawberry champagne trifle. Afternoon tea 'on the house' is served in the garden in good weather.

Rooms	3 doubles, 4 twin/doubles: £205-£245. 4 suites for 2: £260-£275. Price includes dinner for 2.
Meals	Dinner, 4 courses, included in price; non-residents £35.
Closed	November – March.
Directions	M5 junc. 27, A361 to South Molton, then A399 north. Right at Blackmoor Gate onto A39 for Lynton. Left after 3 miles, signed Martinhoe. In village, next to church.

Huw Rees & Sam Prosser
The Old Rectory Hotel Exmoor
Martinhoe, Parracombe,
Barnstable, EX31 4QT

Tel	+44 (0)1598 763368
Email	info@oldrectoryhotel.co.uk
Web	www.oldrectoryhotel.co.uk

Northcote Manor

A small country-house hotel built on the site of a 15th-century monastery. Those who want peace in deep country will find it here. You wind up a one-mile drive, through a wood that bursts with colour in spring, then emerge onto a lush plateau of rolling hills; the view from the croquet lawn drifts east for ten miles. As for the house, wisteria wanders along old stone walls, while the odd open fire smoulders within. There's an airy hall that doubles as the bar, a country-house drawing room that floods with light, and a sitting room where you gather for pre-dinner drinks. Super food waits in a lovely dining room, steps lead down to a pretty conservatory, doors open onto a gravelled terrace for summer breakfasts with lovely views. Bedrooms are no less appealing – more traditional in the main house, more contemporary in the garden rooms. Expect padded bedheads, mahogany dressers, flat-screen TVs, silky throws. You can walk your socks off, then come home for a good meal, perhaps white Cornish crab, local lamb, strawberry soufflé with vanilla ice-cream. Exmoor and North Devon's coasts are close.

Rooms	9 twin/doubles, 7 suites for 2: £170-£280. Singles from £120. Dinner, B&B from £130 p.p.p.n. Extra bed/sofabed £15-£25 p.p.p.n.
Meals	Light dishes from £6.50. Lunch £22.50-£25.50. Dinner, 3 courses, £45. Tasting menu £90. Sunday lunch £28.50.
Closed	Never.
Directions	M5 junc. 27, A361 to S. Molton. Fork left onto B3227; left on A377 for Exeter. Entrance 4.1 miles on right, signed.

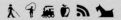

Richie Herkes
Northcote Manor
Burrington,
Umberleigh, EX37 9LZ
Tel +44 (0)1769 560501
Email rest@northcotemanor.co.uk
Web www.northcotemanor.co.uk

The Lamb Inn

This 16th-century inn is adored by locals and visitors alike. It's a proper inn in the old tradition with gorgeous rooms and the odd touch of scruffiness to add authenticity to its earthy bones. It stands on a cobbled walkway in a village lost down tiny lanes, and those lucky enough to chance upon it leave reluctantly. Inside there are beams, but they are not sandblasted, red carpets with a little swirl, sofas in front of an open fire. Boarded menus trumpet irresistible food – carrot and orange soup, haunch of venison with a port jus, an excellent rhubarb crumble. You can eat wherever you want: in the bar, in the fancy restaurant, or out in the walled garden in good weather. There's a cobbled terrace, a skittle alley, maps for walkers and well-kept ales. Upstairs, seven rooms have a chic country style. Two have baths in the room, those in the barn have painted stone walls, the suite has a wood-burner and a private terrace. All are lovely with comfy beds, white linen, good power showers and flat-screen TVs. Kind staff chat with ease. Dartmoor waits, but you may well linger. Brilliant.

Rooms	5 doubles, 1 twin/double: £69-£130. 1 suite for 3: £150.
Meals	Lunch from £9. Dinner, 3 courses, £20-£30. Sunday lunch from £8.90.
Closed	Rarely.
Directions	A377 north from Exeter. 1st right in Crediton, left, signed Sandford. 1 mile up & in village.

Mark Hildyard & Katharine Lightfoot
The Lamb Inn
Sandford,
Crediton, EX17 4LW

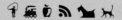

Tel +44 (0)1363 773676
Email thelambinn@gmail.com
Web www.lambinnsandford.co.uk

Mill End

This is a delightful small hotel that sits in a glorious patch of Dartmoor. Outside, birds sing, rabbits hop, and mere mortals sit in the colourful garden digging into afternoon tea. Inside, you find timber frames, nooks and crannies, pretty art and games galore. There's a small bar for pre-dinner drinks, a sitting room with sofas and an open fire, then a stylish restaurant for excellent food, perhaps wood pigeon with rhubarb and shallots, wild bass with lemon and herbs, an orange meringue tart with chocolate ice cream. Beautiful bedrooms are emerging by the dozen due to an on-going refurbishment. You'll find quirky wallpapers, colourful fabrics, cushioned window seats, beds dressed in crisp white linen. A couple have baths in the room, several have balconies, dog-friendly rooms open onto the garden. Outside, the river Teign potters past on one side flanked by the Two Moors Way; Castle Drogo, Fernworthy Reservoir and Buckland Abbey – home to Sir Francis Drake – are close, too. There's high tea for children, porridge for breakfast, and your pooch is very welcome. A great place to escape the city.

Rooms	15 twin/doubles: £105-£200. 6 suites for 2: £190-£260. Singles from £80. Extra beds from £25.
Meals	Lunch from £6. Dinner, 3 courses, £30-£40. Sunday lunch £22-£26. Afternoon tea £18.95.
Closed	Rarely.
Directions	M5, then A30 to Whiddon Down. South on A382, through Sandy Park, over small bridge and on right.

Tara & Nick Culverhouse
Mill End
Chagford,
Newton Abbot, TQ13 8JN

Tel +44 (0)1647 432282
Email info@millendhotel.com
Web www.millendhotel.com

Lewtrenchard Manor

A magnificent Jacobean mansion, a wormhole back to the 16th century. Inside, the full aristocratic monty is on display: a spectacular hall with a cavernous fireplace, a dazzling ballroom with extraordinary plasterwork. There are priest holes, oak panelling, oils by the score. Best of all is the 1602 gallery with its stunning ceiling and grand piano, while *Onward Christian Soldiers* was written in the library. Bedrooms are large. Some are grandly traditional (the four-poster belonged to Queen Henrietta Maria, wife of Charles I); others are more contemporary with airy colours and modern bathrooms. All have jugs of iced water, garden flowers and bathrobes. Delicious food waits downstairs – perhaps smoked haddock risotto, thyme-roasted Lewdown venison, salted caramel and chocolate delice with banana ice cream; there's a chef's table, too, where you watch the kitchen at work on a bank of TVs. Outside, a beautiful courtyard that's home to an ancient wisteria, a Gertrude Jekyll parterre garden, and an avenue of beech trees that makes you feel you're in a Hardy novel. Dartmoor is close. *Minimum stay: 2 nights at weekends.*

Rooms	4 doubles, 6 twin/doubles: £180-£320. 4 suites for 2: £235-£340.
Meals	Lunch, bar meals from £5.95; restaurant from £21. Dinner, 3 courses, £49.50. Children over seven welcome in restaurant.
Closed	Never.
Directions	From Exeter, exit A30 for A386. At T-junc., right, then 1st left for Lewdown. After 6 miles, left for Lewtrenchard. Keep left, house on left after 0.5 miles.

Sue, James, Duncan & Joan Murray
Lewtrenchard Manor
Lewdown,
Okehampton, EX20 4PN

Tel	+44 (0)1566 783222
Email	info@lewtrenchard.co.uk
Web	www.lewtrenchard.co.uk

The Horn of Plenty

The Horn of Plenty is one of those clever hotels that has survived the test of time by constantly improving itself. The latest addition is six gorgeous new rooms, four of which have terraces or balconies that give 40-mile views over the Tamar Valley. Potter about outside and find six acres of gardens, then a path that leads down through bluebell woods to the river. Inside, beautiful simplicity abounds: stripped floors, gilt mirrors, fine art, fresh flowers everywhere. Bedrooms in the main house come in country-house style, those in the garden have a contemporary feel. All have smart colours, big comfy beds, perhaps a claw-foot bath or a ceiling open to the rafters; ten have a terrace or a balcony. Despite all this, the food remains the big draw, so come to eat well, perhaps beetroot mousse with goat's cheese parfait, grilled duck with chicory and orange, chocolate cannelloni with banana sorbet; views of the Tamar snaking through the hills are included in the price. Afternoon tea is served on the patio in summer. Tavistock, Dartmoor and the Eden Project are close.

Rooms	16 twin/doubles: £120-£265. Singles from £110. Dinner, B&B £100 p.p. Extra bed/sofabed £25 p.p.p.n.
Meals	Lunch from £19.50. Dinner, 3 courses, £49.50. Tasting menu £65.
Closed	Never.
Directions	West from Tavistock on A390 following signs to Callington. Right after 3 miles at Gulworthy Cross. Signed left after 0.75 miles.

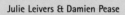

Julie Leivers & Damien Pease
The Horn of Plenty
Gulworthy,
Tavistock, PL19 8JD

Tel +44 (0)1822 832528
Email enquiries@thehornofplenty.co.uk
Web www.thehornofplenty.co.uk

Glazebrook House Hotel

The front door at Glazebrook may well be a rip in the space-time continuum. Outside, English decorum reigns; inside, a wonderland for your senses waits. You don't really find a hotel, more a contemporary art installation that you get to live in for a day or two. It's a reinvention of a 19th-century collector's house and it overflows with pink flamingos, enormous chandeliers, ancient maps, a bust of the queen with a halo instead of a crown. There's a dinosaur in the library, a tasting room for whisky and wine, a red-marbled bar with sofas and armchairs, then doors onto a terrace for afternoon tea. Rooms come fully loaded: vast beds, the loveliest linen, cool design, quirky art. You get iPads, smart TVs and minibars 'on the house'. Black marble bathrooms are flawless, with walk-in showers, fluffy robes, perhaps a free-standing bath. Ambrosial food waits downstairs, maybe goat's cheese mousse, rack of lamb, hake with shellfish butter, chocolate delice with popcorn. The A38 passes nearby, a distant hum when you're outside, so don't let that put you off visiting this exceptional hotel. Dartmoor waits.

Rooms	6 doubles, 1 twin: £229-£289. 1 single: £199.
Meals	Lunch from £7. Dinner: 3 courses, about £40; 5-course tasting menu £45; 8-course tasting menu £64. Afternoon tea £7-£15.
Closed	Rarely.
Directions	From Exeter, A38 for Plymouth. Signed Avonwick/South Brent. Follow South Brent & hotel signs. Pass London Inn on right, second right to hotel.

Pieter & Fran Hamman
Glazebrook House Hotel
South Brent, TQ10 9JE

Tel +44 (0)1364 73322
Email enquiries@glazebrookhouse.com
Web www.glazebrookhouse.com

Inspected & Selected Sawday's British Hotel Awards 2018

Hotel of the Year

Plantation House

This lovely small hotel delivers what so many of us want: a warm welcome, lovely food, rooms that spoil us rotten. Downstairs, a fire smoulders in the sitting-room bar; upstairs, fine Georgian windows frame views of hill and forest. Stylish bedrooms are full of comforts. They come with excellent bathrooms, lovely beds, crisp linen and warm colours. You get padded bedheads, sound systems, bowls of fruit, white robes to pad about in. Back downstairs, you'll succumb to a pre-dinner drink – in front of the fire in the bar in winter, out on the pretty terrace in summer. As for Richard's food, it bursts with flavour, so expect to eat well, perhaps Thai-style sea bass with ginger and lemongrass, local lamb with a Merlot jus, chocolate terrine with hazelnut ice cream. Soft fruits, vegetables and potatoes come from the garden in summer, as do home-laid eggs at breakfast. The river Erme passes across the road – follow it down to the sea and discover wonderful Wonwell Beach. There's lots to see around you: Dartmoor to the north, Totnes, Dartmouth, Salcombe and Slapton Sands to the south. Brilliant.

Rooms	5 doubles, 1 twin: £125-£185. 1 suite for 2: £195-£230. 1 single: £75-£80.
Meals	Dinner, 5 courses, £39.50.
Closed	Never.
Directions	A38, then A3121 for Ermington. In village on western fringe.

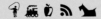

Richard Hendey
Plantation House
Totnes Road, Ermington,
Ivybridge, PL21 9NS
Tel +44 (0)1548 831100
Email info@plantationhousehotel.co.uk
Web www.plantationhousehotel.co.uk

Burgh Island Hotel

Burgh is unique – grand English Art Deco trapped in aspic. Noël Coward loved it, Agatha Christie wrote here. It's more than a hotel – you come to join a cast of players – so bring your pearls and come for cocktails under a stained-glass dome. By day you lie on steamers in the garden, watch gulls wheeling overhead, dip your toes into Mermaid's pool or try your hand at croquet. At night you dress for dinner, sip vermouth in a palm-fringed bar, then shuffle into the ballroom to dine on super organic food while serenaded by the sweet sounds of swing and jazz. Potter about and find flowers in vases four-feet high, bronze ladies thrusting globes into the sky, walls clad in Vitrolite, a 14th-century smugglers inn. Art Deco bedrooms have Bakelite telephones, ancient radios, bowls of fruit, panelled walls. Some have balconies, others have claw-foot baths, the Beach House suite juts out over rocks and has a sofa that looks out to sea. There's snooker, tennis, a sauna and a treatment room, then a sea tractor that can often outwit the tide. On sunny mornings, you may need your dark glasses at breakfast! *Minimum stay: 2 nights at weekends.*

Rooms	10 doubles, 3 twin/doubles: £420-£480. 12 suites for 2: £490-£680. Price includes dinner for 2.
Meals	Lunch from £16.50. Dinner included; non-residents £75. Afternoon tea £18.50. Sunday lunch £62. 24-hour residents' menu from £16.
Closed	2 weeks in January.
Directions	Drive to Bigbury-on-Sea. At high tide you are transported by sea tractor, at low tide by Landrover. Walking across the beach takes 3 minutes. Eco-taxis can be arranged.

Deborah Clark & Tony Orchard
Burgh Island Hotel
Burgh Island, Bigbury-on-Sea,
Kingsbridge, TQ7 4BG

Tel	+44 (0)1548 810514
Email	reception@burghisland.com
Web	www.burghisland.com

The Henley Hotel

A small house above the sea with fabulous views, super bedrooms and some of the loveliest food in Devon. Despite these credentials, it's Martyn and Petra who shine most brightly, their kind, generous approach making this a memorable place to stay. Warm interiors have wooden floors, Lloyd Loom furniture, the odd potted palm, then big windows to frame the view. Below, the Avon estuary slips gracefully out to sea. At high tide surfers ride the waves, at low tide you can walk along the sands. There's a pretty garden with a path tumbling down to the beach, binoculars in each room, a wood-burner in the snug and good books everywhere. Bedrooms are a steal (one is huge). Expect warm colours, crisp linen, tongue-and-groove panelling and robes in super little bathrooms. As for Martyn's table d'hôte dinners, expect to eat very well. Fish comes daily from Kingsbridge market, you might find grilled figs with goat's cheese and Parma ham, roast monkfish with a lobster sauce, then hot chocolate soufflé with fresh raspberries. Gorgeous Devon is all around. Better than the Ritz! *German spoken. Minimum stay: 2 nights at weekends.*

Rooms	2 doubles, 2 twin/doubles: £120-£137. 1 suite for 2: £150. Singles from £85. Dinner, B&B £87-£97p.p. (2 night minimum).
Meals	Dinner £36.
Closed	November – March.
Directions	From A38, A3121 to Modbury, then B3392 to Bigbury-on-Sea. Hotel on left as road slopes down to sea.

Martyn Scarterfield & Petra Lampe
The Henley Hotel
Folly Hill, Bigbury-on-Sea,
Kingsbridge, TQ7 4AR

Tel +44 (0)1548 810240
Email thehenleyhotel@btconnect.com
Web www.thehenleyhotel.co.uk

South Sands Hotel

Two coves west from the bustle of town, this smart hotel stands above the beach with views of water, hill and sky. Interiors have a New England feel – seaside colours, softly painted wood, walls of glass that bring in the view. Doors in the restaurant open onto a decked terrace, where at high tide the beach disappears and the sea laps against the wall below. Pull yourself away to walk in the hills, sail on the water, hire a kayak or try your hand at paddle boarding. If that sounds too energetic, then drop down to the beach for family fun. Children are very welcome and you'll find beach towels, buckets and spades, even crabbing nets for excursions to rock pools. Back at the hotel, you dine on lovely local food, perhaps Salcombe crab cakes with foraged leaves, moorland beef with a red wine sauce, chocolate fondant with pistachio ice cream. Rooms at the front have watery views, a couple have terraces, all have comfy beds, a smart style and swish bathrooms. One has 'his and hers' claw-foot baths that look out to sea, while the family suites have kitchens and separate bedrooms for kids. Brilliant. *Minimum stay: 2 nights at weekends.*

Rooms	16 doubles, 6 twin/doubles: £170-£385. 5 suites for 4: £340-£475.
Meals	Lunch from £17.95. Dinner £15.95-£40.
Closed	Rarely.
Directions	A381 to Salcombe, then signed right to South Sands. Follow road down hill, then along water. On left.

Antoine Gay
South Sands Hotel
Bolt Head,
Salcombe, TQ8 8LL

Tel +44 (0)1548 859000
Email enquiries@southsands.com
Web www.southsands.com

Bayards Cove Inn

In 1620 the Mayflower stopped in Bayards Cove before sailing for America. It docked just outside this cool little inn, one of the oldest buildings in Dartmouth. But if its timber frames are ancient, then its jaunty interiors are the polar opposite with a warm contemporary feel that spreads itself far and wide. Once inside you realise you're in a small and quirky café/restaurant that does a good line in world wines and local ale. You also realise you've landed in heaven and soon you're planning an invasion of one of the bay windows, where you can sink into comfy armchairs and survey life inside and out. Interiors have warm colours, low beams, white stone walls and ancient wood everywhere. There are fairy lights, too, a bar weighted down by freshly baked cakes, and cool tunes float in the air. Cosy rooms have timber frames, padded bedheads, pretty fabrics, comfy beds. Most have compact shower rooms, but you won't mind for a minute; some have views of the water or wildly wonky floors. There's great food, perhaps crispy squid, moules frites, local ice creams. Dartmouth waits at the front door. *Minimum stay: 2 nights at weekends.*

Rooms	4 doubles, 1 twin/double: £90-£155. 1 suite for 2: £130-£180. 1 family room for 4: £110-£160. Singles £95-£150.
Meals	Lunch from £5.95. Dinner from £9.95 (not Mon-Wed off season).
Closed	Never.
Directions	In Dartmouth south along sea front for lower ferry. Follow road right for 200m and on left at T-junction.

Charlie & Zuzana Deuchar
Bayards Cove Inn
Lower Street,
Dartmouth, TQ6 9AN

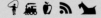

Tel +44 (0)1803 839278
Email info@bayardscoveinn.co.uk
Web www.bayardscoveinn.co.uk

The Cary Arms at Babbacombe Bay

The Cary Arms is a chic little inn that hovers above Babbacombe Bay with huge views of sea and sky. But it's not like other inns. Its determination to spend money creating the lap of luxury is matchless. Which explains the spectacular new suites and beach huts that have recently taken root in the garden. Walls of glass frame the views, bedrooms look out to sea, bathrooms with walk-in showers are hard to beat. Best of all is your terrace, metres from crystal clear waters, with views that stretch for miles; don't expect to move too far. As for the inn, you can eat fresh seafood on terraces that drop downhill towards a small jetty, where locals fish. The pub has six moorings in the bay, you can charter a boat and explore the coast. Inside, you find stone walls, wooden floors and a fire that burns every day. Rooms in the main house have a New England style, all but one with a private terrace or balcony. You get fabulous beds, super bathrooms (one has a claw-foot bath that looks out to sea). Finally, you can snorkel and kayak, there's a treatment room, and a small spa with an infinity pool is on its way. *Minimum stay in cottages: 2 nights.*

Rooms	7 doubles: £195-£295. 1 suite for 4, 9 suites for 2: £375-£475. 1 family room for 4: £395. 1 cottage for 6; 1 for 8; 1 for 9: from £550; £2,750-£3,250 per week. Extra bed/sofabed £25 p.p.p.n. Dogs £20 per night.
Meals	Lunch from £7.95. Dinner £25-£35.
Closed	Never.
Directions	From Teignmouth south on A379; 5 miles to St Marychurch, through lights, left into Babbacombe Downs Rd. Follow road right; left downhill.

Tom Hughes
The Cary Arms at Babbacombe Bay
Beach Road,
Babbacombe, Torquay, TQ1 3LX

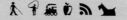

Tel +44 (0)1803 327110
Email enquiries@caryarms.co.uk
Web www.caryarms.co.uk

Southernhay House

A beautiful small hotel on the loveliest square in town, a short stroll from the cathedral. The house dates to 1805 and was built for a major returning from the Raj. These days, it mixes quirky design with all the comforts you'd expect of a small, city hotel. It's central, welcoming, the rooms are lovely, the dining room serves great bistro food and there's a chic bar for cocktails or a pint of local ale. Downstairs, French windows at the back of the house draw you onto a small terrace, where you can eat in good weather, perhaps mussels in a white wine sauce, bangers and mash with a rich gravy, chocolate fondant with vanilla ice cream. Potter about and find electric blue sofas, 50s starlets framed on the wall, old style radiators and beautiful art. Stylish bedrooms wait upstairs – some are bigger, all are lovely. Expect bold colours, sumptuous fabrics, Indian art, hi-tech gadgetry. Cool bathrooms come as standard, bigger rooms have free-standing baths. Exeter has lots to offer: Roman walls, a 12th-century cathedral, the imperious Royal Albert Memorial Museum & Art Gallery. Topsham is close for river walks. *Children over 12 welcome.*

Rooms	10 doubles: £100-£284.
Meals	Lunch from £6.50. Dinner, 3 courses, about £30.
Closed	Rarely.
Directions	M5, junction 29, then B3183 west into city. Left at T-junction. At one-way system, circle round and as if coming back to where you started and Southernhay East is on your left.

Deborah Clark & Tony Orchard
Southernhay House
36 Southernhay East,
Exeter, EX1 1NX

Tel +44 (0)1392 435324
Email home@southernhayhouse.com
Web www.southernhayhouse.com

Sidmouth Harbour Hotel

This lovely spa hotel sits above the town with huge views across Lyme Bay towards Portland Bill. It's a great spot with a terrace that has addictive qualities when the sun shines and a beautiful restaurant with walls of glass to weatherproof the view. You're 200 metres away from two sandy beaches, perfect for sunny days, but the hotel has lots to stop you wandering: a couple of swimming pools, five treatment rooms, a steam room and a sauna. Potter about and find a white marble bar, coastal art in the airy sitting room, then a stylish restaurant, where a vast Chesterfield sofa runs along six tables. Bedrooms are scattered about, some in the main house, others in the courtyard, but all have the same cool style: seaside colours, blond wood furniture, robes for excellent bathrooms, padded headboards and crisp white linen. Several in the main house have sea views, some have balconies, too. By day you take to the coastal path, spin down to the town, or bask on the beach. By night you return for a slap-up meal; start with crab chowder, follow with roast chicken and top it all off with chocolate tart and vanilla ice cream. *Minimum stay: 2 nights at weekends April-October.*

Rooms	48 twin/doubles: £170-£350. 7 singles: £105-£185. Price includes dinner for 2.
Meals	Lunch from £6.50. Dinner, 3 courses, included; non-residents about £30. Afternoon tea from £16.50. Sunday lunch from £17.95.
Closed	Never.
Directions	South from Honiton on A375 into Sidmouth. Right at seafront; hotel on right after 600m.

Ken Cumming
Sidmouth Harbour Hotel
The Westcliff, Manor Road,
Sidmouth, EX10 8RU

Tel	+44 (0)1395 513252
Email	sidmouth@harbourhotels.co.uk
Web	www.sidmouth-harbour-hotel.co.uk

Alexandra Hotel & Restaurant

This chic hotel has rather good views, a clean sweep up the Jurassic coast all the way to Chesil Beach and on to Portland Bill. It sits high on the hill with one foot in town and the other paddling in the water. Directly below, the Cobb curls into the sea, the very spot where Meryl Streep withstood crashing waves in *The French Lieutenant's Woman*. Outside, there's a sun-trapping garden, where guests fall asleep in deckchairs, then a lookout tower with big sea views for a romantic dinner for two. Inside, an easy elegance flows: stripped wood floors, windows everywhere, an airy bar for pre-dinner drinks, an attractive sitting room with lots of books. There's a smart dining room that could double as a ballroom, then a conservatory brasserie that opens onto a terrace for lunch in summer. Both offer tasty, local food, perhaps Lyme Bay scallops, chicken with cavolo nero, a white chocolate mousse. Bedrooms, most with sea views, have warm colours, comfy beds, padded headboards, robes in fine bathrooms. Lyme, the beach, and the fossil-ridden coast, all wait. There's an 18th-century chapel, too.

Rooms	18 twin/doubles: £180-£350. 3 family rooms for 4: £308-£454. 1 single: £95-£130. 1 apartment for 4, 1 apartment for 6: £315-£365.
Meals	Lunch from £9.90. Dinner, 3 courses, about £35. Sunday lunch from £23. Afternoon tea from £7.50.
Closed	1 January to 3 February.
Directions	In Lyme Regis up hill on high street; keep left at bend; on left after 200m.

Kathryn Haskins
Alexandra Hotel & Restaurant
Pound Street,
Lyme Regis, DT7 3HZ
Tel +44 (0)1297 442010
Email enquiries@hotelalexandra.co.uk
Web www.hotelalexandra.co.uk

The Bull Hotel

The Bull was Dorset's first boutique hotel, a cool little place with lovely staff, an informal vibe, tasty food and lots of colour. It was bought by Fullers in 2014, who immediately poured in a small fortune to make it even better. The results are dreamy – airy interiors, big art, some fancy new bathrooms and a chic new restaurant. It remains as friendly as ever and draws a local crowd, who come for coffee and cake, a cool bar that rocks at weekends, even a masked ball on New Year's Eve. All of which makes it a lot of fun for guests passing through. Downstairs, you'll find an open fire, stripped wood floors and a pint of London Pride in the bar; in summer, life decants onto a flower-filled courtyard. Colourful bedrooms – all different – have lots of style: beautiful beds, pashmina throws, chic wallpapers, perhaps a bath at the foot of your bed. Some have sofas, family rooms have bunk beds for kids. You get digital radios, flat-screen TVs, then cool bathrooms, some with big power showers. Don't miss the food, perhaps Portland crab, Dorset lamb, coconut panna cotta. Chesil Beach is close. *Minimum stay: 2 nights at weekends.*

Rooms	10 doubles, 1 twin, 3 four-posters: £100-£230. 1 suite for 2: £235-£265. 3 family rooms for 4: £220-£260. 1 single: £90-£130.
Meals	Lunch, 2 courses, from £12. Dinner, 3 courses, around £35. Sunday lunch £19.
Closed	Never.
Directions	On main street in town. Car park at rear.

Sian Thompson
The Bull Hotel
34 East Street,
Bridport, DT6 3LF

Tel +44 (0)1308 422878
Email info@thebullhotel.co.uk
Web www.thebullhotel.co.uk

The Seaside Boarding House, Restaurant & Bar

You pop up the hill, come to the end of the road, then follow a track along the cliff and down to this lovely and bright small hotel. Rolling hills shoot north towards Dorchester, while the view east follows Chesil Beach, a mere 20 miles round to Portland Bill. The Boarding House's natural beauty comes courtesy of a recent facelift, proving conclusively that cosmetic surgery works. Outside, there's a dining terrace overlooking the sea, then paths that drop down to the beach. Inside, walls of glass flood big rooms with seaside light. There's a bar for cocktails and afternoon tea, a library with books and games for rainy days, then a restaurant for delicious food: perhaps cheese soufflé, whole lemon sole and chocolate and hazelnut delice. Upstairs bedrooms all have sea views and mix period furniture (some from HMS Windsor) with 21st-century design: beautiful beds, Zoffany colours, rugs on wood floors, cushioned window seats. Bathrooms have white robes and vintage tiles, then a big shower, a claw-foot bath, or both. The coastal path passes directly outside, so bring your boots. Brilliant. *Minimum stay: 2 nights at weekends.*

Rooms	8 doubles: £180-£235. Dinner, B&B from £120 p.p.
Meals	Lunch from £14. Sunday lunch £25-£30. Afternoon tea from £10. Dinner, 3 courses, about £30.
Closed	Never.
Directions	East from Bridport on B3157. Downhill into Burton Bradstock; right at garage on left-hand bend; up hill to end of road. On left down track.

Mary-Lou Sturridge
The Seaside Boarding House,
Restaurant & Bar
Cliff Road, Burton Bradstock, DT6 4RB

Tel +44 (0)1308 897205
Email info@theseasideboardinghouse.com
Web theseasideboardinghouse.com

Bridge House Hotel

Beaminster – or Emminster in Thomas Hardy's *Tess* – sits in a lush Dorset valley. From the hills above, you drop through glorious country, rolling down to this old market town, where the church tower soars towards heaven. As for this lovely hotel, it's a 13th-century priest's house and comes with original trimmings: stone flags, mullioned windows, old beams and huge inglenooks. It's intimate, friendly and deeply comfortable, with something beautiful at every turn. There are rugs on parquet flooring, a beamed bar with an open fire, a splendid dining room with Georgian panelling and a Robert Adam's fireplace. Beautiful lighting sets the mood for excellent food, perhaps Witchampton snails, an imperious steak and kidney pie, pear and rosemary tarte tatin. Rooms in the main house are bigger and smarter, those in the coach house are simpler and less expensive; all are pretty with chic fabrics, crisp linen, flat-screen TVs and stylish bathrooms. Breakfast is served in the conservatory, so watch the gardener potter about as you scoff your bacon and eggs. Chesil Beach at West Bay is close. *Minimum stay: 2 nights at weekends.*

Rooms	6 doubles, 3 twin/doubles, 2 four-posters: £95-£200. 2 family rooms for 4: £95-£200. Dinner, B&B £82.50-£145 p.p. (obligatory on Fridays & Saturdays April to September). Extra beds: children under 17 £25; adults £35-£50.
Meals	Lunch from £8.50. Dinner, 3 courses, £25-£35.
Closed	Never.
Directions	From Yeovil A30 west; A3066 for Bridport to Beaminster. Hotel at far end of town as road bends to right.

Mark & Jo Donovan
Bridge House Hotel
3 Prout Bridge,
Beaminster, DT8 3AY

Tel +44 (0)1308 862200
Email enquiries@bridge-house.co.uk
Web www.bridge-house.co.uk

The Greyhound

It's hard to fault this little inn. It sits in one of Dorset's loveliest villages, lost in a lush valley with country views that shoot uphill. Outside, there's a colourful terrace that draws a crowd in summer. Inside, cool, rustic interiors mix old and new to great effect. You find stone walls, old flagstones, gilt mirrors and a wood-burner to keep things cosy. There's a lively locals' bar where you can grab a pint of real ale, then a cosy little restaurant where you dig into delicious food. The feel throughout is informal and you can eat wherever you want, so spin onto the terrace in good weather and try seared scallops, boeuf bourguignon, sticky toffee pudding. Six lovely rooms wait in an old skittle alley. They're not huge, but nor is their price, and what they lack in space, they make up for in comfort and style, with crisp linen, airy colours and pretty furniture. There's a DVD library, too, and wellington boots if you want to walk. The Cerne Abbas giant is close, while the coast is on your doorstep: Lyme Regis for fossil hunters, West Bay for fine walking and fabulous Chesil Beach. *Minimum stay: 2 nights on bank holidays.*

Rooms	5 doubles, 1 twin: £89-£99. Singles from £69.
Meals	Lunch from £5.50. Dinner, 3 courses, about £30 (not Sunday evening).
Closed	Rarely.
Directions	South from Sherborne on A352. Right after 12 miles, for Sydling St Nicholas. In village.

Matthew Martinez
The Greyhound
26 High Street, Sydling St Nicholas,
Dorchester, DT2 9PD

Tel	+44 (0)1300 341303
Email	info@dorsetgreyhound.co.uk
Web	www.dorsetgreyhound.co.uk

The Priory Hotel

The lawns of this 16th-century priory run down to the river Frome. Boats float past, an old church rises behind, a gorgeous garden filled with colour wraps around you. As for this lovely country house, you'll find a grand piano in the drawing room, a first-floor sitting room with garden views, then a new restaurant with walls of glass that jut into the garden giving rather good views. There's a beautiful terrace, too, where you can sit in the sun and watch the river pass. Bedrooms in the main house come in different sizes, some cosy in the eaves, others grandly adorned in reds and golds. You get Zoffany fabrics, padded window seats, bowls of fruit, the odd sofa. Eight have river views, others look onto the garden or church. Chic bathrooms – some dazzlingly contemporary – all come with white robes. Rooms in the boathouse, a 16th-century clay barn, are lavish, with oak panelling, stone walls and sublime views. Outside, climbing roses, a duck pond, banks of daffs and snowdrops in spring. Corfe Castle and Studland Bay are close. A slice of old England with delicious food to boot. *Minimum stay: 2 nights at weekends. Over 14s welcome.*

Rooms	12 twin/doubles: £220-£320. 5 suites for 2: £350-£380.
Meals	Lunch from £14.95. Dinner, 3 courses, £47.50.
Closed	Never.
Directions	West from Poole on A35, then A351 for Wareham and B3075 into town. Through lights, 1st left, right out of square, then keep left. Entrance on left beyond church.

Jeremy Merchant
The Priory Hotel
Church Green,
Wareham, BH20 4ND

Tel	+44 (0)1929 551666
Email	reservations@theprioryhotel.co.uk
Web	https://theprioryhotel.co.uk

Urban Beach Hotel

A quirky little place with surfer-chic interiors, lovely staff and a happy buzz throughout. You're on a residential street 500 meters back from the beach; a short stroll leads down to the promenade which you can follow into town. Back at the hotel a relaxed informality reigns. You'll find circular leather booths, driftwood lamps, a house guitar and surf boards hanging on the wall. There's a bar for cocktails, candle lanterns scattered about, a table laden with cakes, then the daily papers and cool tunes in the air. Outside, a terrace for all seasons waits, with a roof that disappears when the sun shines and a fire pit for cooler nights. Bedrooms upstairs come in different sizes, but even the smaller rooms are lovely with warm colours, crisp linen and smart bathrooms. The beach waits at the end of the road, seven miles of sand with a surf shop on the way down. Come back for a good meal, perhaps cauliflower soup, Cornish mussels, a melting chocolate fondant. Urban Reef, Mark & Fiona's sister restaurant, has a balcony and terrace overlooking the sea, not a bad spot for dinner in summer. *Minimum stay: 2 nights at weekends; 3 nights over bank holidays.*

Rooms	9 doubles, 1 twin/double: £89-£180. 2 singles: £72.
Meals	Lunch from £6. Dinner £25-30. Sunday lunch from £14.
Closed	Never.
Directions	South from Ringwood on A338; left for Boscombe (east of centre). Over railway, right onto Centenary Way. Keep with the flow (left, then right) to join Christchurch Rd; 2nd left (St John's Rd); 2nd left.

Mark & Fiona Cribb
Urban Beach Hotel
23 Argyll Road,
Bournemouth, BH5 1EB

Tel	+44 (0)1202 301509
Email	reception@urbanbeach.co.uk
Web	www.urbanbeach.co.uk

Captain's Club Hotel and Spa

The Captain's Club stands on the banks on the Stour, where a tiny ferry potters along the river dodging swans and ducks. In summer, you decant onto its lovely terrace and watch river life pass by. Inside, walls of glass weatherproof the view. The sprawling bar fills with light and comes with deep sofas, the daily papers and a grand piano. It's smart, stylish and very informal, with live music at weekends. The hotel also has its own boat, so you can take to the high seas and spin over to the Isle of Wight or Brownsea Island. Back on dry land uncluttered bedrooms have river views, low-slung beds, crisp white linen, neutral colours and excellent bathrooms. None are small, some are huge with separate sitting rooms, apartments have more than one bedroom, so perfect for families and friends. There's a spa, too, with a hydrotherapy pool, a sauna and four treatment rooms. Lovely food is on tap all day in the bar, while the mirrored restaurant ensures everyone has the view. Lobster, Dorset crab, sea bass and a good steak all wait. Christchurch is a short walk upstream. Brilliant. *Minimum stay: 2 nights at weekends.*

Rooms	17 doubles: £199-£259. 12 apartments for 6: £289-£649.
Meals	Bar meals all day from £6. Lunch from £15. Dinner £30-£35.
Closed	Never.
Directions	M27/A31 west, then A338/B3073 south into Christchurch. At A35 (lights at big r'bout) follow one-way system left. Double back after 100m. Cross r'bout heading west and 1st left into Sopers Lane. Signed left.

Timothy Lloyd & Robert Wilson
Captain's Club Hotel and Spa
Wick Ferry, Wick Lane,
Christchurch, BH23 1HU
Tel +44 (0)1202 475111
Email reservations@captainsclubhotel.com
Web www.captainsclubhotel.com

The Kings

This is one of those lovely places that delivers what many of us want: lots of style, delicious food, happy staff, attractive prices. The setting is just as good, a slice of Georgian England, with the river Stour to the left, the ruined castle to the right and the old bowling green in between. A riverside path leads down to Christchurch Quay, and another to the gardens at the priory – blissful stuff. As for the hotel, you'll find a cool new bar with big orange armchairs, green leather bar stools and candles everywhere at night – not a bad spot for champagne cocktails. Comfy bedrooms have lots of style: smart colours, fine beds, good bathrooms, perhaps a sofa if there's room. Three overlook the front, those in the eaves have a cute, cosy feel. Back downstairs you find the big draw – excellent food in the candlelit restaurant. Try Dorset cheddar soufflé, turbot with garlic and thyme, lemon meringues with limoncello. It's all local with menus from an amazing £15. Lobster nights bring in the locals, the Christchurch Food Festival comes in May with stalls on the bowling green. Perfect. *Minimum stay: 2 nights at weekends.*

Rooms	14 doubles, 6 twins: £99-£199.
Meals	Lunch from £6.50. Dinner, set menu £18.50; à la carte about £30. Sunday lunch from £15.
Closed	Never.
Directions	West into Christchurch on A35. 2nd left onto High Street, then left at roundabout into Castle Street. On left after 200m. Parking on right in lay-by.

Lukasz Dwornik
The Kings
18 Castle Street,
Christchurch, BH23 1DT

Tel +44 (0)1202 588933
Email kings@harbourhotels.co.uk
Web www.thekings-christchurch.co.uk

10 Castle Street

It may have a humble address, but that is the only humble feature you will find at 10 Castle Street, a stunning Queen Anne mansion that sits in 27 acres of idyllic gardens and parkland. Inside, you discover the re-invention of the English country-house hotel. As tradition demands, it is privately owned and has the feel of home, albeit a deliciously grand one that doubles as a contemporary art gallery. You'll find an elegant drawing room that opens onto a terrace; Ionic columns in the airy bar; a dining room with French windows that frame garden views; a first-floor, sitting-room bar that has the feel of a gentleman's club. Outside, the terrace overlooks a fine English garden, with its trim lawns, wild flowers and an avenue of lime trees. Bedrooms have cool colours, chic fabrics, crisp linen and smart bathrooms; some are huge with garden views, a couple are tiny, but good for a night. Don't miss the food, perhaps Scottish langoustines, haunch of venison, orange and cardamom crème brûlée. There's a bakery, a smokehouse, a cinema and a kitchen garden, with a spa coming soon. Out of this world.

Rooms	9 doubles: £165-£350. Extra bed/sofabed £40.
Meals	Lunch from £15. Dinner, 3 courses, about £40. Afternoon tea from £19.50. Sunday lunch from £24.
Closed	Never.
Directions	North from A31 onto A338. Left in Fordingbridge onto B3078. On left after 5 miles, in village.

Alexander & Gretchen Boon
10 Castle Street
Cranborne, BH21 5PZ

Tel +44 (0)1725 551133
Email enquiries@10castlestreet.com
Web www.10castlestreet.com

Castleman Hotel & Restaurant

It's a little like stepping into the pages of a Hardy novel: an untouched corner of rural Dorset, a 400-year-old bailiff's house, sheep grazing in lush fields, a rich cast of characters pottering about. The Castleman – part country house, part restaurant with rooms – is a true one-off: quirky, intimate, defiantly English (you'll think you've landed in Ambridge). It pays no heed to prevailing fashions, not least because the locals would revolt if it did. Barbara runs the place in great style. Touches of grandeur are hard to miss: a panelled hall, art from Chettle House, a magnificent Jacobean ceiling in one of the sitting rooms. Follow your nose and find a cosy bar, fresh flowers everywhere and books galore. The restaurant has garden views, though your eyes are more likely to be fixed on Barbara's delicious old-school food, perhaps potted shrimp terrine, haunch of local venison, meringues with chocolate mousse and toasted almonds. Homely bedrooms fit the bill: comfortable, delightfully priced, a couple with claw-foot baths. Magical Dorset will fill your days with splendour. Don't miss it.

Rooms	4 doubles, 1 twin/double, 1 twin, 1 four-poster: £95-£110. 1 family room for 4: £95-£110. Singles from £70.
Meals	Sunday lunch £25. Dinner, 3 courses, about £27.
Closed	February.
Directions	A354 north from Blandford Forum. 3rd left (about 4 miles up) and on left in village.

Barbara Garnsworthy
Castleman Hotel & Restaurant
Chettle, Blandford Forum, DT11 8DB

Tel +44 (0)1258 830096
Email enquiry@castlemanhotel.co.uk
Web www.castlemanhotel.co.uk

Plumber Manor

Plumber is old school, it pays no heed to passing fashions, it just gets on with doing what it does so well – looking after guests, pouring fine libations, serving delicious food. It is suitably lost in Dorset's mazy lanes, a fine old pile of golden stone that dates to 1650. It sits in a couple of acres of green and pleasant land with the river Divelish flanking one side. Outside, there's a terrace for afternoon tea with beautiful magnolias on show in summer. Inside, a pair of labradors rule the roost. There's an open fire in the sitting-room bar, fresh flowers, old clocks, a snug in cherry red. The first-floor landing has an enormous sofa, a gallery of family portraits, a grand piano for good measure. Bedrooms are split between the main house and converted barns; the latter are big and welcome dogs. Décor is dated – 1980s florals – as are bathrooms, though several now sparkle in travertine splendour. A family triumvirate oversee it all: Brian in the kitchen, Richard behind the bar, Alison everywhere. Hearty food waits, perhaps crab mousseline, rack of lamb, lemon meringue pie.

Rooms	16 twin/doubles: £160-£240. Singles from £120.
Meals	Dinner £30-£38. Sunday lunch £30.
Closed	February.
Directions	West from Sturminster Newton on A357. Across traffic lights, up hill & left for Hazelbury Bryan. Follow brown tourism signs. Hotel signed left after 2 miles.

Richard, Alison & Brian Prideaux-Brune
Plumber Manor
Plumber,
Sturminster Newton, DT10 2AF

Tel	+44 (0)1258 472507
Email	book@plumbermanor.com
Web	www.plumbermanor.com

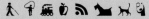

The Stapleton Arms

A quirky village inn: lots of style, lovely staff, super food, excellent prices. The Stapleton started life as a Georgian home, becoming an inn after the war. These days, warm, hip interiors carry a streak of country glamour. Downstairs, you'll find sofas in front of the fire, then a restaurant with shuttered windows and candles in the fireplace. You can eat whatever you want, wherever you want. Delicious pork pies wait at the bar, but it's hard to resist something more substantial, perhaps chilli squid with lime, slow-cooked beef with a red wine jus, chocolate and peanut butter tart. It's a community local with quiz nights, local ales, an excellent Sunday lunch and a wood-fired oven in the garden for pizzas in summer. Cute rooms are soundproofed to ensure a good night's sleep. All have beautiful linen, fresh flowers, cool colours, excellent showers; one has a double-ended bath. You'll find maps and wellies in case you want to walk and a playground for children in the garden. Wincanton is close for the races if you want to lose your shirt. The gardens at Stourhead are nearby, too. One of the best.

Rooms	4 doubles: £90-£120. Singles from £72. Extra beds £15.
Meals	Lunch & bar meals from £7. Dinner, 3 courses, about £30. Sunday lunch from £13.
Closed	Rarely.
Directions	A303 to Wincanton, B3081 into town. Right after fire station, signed Buckhorn Weston. Left at T-junction after 3 miles. In village, pub on right.

Steve & Teela Philpot
The Stapleton Arms
Church Hill, Buckhorn Weston,
Gillingham, SP8 5HS

Tel +44 (0)1963 370396
Email relax@thestapletonarms.com
Web www.thestapletonarms.com

Rose & Crown

Romaldkirk is one of those lovely villages where little has changed in 200 years. It sits peacefully in the north Pennines, lost to the world and without great need of it. As for the Rose & Crown, it dates to 1733 and stands on the village green next to a Saxon Church. Roses ramble across stone walls at the front, so grab a pint of local ale, then sit in the sun and watch life pass by. Inside, you can roast away in front of a fire in the wonderfully old-school bar while reading the *Teesdale Mercury*. There's a peaceful sitting room for afternoon tea, then a panelled restaurant for excellent food, perhaps honey-glazed goats cheese with apple and hazelnut, shoulder of pork wrapped in Parma ham, banana Bakewell tart. Thomas and Cheryl bought the place in 2012 and have been spending money on it ever since: it has never looked better. Stylish rooms – some in the main house, others out back, a couple in a cottage next door – have warm colours, comfy beds, Bose sound systems and super bathrooms. Don't miss High Force waterfall, the magnificent Bowes Museum or the sausage sandwich at lunch. Dogs are very welcome.

Rooms	8 doubles, 3 twins: £115-£160. 3 suites for 2: £180-£200. Singles £95. Dinner, B&B from £79 p.p.
Meals	Lunch from £10.50. Dinner, 3 courses, from £27. Sunday lunch £19.50.
Closed	23-27 December; 1 week in January.
Directions	From Barnard Castle B6277 north for 6 miles. Right in village towards green. Inn on left.

Thomas & Cheryl Robinson
Rose & Crown
Romaldkirk,
Barnard Castle, DL12 9EB

Tel +44 (0)1833 650213
Email hotel@rose-and-crown.co.uk
Web www.rose-and-crown.co.uk

Houndgate Townhouse

This is a deliciously hip hotel inside a beautiful Georgian townhouse. It's the sort of place the word 'boutique' was coined to define: small and friendly with good food and lots of style. It's subtle, cleverly conceived, a design hotel with a level of craftsmanship you rarely find in small hotels. It's a very welcoming place, too, a cool little café/bar where you can pop in for coffee, grab a bowl of soup or come down for cocktails before dinner; the Alice in Wonderland afternoon tea is not to be missed. Potter about and find a mirrored ceiling in the chic bar, a stylish restaurant with green leather booths, then a terraced courtyard for lunch in the sun. Rooms are excellent: comfy beds, beautiful linen, smart TVs, robes in sparkling bathrooms. Two have a free-standing bath in the room, another a panel of original wallpaper that was discovered when refurbishing. Bistro-style food waits downstairs, perhaps beetroot with goats cheese and grapefruit, pork belly with a herb jus, peanut butter parfait. Don't miss the Bowes Museum in Barnard Castle, a jewel of the North. Durham is close. *Complimentary access to the local swimming pool and gym available.*

Rooms	6 twin/doubles, 2 four-posters: £90-£145. Singles from £72. Cots & extra bed/sofabed available at no charge.
Meals	Lunch from £5. Dinner, 3 courses, £25. Afternoon tea £16.
Closed	12pm onwards on Sundays.
Directions	A1(M), then A167 into Darlington. Take the ring road to its southeastern roundabout and exit into Beaumont Street for its car park. Houndgate runs above, a 2-minute walk.

Natalie Cooper
Houndgate Townhouse
11 Houndgate,
Darlington, DL1 5RF

Tel +44 (0)1325 486011
Email info@houndgatetownhouse.co.uk
Web www.houndgatetownhouse.co.uk

Maison Talbooth

The outdoor swimming pool is heated to 29°C every day, a chauffeur is on hand to whisk you down to the hotel's riverside restaurant, a grand piano waits in the sitting room, where guests gather for a legendary afternoon tea. They don't do things by halves at Maison Talbooth, a small-scale pleasure dome with long views across Constable country. The house, an old rectory, stands in three acres of manicured grounds; the pool house is a big draw with its open fire, honesty bar, beautiful art and treatment rooms. Interiors are equally impressive. There are no rooms, only suites, each divine. Some on the ground floor have doors onto terraces where hot tubs wait, but all pamper you rotten with flawless bathrooms, fabulous beds, cool colours and hi-tech excess. At dinner you're chauffeured to the family's restaurants (both within half a mile): Milsoms for bistro food served informally; Le Talbooth on the river Stour for more serious fare, perhaps poached lobster with orange and fennel, saddle of venison with plums and bitter chocolate, pineapple and coconut soufflé with piña colada ice cream. A great escape.

Rooms	12 suites for 4: £210-£420. Singles from £170.
Meals	Dinner at Milsoms £25; at Le Talbooth £35-£50.
Closed	Never.
Directions	North on A12 past Colchester. Left to Dedham, right after S bend. Maison Talbooth is on right; follow brown signs.

Paul & Geraldine Milsom
Maison Talbooth
Stratford Road,
Dedham, Colchester, CO7 6HN

Tel +44 (0)1206 322367
Email maison@milsomhotels.com
Web www.milsomhotels.com

The Sun Inn

This perennial favourite sits in an idyllic village made rich by mills in the 16th century. You're also in Constable country – the artist attended school in the village and often returned to paint the church. Best of all is the river – you can hire boats, grab a picnic from the inn, float down the sleepy Stour, then tie up on the bank for lunch al fresco. As for The Sun, you couldn't hope to wash up in a better spot. Inside, you find open fires, boarded floors, timber frames and an easy elegance. A panelled lounge comes with sofas and armchairs, the bar is made from a slab of local elm and the airy, beamed dining room offers fabulous food inspired by Italy, perhaps crab ravioli, squid with chilli and garlic, monkfish with truffle mash, chocolate mousse with Morello cherries. Rooms are gorgeous: creaking floorboards, timber-framed walls, a panelled four-poster. Those at the back are bigger and come in grand style, but all are lovely with crisp linen, local art and power showers in excellent bathrooms. There's afternoon tea on arrival if you book in advance and a garden for a pint in summer.

Rooms	5 doubles, 1 twin/double, 1 four-poster: £90-£145. Singles £90-£130. Dinner, B&B £97 p.p.
Meals	Lunch from £10.95 (not Monday). Dinner from £16.95.
Closed	Christmas.
Directions	A12 north past Colchester. 2nd exit, signed Dedham. In village opposite church.

Piers Baker
The Sun Inn
High Street,
Dedham, Colchester, CO7 6DF

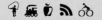

Tel +44 (0)1206 323351
Email office@thesuninndedham.com
Web www.thesuninndedham.com

The Mistley Thorn

This welcoming inn fits the Sawday bill perfectly – lovely owners with fingers dipped into delicious local pies. Their kitchen shop and cooking school stand four doors down the street; Lucca, their popular wood-fired pizzeria, waits in Manningtree. As for their inn, it stands on the high street and dates to 1746. Interiors have an airy feel, the mood is laid-back with a great little bar, the food is local and utterly delicious. Expect tongue-and-groove panelling, a roaring wood-burner, padded benches and a happy vibe. Nicely-priced rooms (two above the kitchen shop) have a similar feel: pretty fabrics, warm colours, crisp linen on comfy beds, REN lotions for power showers and double-ended baths. There's good art, homemade shortbread and fresh fruit, too; the rooms at the front have views of the Stour estuary. As for the food, it's delicious stuff, perhaps smoked haddock chowder, mussels with garlic and herbs, sticky toffee pudding. The Witchfinder General lived here, you can walk along the river to Dedham, the Beth Chatto Gardens are close.

Rooms	5 doubles, 3 twin/doubles: £110-£125. Singles from £90. Dinner, B&B from £75 p.p.
Meals	Lunch from £4.95. Set lunch, 2-3 courses, £12.50-£15. Dinner, 3 courses, about £30.
Closed	Rarely.
Directions	A12 Hadleigh/East Bergholt exit north of Colchester. Through East Bergholt to A137; signed Manningtree; continue to Mistley High St. 50 yds from station.

David McKay & Sherri Singleton
The Mistley Thorn
High Street, Mistley,
Manningtree, CO11 1HE

Tel +44 (0)1206 392821
Email info@mistleythorn.co.uk
Web www.mistleythorn.co.uk

The Pier at Harwich

They don't do things by halves at the Pier – a cool £1.5 million has recently been spent on a 21st-century makeover for this iconic coastal hotel. It sits on the harbourside with views of town and water, its front terrace a big draw in good weather. Inside, a cool new look captivates. A chic warehouse feel waits in the bar – stripped walls, hanging lamps, leather bar stools, big windows to frame the view. You get craft beers and cask ales, a gin library and Prosecco cocktails, then small plates of Nordic design if you fancy a light bite. Hungry souls fly upstairs to the famous first-floor brasserie, where mirrored booths and leather banquettes now come as standard, and doors open onto a balcony, where you can tuck into your lobster Thermidor while gazing out onto the estuary. Bedrooms – some above, others next door in a former inn – have fancy bedheads, seaside colours, crisp white linen and super bathrooms; the suite, with its vast window, has a telescope with which to scan the high seas. Coastal walks and blue flag beaches wait, as does the Electric Palace, the second oldest cinema in Britain.

Rooms	10 doubles, 3 twins: £120-£170. 1 suite for 2: £200-£230. Singles from £95. Dinner, B&B from £100 p.p.
Meals	Lunch from £6.50. Dinner à la carte £25-£40. Sunday lunch from £19.50.
Closed	Never.
Directions	M25 junc. 28, A12 to Colchester bypass, then A120 to Harwich. Head for quay. Hotel opposite pier.

Paul & Geraldine Milsom
The Pier at Harwich
The Quay,
Harwich, CO12 3HH

Tel +44 (0)1255 241212
Email pier@milsomhotels.com
Web www.milsomhotels.com

The Old Stocks Inn

Stow, a pretty market town, is nicely positioned for exploring the Cotswolds, with Stratford to the North, Cheltenham to the west, Oxford and Blenheim Palace to the east and the early stretches of the Thames to the south. As for this 17th-century inn, it's just been refurbished from top to toe. It sits on the market square with golden stone walls inside and out. Interiors mix original beams and timber frames with a big dollop of contemporary style – leather banquettes and hanging lamps in the stylish restaurant; panelled walls and an open fire in the cool little bar; a pretty coffee shop that overlooks the square. In summer, you spin onto a beautiful terrace for wood-fired pizzas in the sun. Super-comfy beds in beautiful rooms are wrapped in the crispest linen. You get coffee machines, iPod docks, Bakelite telephones, old Penguin books. All have chic bathrooms, some with claw-foot baths (a couple in the room). Three are dog-friendly, the family room has bunk beds and an Xbox. Good food waits downstairs, perhaps cured salmon, a chargrilled steak, then lemon and lime mousse.

Minimum stay: 2 nights at weekends in high season.

Rooms	9 doubles, 6 twin/doubles: £119-£279. 1 family room for 4: £159-£209. Extra bed/sofabed £10-£20 p.p.p.n.
Meals	Lunch & dinner £5-£35.
Closed	Never.
Directions	A429 to Stow-on-the-Wold. Inn on northeast corner of square in town.

Charlotte Knowles
The Old Stocks Inn
The Square,
Stow-on-the-Wold, GL54 1AF

Tel +44 (0)1451 830666
Email info@oldstocksinn.com
Web www.oldstocksinn.com

No. 38 The Park

This grand old Georgian house has been reborn as a designer B&B and it offers a level of style and service few hotels can match. It's a treasure trove of beautiful things: striking contemporary interiors, bedrooms you won't want to leave, cool tunes afloat in the air. Downstairs, an elegant sitting room comes with wood floors, deep sofas, fresh flowers and a smouldering fire. Contemporary art fills the room, sparkling chandeliers hang from on high, Peggy the dog rules the roost. There's an honesty bar where drinks are chilled in antique refrigerators, then a breakfast room with walls of glass that open onto a terrace when the sun shines. Bedrooms are flawless. Smaller rooms have beautiful beds, mohair throws, smart TVs and walk-in showers. Bigger rooms have that and more, perhaps a shower for two, a vast wet room, a zinc bath at the end of your bed. The racecourse is up the road, a shuttle whisks you over to their sister hotel for cocktails and a slap-up dinner. Take the whole place and a chef will come to cook; you can get married here too. Dogs are welcome; you can walk them in Pittville Park across the road. *Minimum stay: 2 nights at weekends.*

Rooms	13 doubles: £120-£280.
Meals	Continental breakfast included; cooked items from £4. Dinner for groups by arrangement. Restaurants within 500m. Free taxis provided to their sister restaurant.
Closed	Never.
Directions	South into Cheltenham on A345. Pick up Pittville Park on left. House on right at end of park.

Lee-Anna Rennie
No. 38 The Park
38 Evesham Rd, Cheltenham, GL52 2AH

Tel +44 (0)1242 822929
Email reservations@no38thepark.com
Web www.theluckyonion.com/property/no-38-the-park

No. 131

Beautiful hotels have a style all of their own and this chic townhouse is no exception. Outside, its Georgian façade overlooks Imperial Gardens and comes with towering Corinthian columns. Inside, striking interiors mix old and new to great effect. You get high windows, stripped floors, chandeliers and ceiling friezes, then an exciting collection of contemporary art that's conquered every wall. Fat sofas wait in front of smouldering fires, you find blue leather bar stools, vast yellow armchairs, old wooden fridges piled high with hams and cheese. Downstairs, there's a pool table, then a popular bar that turns into a terrace in summer thanks to a retractable roof. Indulging rooms have big beds, the best linen, piles of art books, robes and big walk-in showers in flawless bathrooms; some have a bath in the room, too. Great food waits in the restaurant, perhaps devilled crab on toast, slow cooked lamb with salsa verde, treacle tart with clotted cream. In summer, life spills onto the terrace for afternoon tea. A small spa is coming soon. Don't miss the jazz festival in May. *Minimum stay: 2 nights at weekends.*

Rooms	11 doubles: £150-£220.
Meals	Lunch from £7. Dinner, 3 courses, about £40. Sunday lunch from £21.
Closed	Never.
Directions	Pick up one-way system in the middle of town and follow it to its southwestern corner at Imperial Square; left onto the Promenade, signed 'M5, Gloucester, Oxford'. Hotel on right after 400m, before lights.

Stephen Wadcock
No. 131
131 The Promenade,
Cheltenham, GL50 1NW

Tel +44 (0)1242 822939
Email reservations@no131.com
Web www.no131.com

Three Choirs Vineyards

England's answer to the Napa Valley. After 15 years of tilling the soil (very sandy, good drainage), Thomas's 75 acres of Gloucestershire hillside now produce 300,000 bottles a year. There are regular tastings, a shop in which to buy a bottle or two, and paths that weave through the vines – a perfect stroll after a good meal. What's more, three fabulous lodges wait down by the lake, all with decks and walls of glass. You'll find claw-foot baths and comfy beds, so camp out in grand savannah style and listen to the woodpeckers. Rooms up at the restaurant are smart and spacious with terraces that overlook the vineyard. They come with padded bedheads, walls of colour, leather armchairs, flat-screen TVs and good bathrooms. Finally, the restaurant: claret walls, lovely views, sofas in front of an open fire. Excellent food waits, perhaps twice-baked Gloucester soufflé, fillet of bream with rocket and watercress, rhubarb crème brûlée with lemon shortbread. World wines are on the list, but you'll want something from the vines that surround you; there's a microbrewery, too. Perfect. *Minimum stay: 2 nights at weekends.*

Rooms	6 doubles, 3 vineyard lodges, 2 twins: £140–£195. Singles from £135.
Meals	Lunch from £7.50. Dinner à la carte about £35.
Closed	Christmas & New Year.
Directions	From Newent north on B4215 for about 1.5 miles. Follow brown signs to vineyard.

Thomas Shaw
Three Choirs Vineyards
Castle Tump,
Newent, GL18 1LS

Tel +44 (0)1531 890223
Email info@threechoirs.com
Web www.three-choirs-vineyards.co.uk

Tudor Farmhouse Hotel

A gorgeous small hotel, one of the best. It sits on the edge of the Forest of Dean, a magical world of woodland walks, medieval castles, meandering rivers and bleating sheep. You're in the middle of a tiny village with country views all around. Step inside to find sparkling interiors – Colin and Hari have spent a small fortune turning their realm into something very special indeed. An airy elegance mixes with golden stone walls and original timber frames, the house bearing testament to its Tudor roots. Big or small, bedrooms are divine – stylishly uncluttered with smart fabrics, robes in fine bathrooms and super-comfy beds. Those in the main house have ancient beamed ceilings, those in the old barns have original stone walls. The bigger rooms are faultless: the best beds, claw-foot baths, enormous showers, the lap of luxury. Lovely local food waits downstairs, perhaps cider-cured salmon, haunch of venison, rhubarb Bakewell tart; there are home-laid eggs for breakfast, too. You can kayak on the Wye, forage in the forest, take to cycle tracks. Don't miss Puzzlewood or Clearwell Caves. *Minimum stay: 2 nights at weekends.*

Rooms	10 doubles, 3 twins, 2 four-posters: £100-£230. 5 suites for 2: £180-£230. Singles £90-£220. Extra bed/sofabed £25 p.p.p.n.
Meals	Lunch from £6.95. Dinner, 3 courses, £30-£40. Sunday lunch from £14.50.
Closed	Never.
Directions	South from Monmouth on A466. Clearwell signed left after 3 miles.

Colin & Hari Fell
Tudor Farmhouse Hotel
High Street,
Clearwell, GL16 8JS

Tel	+44 (0)1594 833046
Email	info@tudorfarmhousehotel.co.uk
Web	www.tudorfarmhousehotel.co.uk

The Master Builder's House Hotel

The position here is hard to beat: lawns run down to the river, yacht masts flutter in the breeze, ancient woodland runs along the water, soundproofing this beautiful landscape. As for the house, it dates to 1729 and was home to the shipwrights who built Nelson's fleet; several ships built here saw action at Trafalgar. These days peace reigns. A chic sitting room opens onto a smart garden, where gravel paths weave past colourful beds to tables for lunch in the sun. There's a lovely old bar and an airy restaurant – both have terraces that drink in the view, and both serve tasty local fare, too, perhaps a pizza or posh fish and chips in the bar, perhaps smoked rabbit chorizo, pot au feu with local veg, salted butterscotch crème brûlée in the restaurant. Bedrooms in the main house have big views, Indian furniture, then colour and character in spades. Those in the annexe, recently refurbished (a few await their turn), come in crisp blues and whites, with a wall of wood, Bose sound systems and excellent walk-in showers. As for the New Forest, walk, cycle or kayak though it. A great forest base.

Rooms	17 doubles, 9 twin/doubles: £95-£320. 2 cottages for 4: £500-£1,400 per week. Singles from £100.
Meals	Lunch from £5. Dinner: in the bar from £12; in the restaurant, 3 courses, £30-£35. Afternoon tea from £15. Sunday lunch £19.95-£23.95.
Closed	Never.
Directions	From Lyndhurst B3056 south past Beaulieu turn-off. 1st left, signed Buckler's Hard. Signed left after 1 mile.

Paul Brown
The Master Builder's House Hotel
Bucklers Hard, Beaulieu,
Brockenhurst, SO42 7XB

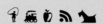

Tel +44 (0)1590 616253
Email enquiries@themasterbuilders.co.uk
Web www.themasterbuilders.co.uk

The Montagu Arms

Beaulieu, an ancient royal hunting ground, was gifted to Cistercian monks by King John in 1204. Their abbey took 40 years to build and you can visit its ruins in the nearby grounds of Palace House, seat of the Montagu family since 1538. As for the village, its tiny high street is a hotchpotch of 17th-century timber-framed houses that totter by the tidal estuary drinking in the view. The hotel dates to 1742, but was re-modelled in 1925, giving interiors an Arts & Crafts country-house feel. You'll find roaring fires and deep sofas, then a library bar and a courtyard garden where you can eat in summer. Chic bedrooms come with period furniture, smart fabrics, fresh flowers and robes in spotless bathrooms. Downstairs, ambrosial food is the big surprise, perhaps truffle risotto with wild mushrooms, saddle of roe deer with parsnip purée, Seville orange soufflé with pepper ice-cream. There's a gastro pub if you want something lighter: local fish pie, ham and chips with poached eggs from resident hens. A kitchen garden provides much for the table, too. Beautiful walks start from the front door. *Minimum stay: 2 nights at weekends.*

Rooms	7 doubles, 3 twin/doubles, 4 four-posters: £157-£317. 5 suites for 2: £257-£377. Singles from £129. Dinner, B&B from £140 p.p.
Meals	Lunch from £25. Dinner, 3 courses, £70; 7-course tasting menu £90. Sunday lunch from £32.50.
Closed	Never.
Directions	South from M27, junc. 1 to Lyndhurst on A337, then B3056 for Beaulieu. Left into village and hotel on right.

Sunil Kanjanghat
The Montagu Arms
Palace Lane, Beaulieu,
Brockenhurst, SO42 7ZL

Tel +44 (0)1590 612324
Email reservations@montaguarmshotel.co.uk
Web www.montaguarmshotel.co.uk

Daisybank Cottage Boutique B&B

This chic B&B in the New Forest mixes a warm contemporary style with some fine, old-fashioned hospitality – Ciaran and Cheryl go out of their way to make your stay special. As for their lovely Arts & Crafts house, it sits peacefully on the southern fringes of Brockenhurst with pretty gardens front and back. There's a juke box in the breakfast room, then an honesty bar for pre-dinner drinks. Spoiling bedrooms have airy colours, plantation shutters, Vi-Spring mattresses for lovely beds, then robes in stylish bathrooms. One has a claw-foot bath, another at the back opens onto the garden; keep going you'll find a shepherd's hut with its own wood-burner and a small terrace. All rooms have coffee machines, silent fridges in which to chill drinks, iPod docks and flat-screen TVs; a reading room is coming for 2018. Breakfast is a feast: local eggs, artisan jams, home-baked soda bread, bacon and sausages from a local farm. You can walk by the sea or explore the forest by foot, bike or horse. Good restaurants wait in town (a gentle ten-minute stroll), perhaps Thai, French or an excellent pizza. *Minimum stay: 2 nights at weekends. Over 10s welcome.*

Rooms	4 doubles: £120-£155. 2 cottages for 2; 1 shepherd's hut for 2: £120-£155. Extra bed/sofabed £35-£40 p.p.p.n.
Meals	Local restaurants within half a mile.
Closed	One week over Christmas.
Directions	M27, junc. 1, then A337 south for Lymington. Right onto B3055 as you approach Brockenhurst. Over x-roads and signed left after half a mile.

Cheryl & Ciaran Maher
Daisybank Cottage Boutique B&B
Sway Road,
Brockenhurst, SO42 7SG

Tel +44 (0)1590 622086
Email info@bedandbreakfast-newforest.co.uk
Web www.bedandbreakfast-newforest.co.uk

The Manor at Sway

A big house in a small village in the middle of the New Forest – lovely gardens run down to woodland, the odd deer comes in to nibble the roses. Inside, country-house interiors have a distinctly contemporary feel – airy and nicely stylish with wood floors, pretty wallpapers and a relaxed feel. You'll find smart sofas in the sitting room, then a chic bar with a wall of glass that opens onto the terrace, perfect for afternoon tea in the sun. Bedrooms are lovely. They come in different shapes and sizes, but all have the same comforts: excellent beds, crisp linen, warm colours, sparkling bathrooms. Three are dog-friendly, those in the eaves are warmly cosy, larger rooms have armchairs, most have garden views. The big surprise is the delicious food, so work up an appetite in the forest by day, then come home for a feast, perhaps scallops with curried cauliflower, local venison in a port sauce, Bakewell tart with blackberry jam. There are simpler dishes, too: posh fish and chips, pork belly with buttered greens, beetroot tarte tatin. Fabulous walking, mountain bike trails and sun loungers in the garden wait. *Minimum stay: 2 nights at weekends.*

Rooms	12 doubles, 3 twin/doubles: £90-£210.
Meals	Lunch from £6. Dinner, 3 courses, £30-£40. Sunday lunch £19.50-£24.50.
Closed	Rarely.
Directions	South from Brockenhurst on B3055 for 3 miles. In village, right at Skoda garage, then right at x-roads, for station. On left after 500m.

Tim Holloway
The Manor at Sway
Station Road, Sway,
Lymington, SO41 6BA

Tel +44 (0)1590 682754
Email info@swaymanor.com
Web www.themanoratsway.com

Chewton Glen

Chewton Glen is one of the loveliest country-house hotels in the land. It opened in 1964 with eight bedrooms, and even though it now has over 70, it remains delightfully intimate. Fifty years of evolution have brought a pillared swimming pool, a hydrotherapy spa, a golf course and a tennis centre. The most recent addition is The Kitchen, an informal foil to the main restaurant, where you can also come for cookery classes. As for the hotel, expect beautiful sitting rooms, roaring fires, busts and oils, a bar that opens onto a sun-trapping terrace. Bedrooms mix country-house style with contemporary flair. Expect marble bathrooms, private balconies, designer fabrics, flawless housekeeping. You'll also find 13 treehouses that sit peacefully in their own valley with hot tubs on balconies and wood-burners within. Beyond, nine gardeners tend 130 acres of lawns and woodland, with a kitchen garden that serves both restaurants. The food is exceptional, perhaps twice-baked cheese soufflé, Thai lobster curry, pineapple and black pepper tarte tatin. Beach and forest wait, there's croquet on the lawn in summer. *Minimum stay: 2 nights at weekends.*

Rooms	5 doubles, 30 twin/doubles: £325-£695. 23 suites for 2: £800-£1,495. 13 treehouses for 2: £850-£1500.
Meals	Breakfast £21-£26. The Kitchen: lunch & dinner from £10. Main restaurant: lunch, 3 courses, £26.50. Dinner, 3 courses, £50-£70. Tasting menu £70. Afternoon tea £29.50. Sunday lunch £39.50.
Closed	Never.
Directions	A337 west from Lymington. Through New Milton for Christchurch. Right at r'bout, for Walkford. Right again; on right.

Andrew Stembridge
Chewton Glen
Christchurch Road,
New Milton, BH25 6QS

Tel +44 (0)1425 275341
Email reservations@chewtonglen.com
Web www.chewtonglen.com

The Verzon

This English auberge has a cute rustic style and serves some seriously good food. It sits on the Hereford to Ledbury road and is owned by Will and Kate Chase, farmers who turn their potatoes and apples into Chase vodka and gin. Not that this is the limit of their world. They also rear cattle and pigs and have a vineyard in the Lubéron. The Verzon exists to bring it all together – a gin and tonic on the terrace in summer, then a lovely dinner washed down by French wines. Most of the food is sourced within 30 miles, perhaps a hoppy Hereford rarebit, a perfect Chase steak, an ambrosial pecan tart with espresso mousse. Interiors mix old and new playfully, with timber frames and Union-Jack sofas in the bar, then a white marble fireplace in the theatrical dining room. Bedrooms have warm colours, crisp linen and robes in fine bathrooms. Two have baths in the room, those at the back have views over fields to the Malvern Hills. Local ales and a roaring fire wait in the bar, while the Chase distillery is up the road, with tours easily arranged. Don't miss Hereford cathedral for the Mappa Mundi.

Rooms	4 twin/doubles: £90-£140. 3 suites for 2: £160-£180. 1 single: £80. Extra beds £15.
Meals	Lunch from £12. Dinner, 3 courses, £30-£40. Sunday lunch £22-£27. Afternoon tea from £15.
Closed	Never.
Directions	A438 west from Ledbury for 4 miles. On right, signed.

Will & Kate Chase
The Verzon
Hereford Road, Trumpet,
Ledbury, HR8 2PZ

Tel +44 (0)1531 670381
Email info@verzonhouse.com
Web www.verzonhouse.com

Castle House

Hereford's loveliest hotel stands 200 paces from the city's magnificent 11th-century cathedral, home to the Mappa Mundi. It's English to its core with a beautiful garden that overlooks what remains of the castle moat – in summer you can eat here watching ducks glide by. Inside, the lap of luxury: a fine staircase, painted panelling, a delicious restaurant for the best food in town. Big bedrooms are lavish. Those in the main house are more traditional (the top-floor suite runs all the way along the front of the house); those in the townhouse (a 30-second stroll) are distinctly 21st century. All have a smart country-house feel with beautiful fabrics, super-comfy beds, crisp white linen, excellent bathrooms. Seriously good food, much from the owner's nearby farm, waits in the restaurant, perhaps beetroot panna cotta, roast bream with saffron mash, banana mousse with chocolate brownies. You can walk it off along the river Wye, which runs through the park behind. Hereford has lots to offer: pop-up opera, guided walks, Evensong in the cathedral, the Three Choirs Festival in July.

Rooms	4 doubles: £150-£190. 16 suites for 2: £195-£250. 4 singles: £130.
Meals	Lunch from £5. Sunday lunch from £18.50. Dinner, 3 courses, about £35.
Closed	Never.
Directions	Follow signs to Hereford city centre, then City Centre east. Right off Bath St into Union St, through St Peters Sq to Owen's St, then right into St Ethelbert St. Hotel on left as road veers right.

Michelle Marriott-Lodge
Castle House
Castle Street,
Hereford, HR1 2NW

Tel	+44 (0)1432 356321
Email	info@castlehse.co.uk
Web	www.castlehse.co.uk

Brooks Country House

Led Zeppelin used to stay here when recording at studios on a nearby farm, and there's definitely a bit of a rock-star feel to the place. A big house in the country, a swimming pool in the kitchen garden and its own vineyard that produces wine for the restaurant... There's a rather good view, too, a clean sweep over ten miles of rolling country to rising mountains. The house once stood in 1,000 acres and now has a mere 12, but the land beyond is owned by the National Trust and you can walk straight out, skirt a copse and find yourself at a 14th-century church. As for the hotel, it's going to make a small splash – Andrew and Carla are far too down-to-earth for anything bigger. It's a total refurbishment – smart, but relaxed, a place to feel at home. Expect an open fire in the sitting room, wood floors in the restaurant, then cowhide rugs in a bar that opens onto a sun-trapping garden. Nicely priced rooms are scattered about, some grander, others smaller, all with good beds, warm colours and lovely bathrooms. As for the food, it's earthy stuff; homemade soups, a local rib-eye, a sinful chocolate tart. Hard to beat. *Minimum stay: 2 nights at weekends.*

Rooms	14 twin/doubles, 6 four-posters: £79-£169. 2 suites for 2: £99-£169. 3 trucks for 2: £99-£139. Singles £89-£119. Dinner, B&B £60-£80 p.p. Extra bed/sofabed £10-£20 p.p.p.n.
Meals	Dinner £19.50-£25.
Closed	Never.
Directions	West from Ross-on-Wye on A49. Through Peterstow and hotel signed right after 1 mile.

Carla & Andrew Brooks
Brooks Country House
Pengethley Park,
Ross-on-Wye, HR9 6LL

Tel	+44 (0)1989 730211
Email	info@brookscountryhouse.com
Web	www.brookscountryhouse.com

The Bridge House

Kevin and Kathryn left high-flying jobs to cook, clean, polish and shine; extraordinarily, they couldn't be happier. Their new home is this attractive 17th-century merchant's house with the best view in town. Lawns run down to the river Wye, then views shoot up the other side to St Mary's church. Inside, you find original elm floors and painted beamed ceilings, but the feel is contemporary, with cool colours, beautiful armchairs and antler chandeliers in the sitting room. Bedrooms have an easy elegance: comfy beds, crisp linen, pretty art, the odd timber frame. Five have the view, two have a claw-foot bath, others have power showers, a couple on high can be taken together. Breakfast is delicious, with doors in the sun room that fold back to drink in the view. Walk in the hills, kayak on the Wye, cycle in the Forest of Dean. Come home to an honesty bar in the sitting room and three terraces in the gorgeous garden, where colourful beds flourish. Wilton Castle, a 12th-century ruin, stands across the field; Hereford is close for the Mappa Mundi; good local restaurants wait. Dogs are welcome. *Minimum stay: 2 nights at weekends.*

Rooms	6 doubles, 2 twin/doubles: £95–£130. Singles £80.
Meals	Restaurants within walking distance.
Closed	15 December to 1 February.
Directions	Leave A40 in Wilton for B4260, signed Ross-on-Wye. On left after 250m.

Kevin & Kathryn Whyte
The Bridge House
Wilton,
Ross-on-Wye, HR9 6AA

Tel +44 (0)1989 562655
Email info@bridgehouserossonwye.co.uk
Web www.bridgehouserossonwye.co.uk

Wilton Court Restaurant with Rooms

This Grade-II listed house dates to 1510 and looks across the lane to the river Wye: herons dive, otters swim, kingfishers nest. Roses ramble outside, happy guests potter within. This is a small hotel with pretty rooms, good food and owners that care. Bedrooms upstairs come in different shapes and sizes, but all have style. Those at the front have watery views, William Morris wallpaper, lots of space, perhaps a four-poster. A couple of rooms are small (as is their price), but, along with several others, have recently been refurbished. Expect lots of colour, a wall of paper, white bathrooms and sofas in the bigger rooms. Back downstairs there's a bar for pre-dinner drinks, a wood-burner in the panelled library, then a conservatory restaurant for tasty food, perhaps Shropshire blue cheese soufflé, Herefordshire beef with savoy cabbage, caramel panna cotta with vanilla ice cream. Berries from a Grade-I listed mulberry tree in the garden are turned into sorbets and pies. You can cross the lane to a second garden for drinks by the river in summer. Ross is a five-minute stroll. *Minimum stay: 2 nights at weekends.*

Rooms	4 doubles, 5 twin/doubles, 1 four-poster: £135-£185. 1 family room for 4: £165-£205. Singles from £100.
Meals	Lunch snacks from £6.95. Lunch, 2 courses, £16.95; 3 courses, £19.95. Dinner, 2 courses, £27.50; 3 courses, £32.50; 3 courses à la carte £35-£40.
Closed	Rarely.
Directions	South into Ross at A40/A49 Wilton roundabout. 1st right into Wilton Lane. Hotel on right.

Roger & Helen Wynn
Wilton Court Restaurant with Rooms
Wilton Lane, Wilton,
Ross-on-Wye, HR9 6AQ

Tel	+44 (0)1989 562569
Email	info@wiltoncourthotel.com
Web	www.wiltoncourthotel.com

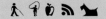

Hillside

Is it an art gallery, a small holding or just a cool hotel? Whatever it is, Hillside is a great little place to wash up for a couple of nights. It stands at the foot of forested hills with views over Ventnor and out to sea. Outside, five acres of lawn, field and woodland are home to Hebridean sheep, free-range chickens, red squirrels and white doves; there are beehives, too, and a stunning kitchen garden that provides much for the table. Inside, you find a wonderland in white. There's a cute bar with a wood-burner, a sitting room with Danish leather sofas, an airy restaurant for the freshest food, then a conservatory that opens onto a terrace for afternoon tea in the sun. Inside, 286 pieces of art hang on the walls, but it's the food that counts most; the hotel has its own fishing boat and rears its own cattle in nearby fields. And it's delicious stuff, as fresh as can be, perhaps Ventnor Bay scallops with chorizo and Hillside honey, local rack of lamb with a red wine jus and garden greens, pear tarte tatin with edible wild flowers. Uncluttered bedrooms are a treat, those at the front have the view. *Minimum stay: 2 nights at weekends.*

Rooms	6 doubles, 2 twin/doubles, 1 twin: £156-£206. 3 singles: £78-£143. 2 apartments for 4: £206-£292. Dinner, B&B from £108 p.p.
Meals	Lunch, 2 courses, £20. Dinner £24-£28.
Closed	Never.
Directions	South to Ventnor on A3055, then right (on approach to town) onto B3277. Past tennis courts, up hill, on right.

Gert Bach
Hillside
151 Mitchell Avenue,
Ventnor, PO38 1DR

Tel +44 (0)1983 852271
Email mail@hillsideventnor.co.uk
Web www.hillsideventnor.co.uk

Hever Castle Luxury Bed & Breakfast

Hever is out of this world, a 13th-century moated castle that was home to Anne Boleyn, second wife to Henry VIII, mother of Elizabeth I. It is one of those places that thrills adults and children alike. It has all the regal trimmings: 625 acres of green and pleasant land with formal gardens and a 38-acre lake. You stay in the Astor wing or the Anne Boleyn wing, both built in Tudor style in 1903. Family-friendly rooms are fit for a queen. Expect period colours, panelled walls, perhaps a golden chaise longue or a glimpse of the castle through leaded windows. One has a vaulted ceiling, bigger rooms have sofas, several have four-poster beds. Bathrooms are faultless, some with claw-foot baths, others with walk-in power showers; a few have both. There's a panelled sitting room, a timber-framed billiard room, and a small courtyard for summer sun. Entrance to the castle and gardens is included in your room price. You can wander the grounds, boat on the lake, watch the odd spot of jousting, while a moated castle playground is a big hit with kids. A village pub for good food is a short stroll. Unbeatable.

Rooms	22 doubles, 3 twins: £168-£295. 2 singles: £105-£120. Extra beds £50 p.p.p.n.
Meals	Restaurants within 0.25 miles.
Closed	Rarely.
Directions	Castle signed west out of Edenbridge.

Roland Smith
Hever Castle Luxury Bed & Breakfast
Hever,
Edenbridge, TN8 7NG

Tel	+44 (0)1732 861800
Email	stay@hevercastle.co.uk
Web	www.hevercastle.co.uk

The Milk House

The gardens at Sissinghurst Castle were designed by Vita Sackville-West. They're some of the loveliest in the land and if you stay at this charming village pub, you can stroll over after breakfast, through apple orchards and bluebell woods. As for the Milk House, it's a great base from which to explore – stylish, welcoming, nicely priced. It's also a place for excellent food, with seasonal produce mostly sourced within 20 miles. In summer, you decant onto a big terrace with an outside bar and a wood-fired pizza oven, not a bad spot for a crispy margherita and a glass of Pimm's. There's a duck pond, a lawned garden, views over open country, even a four-day festival in August (local bands, theatre, face painting, lots of food). Interiors have an easy style: woven willow lampshades, a sofa in front of the fire, a timber-framed dining room for fabulous food, perhaps twice-baked Stilton soufflé, grilled mackerel with roasted fennel, After Eight crème brûlée with brandy butter brioche. Beautiful bedrooms are crisply uncluttered. Expect chic fabrics, super beds, excellent bathrooms, a sofa if there's room.

Rooms	3 doubles, 1 twin: £80-£140. Extra bed/sofabed £10 p.p.p.n.
Meals	Lunch from £6. Dinner, 3 courses, about £30. Sunday lunch from £15.
Closed	Rarely.
Directions	East into Sissinghurst on A262. In village, on left.

Dane & Sarah Allchorne
The Milk House
The Street, Sissinghurst,
Cranbrook, TN17 2JG

Tel +44 (0)1580 720200
Email fresh@themilkhouse.co.uk
Web www.themilkhouse.co.uk

The Barrow House

You get a little time travel at the Barrow House: a 14th-century inn, 17th-century timber frames, 21st-century comfort and design. It's a great little place – friendly and stylish with super food and all sorts of libations waiting at the bar. It sits in a pretty village surrounded by open country with Leeds Castle up the road. Known as the George for centuries, it changed its name in deference to the Bronze Age barrow that rises in a field on the edge of the village; great walking waits. Back at the inn, there's a smart terrace for lunch in the sun, then a couple of open fires inside to keep things cosy. The bar mixes old-fashioned conviviality with chic design. They serve their own ale, craft beers and well-priced wines, but you can pop in for an espresso, too. Lovely rooms have big beds, pretty fabrics and smart TVs, perhaps timber frames or a wonky floor; bathrooms are a treat. As for the food, most is sourced within 20 miles. You'll find soups and sharing plates, burgers and fish and chips, or a three-course feast, perhaps smoked salmon, slow-cooked beef, marmalade Bakewell tart.

Rooms	2 doubles, 1 twin/double: £80-£140. Extra bed £10 p.p.p.n.
Meals	Lunch from £6. Dinner, 3 courses, about £25.
Closed	Never.
Directions	M20, junction 8, then A20 south. Right, signed Egerton, two miles south of Lenham. Keep straight for 2 miles. In village, on left.

Dane & Sarah Allchorne
The Barrow House
The Street,
Egerton, TN27 9DJ

Tel +44 (0)1233 756599
Email digin@thebarrowhouse.co.uk
Web www.thebarrowhouse.co.uk

The Relish

It's not just the super-comfy interiors that make The Relish such a tempting port of call. There's a sense of generosity here: a drink on the house each night in the sitting room; tea and cakes on tap all day; free internet throughout. This is a grand 1850s merchant's house on the posh side of town – lovely old bricks and mortar, softly contemporary interiors. Laura and Rakesh took over recently and have already pulled out the paintbrushes, so wind up the cast-iron staircase to find bedrooms that make you smile. You get Hypnos beds with padded headboards, crisp white linen and pretty throws. There's a sense of space, a sofa if there's room, big mirrors and lovely bathrooms. All are great value for money. Downstairs candles flicker on the mantelpieces above open fires, the high-ceilinged dining room comes with stripped floors and padded benches and in summer you can decamp onto the terrace for breakfast, a communal garden stretching out beyond. You're one street back from Folkestone's cliff-top front for big sea views. Steps lead down to smart gardens, the promenade and waterside restaurants. *Minimum stay: 2 nights at weekends in summer.*

Rooms	9 doubles: £88-£150. 1 single: £70-£75.
Meals	Restaurants nearby.
Closed	22 December to 2 January; last week of January.
Directions	In centre of town, from Langholm Gardens, head west on Sandgate Road. 1st right into Augusta Gardens/Trinity Gardens. Hotel on right.

Laura & Rakesh Sharma
The Relish
4 Augusta Gardens,
Folkestone, CT20 2RR

Tel +44 (0)1303 850952
Email reservations@hotelrelish.co.uk
Web www.hotelrelish.co.uk

Albion House

This is quite some house, a Regency pile that dates to 1790, with huge rooms, high ceilings and grandeur at every turn. It stands at the top of a hill in the middle of town with fine views over the Royal Harbour. Incredibly, it was left to decay by its last inhabitants, Ramsgate Town Council, whose headquarters this was until 2008. Now, after a long renovation, interiors shine, mixing contemporary design with the feel of a colonial gentleman's club. There's a fire in reception, watery views through big windows in the restaurant, then a fabulous bar with a grand piano, exotic pot plants, a roaring fire, and sofas everywhere. Classical prints are jammed on the wall, the bar itself came from the town hall. The whole place is a work of art, nothing is here by accident. A treatment room, a steam room and a vaulted cavern for wine tastings are coming for summer 2018. Big bedrooms get smaller as you climb the house, but the best views are at the top. Expect good beds, crisp linen, neutral colours, robes in white marble bathrooms. Beaches, gardens and cliff-top walks wait, but don't miss afternoon tea. *Minimum stay: 2 nights at weekends April-September.*

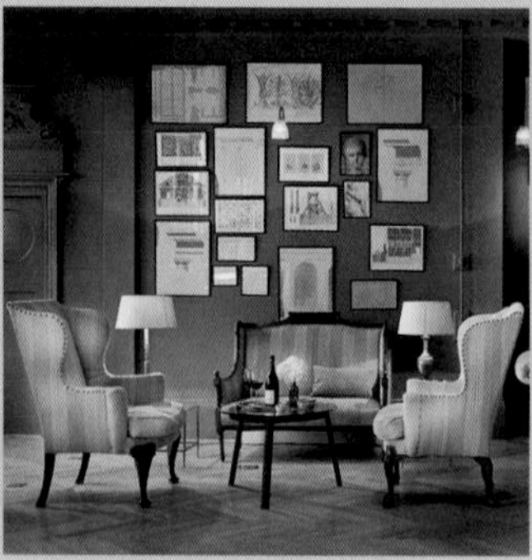

Rooms	13 twin/doubles: £89-£245. 1 suite for 2: £180-£345. Dinner, B&B from £80 p.p.
Meals	Lunch from £5. Dinner, 3 courses, £25-£35. Sunday lunch from £16. Afternoon tea £16.
Closed	Never.
Directions	M2, A299, then B2054 into Ramsgate. Follow signs for town centre, pick up coast on right, down hill, up the other side, on left at top.

Ben & Emma Irvine
Albion House
Albion Place,
Ramsgate, CT11 8HQ

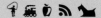

Tel +44 (0)1843 606630
Email enquiries@albionhouseramsgate.co.uk
Web www.albionhouseramsgate.co.uk

Sands Hotel Margate

Hoteliers don't do things by halves, and Nick is a case in point. He bought a crumbling pile, knocked the place down, then built it back up again. The result is a delicious hotel with huge views of beach and sea, a view framed triumphantly by walls of glass in the enormous restaurant and bar. Coastal light floods the room, there's a balcony for afternoon tea, three chandeliers hanging above the bar, crushed velvet banquettes to salute Victorian roots and, with Turner Contemporary a five-minute stroll along the seafront, big canvases that pay homage to the great man's work. Bedrooms have bags of style; nine have sea views, six have balconies and all have chic fabrics, padded bedheads, smart TVs and robes in fine bathrooms. There's a roof terrace above for the best views in town and an ice-cream parlour and pizzeria below, but you'll want to stop in the middle for the food as well as the view; perhaps gin and juniper-cured salmon, or confit pork belly with candied apple, finished off with a spiced pineapple tarte tatin. Canterbury, Broadstairs and Ramsgate are close and the train from Victoria takes less than two hours. *Minimum stay: 2 nights at weekends in high season.*

Rooms	10 doubles, 10 twin/doubles: £120-£210. Dinner, B&B £95-£130 p.p. Extra bed/sofabed available £20-£40 p.p.p.n.
Meals	Lunch from £11.50. Cream tea £6.50. Afternoon tea £14.95. Dinner, 3 courses, £35.
Closed	Never.
Directions	A28 into Margate. Keep straight ahead with the coast on your left and hotel on right at end of beach.

Nick Conington
Sands Hotel Margate
16 Marine Drive,
Margate, CT9 1DH

Tel +44 (0)1843 228228
Email info@sandshotelmargate.co.uk
Web www.sandshotelmargate.co.uk

Read's Restaurant with Rooms

For the last 40 years David and Rona have been whisking up ambrosial food for the world and his wife to eat. On its own that's an incredible achievement, but to do so at the highest level is extraordinary. What's more, they make no fuss about it, just come to work every day and excel at what they do, a testament to their dedication and love of good food. As for Read's, it's a restaurant with rooms that happens to be a country house set in five acres of lawned gardens that include – no surprise – a productive kitchen garden. Inside, elegance at every turn. There's a sitting-room bar for pre-dinner drinks, then three dining rooms, where you eat at clothed tables, perhaps a Montgomery Cheddar soufflé, wild mallard with blackberries, Cox apple mousse with toffee apple jelly and cinnamon ice cream. Bedrooms are just as good, country-house splendour in spades. Expect decanters of sherry, Roberts radios, beds dressed in crisp white linen, smart bathrooms with white robes. Don't miss the orchards at Brogdale, where thousands of varieties of apples, pears, plums and cherries are on show.

Rooms	5 doubles, 1 twin/double: £165-£195. Singles from £125. Dinner, B&B from £135 p.p.
Meals	Lunch £28. Dinner £60.
Closed	Sunday & Monday. 1st 2 weeks in Jan, 1st 2 weeks in Sept. 25-27 December.
Directions	M2, junc. 7, then A2 west into Faversham. Past petrol station and signed left after 400m.

David & Rona Pitchford
Read's Restaurant with Rooms
Macknade Manor, Canterbury Road,
Faversham, ME13 8XE

Tel	+44 (0)1795 535344
Email	enquiries@reads.com
Web	www.reads.com

The Cartford Inn

This quirky inn is full of its own delights, not least its stylish interiors, fabulous food and helpful staff. This might explain why it was named Best Inn in Britain in 2016, a richly deserved award. Julie and Patrick love their world and can't stop spending money on it. Last year they opened a gorgeous deli on the terrace, this year, they've built two gob-smacking suites on stilts overlooking the river. It's a mecca for locals, who come to eat, drink and gossip. Outside, views stretch across to the Trough of Bowland. Inside, delicious food waits, perhaps fresh crab gnocchi, roasted Lytham poussin, Ovaltine panna cotta with dark chocolate mousse. The bar, with its cool art and roaring fire, is a great place to linger over a pint of local ale, but a courtyard garden will draw you out in good weather. Bedrooms have style in spades: gilded sleigh beds, signature wallpapers, river views, perhaps a roll-top bath in the room; the penthouse has a rooftop terrace, too. You can follow the river on a two-mile circular walk. Don't miss Blackpool, a proper northern town. Brilliant.

Rooms	11 doubles: £125-£230. 1 suite for 2: £230. 2 family rooms for 3-4: £150. Singles £80.
Meals	Lunch from £8.50 (not Mon). Dinner, 3 courses, £25-£35.
Closed	Christmas Day.
Directions	M6 junc. 32, M55 junc. 3, then A585 north. Right at T-junc. onto A586 for Garstang. Little Eccleston signed left.

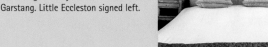

Patrick & Julie Beaume
The Cartford Inn
Cartford Lane, Little Eccleston,
Preston, PR3 0YP

Tel +44 (0)1995 670166
Email info@thecartfordinn.co.uk
Web www.thecartfordinn.co.uk

The Inn at Whitewell

It is almost impossible to imagine a day when a better inn will grace the English landscape. Everything here is perfect. The inn sits just above the river Hodder, and doors in the bar lead onto a terrace where guests can enjoy five-mile views across parkland to rising fells. Inside, fires roar, newspapers wait, there are beams, sofas, maps and copies of *Wisden*. Bedrooms, some in the Coach House, are exemplary and come with real luxury, perhaps a peat fire, a lavish four-poster, a fabulous Victorian power shower. All have beautiful fabrics, top linen and gadgets galore; many have the marvellous view – you can fall asleep at night to the sound of the river. There are bar meals for those who want to watch their weight (the Whitewell fish pie is rightly famous) or a restaurant for splendid food, so dig into seared scallops, Bowland lamb, a plate of local cheese (the Queen once popped in for lunch). Elsewhere, a wine shop in reception, seven miles of private fishing and countryside as good as any in the land. Dogs and children are very welcome. Magnificent.

Rooms	17 doubles, 5 twin/doubles: £120-£215. 1 suite for 2: £210-£240. Singles from £92.
Meals	Lunch & bar meals from £8. Dinner £25-£35.
Closed	Never.
Directions	M6 junc. 31A, B6243 east through Longridge, then follow signs to Whitewell for 9 miles.

Charles Bowman
The Inn at Whitewell
Dunsop Road, Whitewell,
Clitheroe, BB7 3AT

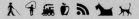

Tel +44 (0)1200 448222
Email reception@innatwhitewell.com
Web www.innatwhitewell.com

Washingborough Hall

In its day Lincoln was one of the most important cities in England. Its castle holds a copy of the Magna Carta and was built by William the Conqueror in 1068; its cathedral dates to 1090 and remains one of the finest in Europe. All of which makes it a great city to visit, and if you want to beat a peaceful retreat into the country at the end of the day, this is the place to stay. It sits two miles east of town in a small village on the river Witham – footpaths by the water lead back into town. As for this Georgian rectory, you'll find smart lawns to the front, then a big welcome within – Edward and Lucy go out of their way to make your stay special. There's a wood-burner in the hall, a breakfast room with garden views, a sitting-room bar for afternoon tea, then a light-filled orangery restaurant. Stylish bedrooms offer unstinting comforts. Rooms at the front are bigger and have the view, all have good beds, bold wallpapers, excellent bathrooms, a sofa if there's room. As for the food, there's posh fish and chips in the bar or sea bass with spring greens in the orangery.

Rooms	6 doubles, 3 twin/doubles, 2 four-posters: £85-£175. 1 suite for 2: £175-£195. 2 singles: £65-£85.
Meals	Lunch from £5.50. Dinner, 3 courses, £25-£35. Sunday lunch from £18.50.
Closed	Never.
Directions	East out of Lincoln on B1190. In village, right at mini r'bout onto Church Hill. On left after 500m.

Lucy & Edward Herring
Washingborough Hall
Church Hill,
Washingborough, LN4 1BE

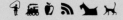

Tel +44 (0)1522 790340
Email enquiries@washingboroughhall.com
Web www.washingboroughhall.com

The William Cecil

This attractive townhouse hotel stands yards from the gates of the Burghley estate. Inside, interiors offer a pleasing mix of English quirkiness and splendour. Downstairs, informality reigns. There are armchairs in front of the fire in the bar, smart wicker tables in the conservatory, doors onto a lovely terrace in summer, then hanging lamps and half-panelling in the colourful restaurant. The food is fresh and local with seasonal delights that include game from the estate. You might find lobster mousse with avocado ice-cream, slow-cooked Burghley venison casserole, lemon curd pie with lime sorbet. You can walk it all off with a stroll through historic Stamford or spin over to Burghley for one of the finest Elizabethan houses in the realm. Come back to country-house bedrooms that mix eclectic Rajasthan furniture with a little English decorum. You'll find beautiful art, a wall of paper, perhaps a day bed or a ceiling rose. Some have views onto the estate, all have good bathrooms, the best with roll top tubs and vast walk-in showers. Dogs don't fare badly either with Union Jack beds.

Rooms	20 doubles, 7 twin/doubles: £100-£180.
Meals	Lunch from £6.50. Dinner from £12. Sunday lunch, 3 courses, £24.50.
Closed	Never.
Directions	A1 north past Easton-on-the-Hill, then B1081 for Stamford. On right as you enter town.

Paul Brown
The William Cecil
St Martins,
Stamford, PE9 2LJ

Tel	+44 (0)1780 750070
Email	enquiries@thewilliamcecil.co.uk
Web	www.thewilliamcecil.co.uk

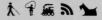

Europa House

Fancy having your own place in a great part of town? These lovely serviced apartments sit around the corner from Abbey Road studios, with the canals of Little Venice at the bottom of the road. Regents Park and Lord's for the cricket are close, while two tube stations whizz you into town. You may spurn the lot for the gorgeous communal gardens that wait behind leafy Randolph Avenue. Find three acres of peace, with well-kept lawns, weeping willows, and benches if you want to read. In summer, there's Shakespeare on the lawn, in autumn a big firework display, you can even have an outside session with a personal trainer. As for the apartments, they're big and airy, nicely stylish and extremely comfy. You get fully-equipped kitchens, big sofas in large sitting rooms, REN oils in sparkling marble bathrooms. You'll also find a mobile phone 'on the house' with free browsing and UK calls and the odd overseas country, too. You can cook for yourself (good local shops), but excellent restaurants will tempt you out; the Formosa, the Prince Albert and The Elgin. There's off-street parking, too. *Minimum stay: 2 nights.*

Rooms	1 apartment for 2, 11 apartments for 4: £199-£450. Extra beds £36. Under 12s free.
Meals	Restaurants 200m.
Closed	Never.
Directions	Tube: Maida Vale, Warwick Avenue. Train: Paddington (to Heathrow). Bus: 6, 16, 46, 98, 187.

Gloria Mabaso
Europa House
79A Randolph Avenue, London, W9 1DW
Tel +44 (0)20 7724 5924
Email sales@europahouseapartments.com
Web www.living-rooms.co.uk/hotel/europa-house

The Portobello Hotel

In 1969, in the days of Bowie and the Rolling Stones, this small hotel opened its doors, making it London's first boutique hotel. It was a new idea, a hip little place, not dull and formal like other hotels, but relaxed and friendly with lots of colour and a bohemian feel. These days, not much has changed, and it remains a popular base for artists, movie stars and musicians, who come for its seductive combination of privacy, informality and style. It stands in the middle of Notting Hill, peacefully hidden away on a side street, with Portobello Road and the shops and cafés of Westbourne Grove a short stroll. The sitting room has a beautiful pine bay window, then fresh flowers, deep sofas and an honesty bar, and you can eat here, too, perhaps a Greek salad, a club sandwich, butternut squash ravioli. Colourful bedrooms hit the spot. Lots have claw-foot baths, you'll find antique furniture, coffee machines, robes in the bathroom, sofas in bigger rooms; those at the back overlook communal gardens. A refurbishment is underway, with six chic rooms already completed. Good restaurants are nearby.

Rooms	19 doubles: £195-£395. 2 singles: £155-£175.
Meals	Continental breakfast included; cooked dishes from £5. Light bites from £8.50. Good restaurants within 500m.
Closed	Never.
Directions	Tube: Notting Hill Gate. Bus: 12, 27, 28, 52, 70, 94. Parking: £25 per 24 hrs.

Douglas Cooper
The Portobello Hotel
22 Stanley Gardens,
Notting Hill Gate, London, W11 2NG

Tel +44 (0)20 7727 2777
Email stay@portobellohotel.com
Web www.portobellohotel.com

Temple Lodge Club

Temple Lodge, once home to the painter Sir Frank Brangwyn, is sandwiched between a courtyard and a lushly landscaped garden. The peace is remarkable making it a very restful place – simple yet human and warmly comfortable, a nourishing experience. Michael and his devoted team run it with quiet energy. You breakfast overlooking the garden, there are newspapers to browse, a library instead of TVs. Bedrooms are surprisingly stylish: pretty art, crisp linen, no clutter, a hint of country chic. They're exceptional value for money, too, so book well in advance. Some rooms have garden views, only two have their own bathrooms and loo; if you don't mind that, you'll be happy. The Thames passes by at the end of the road, the Riverside Studios is round the corner for theatre and film, and the Gate Vegetarian Restaurant is across the courtyard, a well-known eatery, its food so good even committed carnivores can't resist. It was also Brangwyn's studio, hence the artist's window. The house is a non-denominational Christian centre with two services a week, which you may take or leave as you choose.

Rooms	1 double; 2 double with separate bathrooms; 1 double, 2 twins sharing 2 bathrooms: £77-£125. 2 singles with separate showers; 3 singles sharing baths & shower: £59-£73. Extra bed/sofabed £12-£14 p.p.p.n.
Meals	Continental breakfast included. Vegetarian restaurant across courtyard.
Closed	Never.
Directions	Tube: Hammersmith (5-minute walk). Bus: 9, 10, 27, 295.

Michael Beaumont
Temple Lodge Club
51 Queen Caroline Street,
Hammersmith, London, W6 9QL

Tel +44 (0)20 8748 8388
Email templelodgeclub@btconnect.com
Web www.templelodgeclub.com

The Georgian House

Serena's great-great grandfather was commissioned by Thomas Cubitt to build this row of houses and liked the results so much he kept one for himself. They were built to rival Belgravia and have the same august credentials: pillars at the door, porticos and friezes, then high-ceilinged interiors as befits elegant Georgian architecture. Fast forward 160 years and the house, still in the same family, is now a chic B&B hotel, with a friendly brigade of international staff and a lovely sitting room in reception, where you can make a coffee and read the papers. Stylish bedrooms have all been recently refurbished. Expect vibrant colours, period wallpaper, robes in good bathrooms, perhaps a sofa or a bath in the room. You get smart phones, too; free WiFi, UK calls, even calls to the US and several EU countries. A delicious breakfast is served behind a wall of glass downstairs in a cool new dining room with a map of London on one wall; the far end turns into a bar at night. Victoria (and the train to Gatwick) and Buckingham Palace are close. The Harry Potter rooms are popular with younger guests.

Rooms	24 doubles: £114-£199. 9 triples: £159-£364. 3 quadruples: £179-£374. 2 apartments: £239-£394. 11 singles: from £114.
Meals	Pubs/restaurants within walking distance.
Closed	Never.
Directions	Tube: Victoria, Pimlico, Sloane Square. Train: Victoria (for Gatwick). Bus: 6, 11, 16, 24, 38, 52, 73, 82, 185, 211, 239, C10

Adam Rowledge
The Georgian House
35-37 St Georges Drive,
Pimlico, London, SW1V 4DG

Tel	+44 (0)20 7834 1438
Email	reception@georgianhousehotel.co.uk
Web	www.georgianhousehotel.co.uk

Artist Residence London

In the future, if a book is written about London hotels, they will divide it into two periods – before and after Artist Residence London. Because this gorgeous small hotel is a game changer, a new template of British cool, a space designed wholly to exercise your pleasure receptors. It proves resoundingly that small is more beautiful than big ever can be and while large hotels will try to copy it, they'll fail miserably, unable to match its intimacy, or the fantastic staff who look after you all the way. So what do you get? A small slice of heaven between Pimlico and the Kings Road. It's a phoenix from the ashes, a Thomas Cubitt pub recently rescued from neglect. The cellar bar, with pop art and exposed brick walls, must qualify as one of London's coolest; the sitting room has fat sofas in front of a roaring fire; the Cambridge Street Café offers lovely food in a stylish, relaxed setting. Bedrooms are flawless: cool art, chic fabrics, the best beds, power-showered bathrooms. Smaller rooms are divine, bigger rooms have sofas, the suites have free-standing baths. Battersea Park is close.

Rooms	8 doubles: £170-£285. 2 suites for 2: £295-£520.
Meals	Lunch from £9.50. Dinner, 3 courses, about £35.
Closed	Never.
Directions	Tube: Victoria, Pimlico, Sloane Square. Train: Victoria (for Gatwick). Bus: 6, 11, 16, 24, 38, 52, 73, 82, 185, 211, 239, C10.

Charlie & Justin Salisbury
Artist Residence London
52 Cambridge Street,
Pimlico, London, SW1V 4QQ

Tel +44 (0)20 7931 8946
Email london@artistresidence.co.uk
Web www.artistresidencelondon.co.uk

Lime Tree Hotel

You'll be hard pressed to find better value in the centre of town. The Lime Tree – two elegant Georgian townhouses – stands less than a mile from Buckingham Palace, with Westminster, Sloane Square and Piccadilly all a short stroll. Add warm interiors, kind owners and a smart gastropub waiting round the corner and you've unearthed a London gem. The airy dining room serves a mean breakfast and is soon to turn into a café, with light meals served throughout the day. Rooms are just the ticket: smart without being lavish, all with mod cons. Expect warm colours, crisp linen, attractive wallpaper and excellent bathrooms (most have big showers). One on the ground floor has doors onto the garden; others on first floor have high ceilings; those at the top (a few stairs!) are cosy in the eaves; rooms at the back are the quietest. Charlotte and Matt are hands-on and will point you in the right direction, while there's a tiny sitting room for guide books and a computer for guests to use. The Thomas Cubitt pub – 50 paces from the front door – serves great food. A very handy base for the Chelsea Flower Show. *Minimum stay: 2 nights at weekends.*

Rooms	12 doubles, 4 twins: £185-£215. 6 singles: £125-£165. 3 triples: £240.
Meals	Restaurants nearby.
Closed	Never.
Directions	Train: Victoria (to Gatwick). Tube: Victoria or Sloane Square. Bus: 11, 24, 38, 52, 73, C1. Parking: £34 a day off-street.

Charlotte & Matt Goodsall
Lime Tree Hotel
135 Ebury Street,
Belgravia, London, SW1W 9QU

Tel +44 (0)20 7730 8191
Email info@limetreehotel.co.uk
Web www.limetreehotel.co.uk

The Levin Hotel

This is shopaholic heaven – Harrods at one end of the street, Harvey Nicks at the other. As for the Levin, it sits quietly on Basil Street, a peaceful retreat in the middle of Knightsbridge. A lively café/bar/restaurant acts as the hub; you can enjoy breakfast here of freshly backed croissants, nip back early for afternoon tea or a filling lunch; perhaps Cornish mussels in cider cream and parsley to start then a tasty spinach, blue cheese & red onion frittata as your main. If that's not enough, nip next door to the Capital (their sister hotel) where you'll find Outlaw's, a Michelin starred restaurant. Bedrooms are spread over four floors with a lift to carry you up, though you may prefer to walk; a contemporary chandelier with an 18-metre drop fills the stairwell. As for the rooms, some are big, others smaller, but all have the same crisp style: bold colours, hand-stitched beds, marble bathrooms, books galore. Bigger rooms have sofas, all have white robes, crisp linen, Bose radios and flat-screen TVs. You get air conditioning and a handy smartphone, too. There's a full concierge service, iPads are available at reception. Hyde Park is close. *Pets by arrangement.*

Rooms	3 doubles, 8 twin/doubles: £245-£479. 1 suite for 2: £395-£619. Extra bed/sofabed £45 p.p.p.n.
Meals	Lunch from £5.50. Dinner, 3 courses, about £30. Afternoon tea from £22.99.
Closed	Never.
Directions	Tube: Knightsbridge (for Heathrow). Station: Victoria (for Gatwick). Bus: 09, 10, 19, 22, 52, 137, C1. Parking: £45 a day.

Kate Levin
The Levin Hotel
28 Basil Street,
Knightsbridge, London, SW3 1AS

Tel +44 (0)20 7589 628
Email reservations@thelevinhotel.co.uk
Web www.thelevinhotel.co.uk

The One Tun Pub & Rooms

This stylish inn dates to 1759, but its moment of fame came in 1838, when Charles Dickens changed its name to the Three Cripples and made it Bill Sikes' watering hole of choice in *Oliver Twist*. These days it's a thriving local with a restaurant serving pan-Asian food and some beautiful bedrooms above the pub. It sits on peaceful Saffron Hill (home to Fagin and the Artful Dodger), with flower baskets and Victorian lanterns on the outside, then painted panelling and Chesterfield sofas within. You'll find English ales, fancy cocktails, wines from around the world, then some very popular Asian cooking, perhaps chilli salt squid, Asian pork belly with choy sum, vanilla ice cream topped with tamarind caramel. Bedrooms upstairs are delightful – crisp linen, beautiful fabrics, stylish wallpapers, robes in excellent bathrooms. Most are big, none are small, one has a decked terrace, all have comfy beds, coffee machines, smart TVs and super-fast WiFi. Breakfast (7.30am-11am) is brought to your room with a complimentary newspaper. St Pauls, the Barbican and Tate Modern all within easy reach.

Rooms	8 doubles: £140-£215. Extra bed £25.
Meals	Continental breakfast £12. Lunch from £4.50. Dinner, 3 courses, about £30.
Closed	Rarely.
Directions	Tube: Farringdon, Chancery Lane. Train: Farringdon (Thameslink); Liverpool Street (for Stansted). Bus: 17, 45, 46, 55, 63, 243.

Leo Fernandez
The One Tun Pub & Rooms
125 Saffron Hill,
Fitzrovia, London, EC1N 8QS

Tel	+44 (0)20 7405 1521
Email	info@onetun.co.uk
Web	www.onetun.co.uk

The Zetter Townhouse

This is a deliciously quirky hotel, part 19th-century Viennese coffee house, part 20th-century bohemian dive, part 21st-century gentleman's club. It sits peacefully on St John's Square in the epicentre of trendy Clerkenwell, both away from the city and very much a part of it. A formal London exterior gives way to theatrical interiors. Rooms overflow with beautiful things – period furniture, claret wallpaper, glass cabinets filled with curios, a couple of Corinthian columns for good measure. You get rugs on wood floors, cool tunes in the air, then a mirrored cocktail bar where you chat to the barman as he mixes you a Calpis Sour. Rooms have lots of colour, art everywhere and robes in sparkling bathrooms. One has a four-poser with a Union Jack canopy, those in the eaves have painted bedheads; you get Hypnos beds and crisp linen, antique furniture and bluetooth speakers. Downstairs, dig into potted shrimps, shepherd's pie, chocolate and hazelnut brownie or spin across the square to their sister hotel for something more substantial. Farringdon station is close, with Crossrail coming in 2018.

Rooms	5 doubles, 6 twin/doubles: £200-£315. 1 suite for 4: £345-£425. 1 apartment for 4: £475-£500.
Meals	Breakfast £9.50-£10.50. Lunch & dinner from £6.
Closed	Never.
Directions	Tube: Barbican. Train: Farringdon (2 minutes). Also: Kings Cross, Euston & Liverpool Street (for Stansted). Bus: 19, 38, 56, 63, 243, 341.

Angela Ellis
The Zetter Townhouse
49-50 St John's Square,
Clerkenwell, London, EC1V 4JJ

Tel +44 (0)20 7324 4567
Email reservations@thezetter.com
Web www.thezettertownhouse.com/clerkenwell

The Tommyfield

The Tommyfield is a cool little find – a lively pub for a good pint, a restaurant serving tasty food, a small hotel with well-priced rooms that deliver in spades. It sits between Vauxhall and Kennington, with two tube lines to whizz you into town and three buses passing outside. Inside, you find wooden floors, high ceilings and the odd ionic pillar. Lamps hang above the bar, where you can order a pint of Wandle, then dig into posh fish and chips. Leather banquettes run along big windows, an open kitchen is on display, a couple of booths are nicely private. Rooms are the big surprise, some with painted panelling, others with planked walls. You get pop art, good beds, coffee machines and flat-screen TVs. Excellent bathrooms have walk-in power showers, two have claw-foot baths. On weekdays a continental breakfast is left in your fridge, on weekends the full English is on tap below. As for the food – half-price for residents – pies, steaks and burgers sit alongside pumpkin ravioli, Chateaubriand and banoffee pie. Tuesday is quiz night, Oval is close for the cricket. *Cots available.*

Rooms	4 doubles, 2 twin/doubles: £99-£139.
Meals	Continental breakfast included; cooked breakfast on weekends £6-£9. Lunch & dinner from £12.50. Sunday lunch from £13.50. Food half-price for residents.
Closed	Never.
Directions	Tube: Vauxhall, Kennington, Oval (all a 5-minute walk). Bus: 3, 59, 159. Train: Vauxhall (for Gatwick/Victoria).

Alex Cook
The Tommyfield
185 Kennington Lane,
Kennington, London, SE11 4EZ

Tel +44 (0)20 7735 1061
Email info@thetommyfield.co.uk
Web www.thetommyfield.com

The Victoria Inn

A great little pub in a trendy enclave with lovely staff, tasty food and chic rooms that don't cost a fortune. Outside, there's a shaded terrace for sunny days where you can watch local life pass by. Inside, you get a 21st-century makeover of a beautiful Victorian pub: original wood floors and windows, then colourful booths and banquettes. Craft beers and local ales wait at a fine old bar; spin round to the restaurant and find quirky local photos on exposed brick walls. Pull up a chair at one of the smart tables and dig into super food, perhaps pea and lovage soup, shepherd's pie with buttered greens, chocolate fondant with blackberry sorbet. Bedrooms are a steal – most cost £110 or less. They're lovely, too: airy colours, local art, comfy beds, super bathrooms. You get coffee machines, flat-screen TVs and Bose WiFi speakers. Why spend a fortune in central London, when you can hang out with locals in a cool part of town? Sundays are fun – delicious roasts, live jazz in the evening. Peckham Rye station is a three-minute walk. There's a funky market, a lovely common and free parking, too. *No minimum stay.*

Rooms	11 doubles, 3 twin/doubles: £90-£165. 1 family room: £125-£165.
Meals	Lunch from £5. Dinner, 3 courses £25-£30. Sunday lunch from £16.
Closed	Never.
Directions	Station: Peckham Rye (to London Bridge, Victoria, Clapham Junction). Bus: 12, 37, 63, 78, 343.

Joe Sheasgreen
The Victoria Inn
77 Choumert Road,
Peckham, London, SE15 4AR

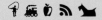

Tel +44 (0)20 7639 5052
Email reservations@victoriainnpeckham.com
Web www.victoriainnpeckham.com

Tulse Hill Hotel

This is a fantastic find, a beautiful hotel close to Herne Hill and its lovely park, Brixton and its hipster groove and Dulwich and its famous art gallery. There's been a hostelry on this spot for over 500 years. The current version is a dream, a delightful mix of old and new. A smart Georgian exterior gives way to beautiful interiors. You'll find open fires, panelled walls, then an airy restaurant with a wall of glass that opens onto a terrace for great food and a good pint. It draws a local crowd – who doesn't love having an excellent pub on their doorstep? Cool tunes float in the air, lights go down at night and candles flicker. Bedrooms upstairs are hard to fault: padded headboards, colourful throws, quirky art, robes in sparkling bathrooms. All have coffee machines, air-conditioning and flat-screen TVs. Spin down for a delicious dinner, perhaps salt cod fritters, a bavette steak, coconut panna cotta with pineapple and rum. Staff are lovely, don't miss Brockwell Park and its wonderful lido, perfect for summer days. Finally, the most coveted possession in London: a car park for guests! *No minimum stay.*

Rooms	6 doubles: £115-£150. 2 family rooms for 4: £150-£165. 1 single: £85-£95.
Meals	Lunch from £7.50. Dinner, 3 courses, about £30. Sunday lunch from £16.
Closed	Never.
Directions	Train: Tulse Hill (to London Bridge). Tube: Brixton. Bus: 2, 68, 196, 322.

Jemma Kiddle
Tulse Hill Hotel
150 Norwood Road,
Tulse Hill, London, SE24 9AY

Tel +44 (0)20 8671 7499
Email sleep@tulsehillhotel.com
Web www.tulsehillhotel.com

Strattons

You arrive to find an exquisite Queen Anne villa that wouldn't look out of place in France, then you step inside and discover a contemporary art gallery with rooms. Strattons is a treasure trove of beautiful things. It is in constant flux, too – the new café/deli overflows with delicious treats and comes with a roof terrace, not a bad spot for afternoon tea. Back inside, you find august busts, contemporary chandeliers, stylish sofas to take the strain. Bedrooms are equally creative: a carved four-poster in priestly red, Botticelli's angels hovering on a wall, bedside lights that hang from the ceiling. Some have double-ended baths in the room, others a roof terrace with sun loungers. You breakfast in the deli on irresistible delights: natural yoghurt and muesli, sweet-smelling bacon rolls, the full cooked works. After which head off to the Brecks for walks thought its magical forest or spin up to King's Lynn to explore its Hanseatic architecture. A very good dinner awaits your return, perhaps smoked haddock soufflé, spiced quail with poached pear, chocolate brownie with banana ice cream. *Minimum stay: 2 nights at weekends. Pets by arrangement.*

Rooms	6 doubles, 1 twin/double: £116-£199. 5 suites for 2: £149-£249. 2 apartments for 2: £175-£275. Singles from £94.
Meals	Lunch from £6. Dinner, 3 courses, £30-£35. Sunday lunch from £14. Afternoon tea £15.50.
Closed	1 week over Christmas.
Directions	Ash Close runs off north end of market place between W H Brown estate agents & fish & chip restaurant.

Vanessa & Les Scott
Strattons
4 Ash Close,
Swaffham, PE37 7NH

Tel +44 (0)1760 723845
Email enquiries@strattonshotel.com
Web www.strattonshotel.com

Chalk & Cheese

Andrew and Bridget's Victorian schoolhouse stands on the village green. If its exterior gives the impression of English decorum, its interiors do the very opposite; the bust of Aristotle draped in a feather boa is a bit of a giveaway. It's all refreshingly original – interior design laced with humour. The big room takes centre stage, its high ceiling and stained glass giving an ecclesiastic feel. You'll find Cambodian lampshades and Vietnamese water puppets, mismatching sofas and a crackling fire, William Morris wallpaper and books by the hundred, then a quirky bar with light descending from on high. Homely bedrooms are warm, simple and nicely priced. One has a four-poster, another a slipper bath, two next door in a cute cottage can be taken together to self-cater. There's even a bunk house and a wheelchair-friendly bolthole in the garden. Pizzas fly from a wood-fired oven, or you could try pea and ham soup, homemade cottage pie, sticky toffee pudding. There's a conservatory breakfast room, a terrace for summer and a farm shop selling the odd antique. Good walks and the coast wait.

Rooms	3 doubles, 1 twin, 1 four-poster: £75-£95. 1 cottage for 2: £105-£125. 1 bunk room for 4: £35 per person. Singles from £65. Extra beds from £10. Self-catering option.
Meals	Lunch from £4.50. Dinner, 3 courses, £20-£25 (not Sun-Wed). Sunday lunch from £9.95.
Closed	Never.
Directions	North of A1122 between Swaffham and Downham Market. In village, on green.

Andrew & Bridget Archibald
Chalk & Cheese
1 Eastgate Street, Shouldham,
King's Lynn, PE33 0DD

Tel	+44 (0)1366 348039
Email	info@chalkandcheesenorfolk.co.uk
Web	www.bed-and-breakfast-west-norfolk.co.uk

Congham Hall

This is a beautiful Georgian merchant's house set in 30 acres of parkland. It's also a cool little spa hotel with an indoor pool and treatment rooms, a perfect blend of old and new. Outside, three gardeners grow flowers for the house, vegetables for the kitchen and keep the gardens looking serene. Inside, country house interiors have an elegant contemporary feel. There's an open fire in the sitting room, a chic bar with low-hanging lampshades, then an airy dining room for excellent local food, perhaps crayfish salad, slow-cooked chicken, hot chocolate fondant with banana ice cream. After which you'll need to atone, so roast away in the sauna before a dip in the pool; there are sunbeds and a hot tub on the decked terrace, too. Refurbished rooms are gorgeous. Bedrooms in the house have beautiful fabrics and excellent beds. The suite has a balcony for breakfast, all have robes in striking bathrooms (one is entered through cupboard doors). Courtyard rooms are big and airy and open onto the kitchen garden. Children are welcome and have their own menu. Sandringham is close. There's tennis and croquet, too. *Minimum stay: 2 nights at weekends.*

Rooms	25 twin/doubles: £135-£260. 1 suite for 2: £275. Dinner, B&B from £110 p.p. Extra beds for children under 12 free.
Meals	Breakfast £8-£15. Lunch from £5. Dinner, 3 courses, about £35. Afternoon tea from £8.75. Sunday lunch, 3 courses, £27.50.
Closed	Rarely.
Directions	A10 to King's Lynn, then A149 north. At second r'bout, A148 east for 500m, then right for Grimston. Hotel signed.

Julie Woodhouse
Congham Hall
Grimston,
King's Lynn, PE32 1AH

Tel +44 (0)1485 600250
Email info@conghamhallhotel.co.uk
Web www.conghamhallhotel.co.uk

The Hoste

This iconic hotel sits a couple of miles back from Norfolk's sparkling north coast. It dates to the early 1600s and had one rather famous local – Nelson used the beautiful timbered bar as a recruiting post and would catch the stage to London from the front door after a good night's sleep. These days it's a social hub on the village green that pulses with life all year round, a great base from which to explore this stretch of heaven. Inside, beautiful bedrooms, delicious food, fine wines and quenching local ales all wait. You can eat in the panelled dining room, the historic bar, the buzzing conservatory or the airy garden room that opens onto a terrace, and the food is delicious, perhaps lobster risotto with Cromer crab, Norfolk venison with red cabbage, warm chocolate fondant with vanilla ice cream. There's a peaceful walled garden, a small spa for treatments, a cute little cinema that shows three films a day. Bedrooms are scattered about: contemporary delights at the Hoste; boutique elegance at Vine House; smart rooms and a vintage train carriage at Railway House; chic cottages for longer stays. A treat.

Rooms	52 twin/doubles: £130-£230. 9 self-catering cottages for 6: £160-£200. 1 train carriage for 2: £170-£230. Singles from £110. Dinner, B&B from £85 p.p.
Meals	Lunch from £6. Dinner, 3 courses, from £25. Sunday lunch from £14.
Closed	Never.
Directions	On B1155 for Burnham Market. By green & church in village centre.

Martin De Sousa
The Hoste
The Green, Burnham Market,
King's Lynn, PE31 8HD

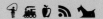

Tel +44 (0)1328 738777
Email reservations@thehoste.com
Web www.thehoste.com

The White Horse

A smart little inn on the North Norfolk coast with beautiful views that shoot across tidal marshes to Scolt Head Island. At high tide boats bob, birds swoop and the water laps at the garden edge; at low tide, the marshes appear and fishermen come to harvest the mussels and oysters. In summer you can eat on the terrace and drink it all in, then drop down to the coastal path at the bottom of the garden and follow your nose. But the view here is weather proofed – a big conservatory restaurant looks out on it all. It's a popular haunt for locals and visitors alike, who come for consistently good food, perhaps oysters from the bay, sea bass with squid risotto, lemon tart with a chocolate macaroon. There's a sunken garden that catches the sun, then an open fire in the locals' bar, where you'll find well-kept ales, the daily papers, bar billiards and sofas for a game of scrabble. Chic, uncluttered bedrooms have seaside colours, robes for spotless bathrooms, good beds and fine linen. Some in the main house have the view, dog-friendly garden rooms have terraces. Sandringham is close. *Minimum stay: 2 nights at weekends.*

Rooms	11 doubles, 4 twins: £100-£230. Extra beds £30. Cots £5. Dogs £10.
Meals	Lunch & bar meals from £8.95. Dinner from £13.95.
Closed	Never.
Directions	Midway between Hunstanton & Wells-next-the-Sea on A149.

Cliff Nye & Family
The White Horse
Brancaster Staithe, PE31 8BY

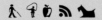

Tel +44 (0)1485 210262
Email reception@whitehorsebrancaster.co.uk
Web www.whitehorsebrancaster.co.uk

The Globe Inn at Wells-next-the-Sea

It's as English as England can be – a beautiful inn on a Georgian green, where Nelson used to catch the coach to London. Potter down to the water and find a sandy beach for family fun, then a small harbour, where day boats land their catch on the quay. As for the Globe, it's an inn for all seasons. Outside, there's a sun-trapping terrace at the front, a flower-filled courtyard where you can eat in summer, then a colourful roof terrace for guests. Inside, wood-burners sit at both ends of the bar, there are sofas and armchairs, games for rainy days, then local ales and excellent wines with which to wash down delicious local food. You eat in an airy restaurant with local art of the walls, perhaps clam linguini with chilli and garlic, dressed Wells crab or a rib-eye steak, then chocolate mousse with pistachio ice cream. Rooms above have the comfiest beds in the land. Those at the front have views of the green, all have crisp linen, padded heads and vintage tiles in sparkling bathrooms. Rooms connect for families, dogs are very welcome, boat trips can be arranged. Sandringham is up the road. *Minimum stay: 2 nights at weekends.*

Rooms	4 doubles, 3 twin/doubles: £110-£170. Extra bed/sofabed £30 p.p.p.n.
Meals	Lunch from £6. Dinner, 3 courses, £25-£30.
Closed	Rarely.
Directions	A149 east into Wells. In village, on green.

Antonia & Stephen Bournes
The Globe Inn at Wells-next-the-Sea
The Buttlands,
Wells-Next-The-Sea, NR23 1EU

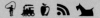

Tel +44 (0)1328 710206
Email hello@theglobeatwells.co.uk
Web www.theglobeatwells.co.uk

The Blakeney Hotel

The view here is matchless, a clean sweep across the salt marshes up to Blakeney Point. The estuary passes five paces from the front door and you can watch the boats slide by from a sun-trapping terrace, a convivial bar, a stylish restaurant and a beautiful first-floor sitting room that comes with binoculars to follow the local wildlife. Bedrooms have a contemporary country-house style: chic fabrics, cool colours, antique furniture, white linen on beautiful beds, sparkling bathrooms with posh oils. Many have views to the front, a couple have balconies, too. Elsewhere, you'll find three open fires, a bar for light lunches and local ales, an elegant drawing room where you can play Scrabble, read the papers, or dig into afternoon tea. There's an indoor pool with a gym, a steam room and a sauna, then glass doors onto the garden; you'll also find a games' room for children. Outside, paths lead down to the marshes, there are seals to spot, birds to watch, links golf at Sheringham and Cromer, a point to point at Fakenham. Sandringham is close, too. Dogs and children are very welcome. *Minimum stay: 2 nights at weekends.*

Rooms	19 doubles, 36 twin/doubles: £208-£386. 8 singles: £104-£193. Price includes dinner for 2.
Meals	Lunch from £9.50. Dinner included; non-residents, 3 courses, £32.
Closed	Never.
Directions	A148 north from Fakenham, then B1156 north to Blakeney. In village on quay.

Stannard Family
The Blakeney Hotel
The Quay, Blakeney,
Holt, NR25 7NE

Tel +44 (0)1263 740797
Email reception@blakeneyhotel.co.uk
Web www.blakeneyhotel.co.uk

Cley Windmill

The setting here is magical: rushes flutter in the salt marsh, raised paths lead off to the sea, a vast sky hangs overhead. The windmill, now with new sails, dates to 1713. It became a house in the 1920s, the family home of James Blunt no less. Square rooms are bigger, a couple have sofas, while round rooms in the tower are impossibly romantic (one is for mountaineers only). Six rooms are in the mill and you really want to go for these, though the cottage is set up for self-catering and visiting dogs. Inside, you find the loveliest drawing room – low ceiling, open fire, stripped floorboards and a cute little window seat. Bedrooms have a chic feel with Farrow & Ball colours, beautiful fabrics, the odd claw-foot bath. Those in the tower (with compact shower rooms) get smaller as you rise, but the view improves with every step; there's a viewing platform halfway up for all. You eat in a pretty dining room, perhaps crab fishcakes, Norfolk lamb, pear tarte tatin with cinnamon ice cream. But plans are afoot to build an orangery and when it's ready, you'll eat there surrounded by the walled garden. *Minimum stay: 2 nights.*

Rooms	6 doubles, 2 twin/doubles: £159-£219. 1 cottage for 4: £390 for 3 days; extra days £50-£130; 7 days £495-£625. Children under 12 £30.
Meals	Dinner, 3 courses, £27.50-£32.50.
Closed	Christmas.
Directions	Head east through Cley on A149. Mill signed on left in village.

Simon Whatling
Cley Windmill
The Quay, Cley,
Holt, NR25 7RP

Tel +44 (0)1263 740209
Email info@cleywindmill.co.uk
Web www.cleywindmill.co.uk

The Kings Head

This small Georgian inn was once the local jail. It is anything but these days, a quirky bolt hole full of creature comforts a few miles south of the North Norfolk coast. Outside, a large garden for barbecues in summer gives way to parkland beyond. Inside, cool interiors mix contemporary design and rustic bricks and mortar to great effect. You'll find cow-hide rugs, skis on the walls, Chesterfield sofas on original wood floors. There's a sitting-room bar for games in front of an open fire, then a restaurant with whitewashed walls and painted beams. Potter about and find cartwheel mirrors, lots of books, curious objects d'art. Bedrooms aren't huge, but nor is their price. You get lovely beds, smart fabrics, period colours, the odd antique; good showers wait in compact bathrooms. Downstairs, you'll find quiz nights, jazz nights and some lovely local food, perhaps corned beef hash with a quail's egg, local partridge with game chips, rhubarb and apple crumble; kids have their own menu, too. There's lots to do: cute villages, medieval Norwich, Fakenham for the races, the glorious north coast.

Rooms	4 doubles: £70-£130.
Meals	Lunch from £5.50. Dinner, 3 courses, £25-£30. Sunday lunch from £15.50.
Closed	Rarely.
Directions	Just off A148 Holt to Fakenham road, 1 mile west of Holt.

Cliff Nye & family
The Kings Head
Holt Road, Letheringsett,
Holt, NR25 7AR

Tel +44 (0)1263 712691
Email info@kingsheadnorfolk.co.uk
Web www.kingsheadnorfolk.co.uk

Saracens Head

Lost in the lanes of deepest Norfolk, an English inn that's hard to match. Outside, Georgian red-brick walls stand to attention at the front, but nip round the back and find them at ease in a beautiful courtyard where you can knock back a pint of Wherry in the evening sun before slipping inside to eat. Tim and Janie upped sticks from the Alps, unable to resist the allure of this lovely old inn. A sympathetic refurbishment has worked its magic, but the spirit remains the same: this is a country-house pub with lovely staff who go the extra mile. Downstairs the bar hums with happy locals who come for Norfolk ales and good French wines, while the food in the restaurant is as good as ever: Norfolk pheasant and rabbit terrine, wild duck or Cromer crab, treacle tart and caramel ice-cream. Upstairs, there's a sitting room on the landing, then six pretty rooms. All have have smart carpets, wooden furniture, comfy beds and sparkling bathrooms. There's masses to do: ancient Norwich, the coast at Cromer, golf on the cliffs at Sheringham, Blickling Hall, a Jacobean pile. Don't miss Sunday lunch.

Rooms	5 twin/doubles: £100-£110. 1 family room for 4: £110-£140. Singles from £70.
Meals	Lunch from £6.50. Dinner, 3 courses, £25-£35. Sunday lunch £19-£24.
Closed	Christmas.
Directions	From Norwich A140 past Aylsham, then 3rd left for Erpingham. Right into Calthorpe, through village, straight out the other side (not right). On right after about 0.5 miles.

Tim & Janie Elwes
Saracens Head
Wolterton,
Norwich, NR11 7LZ

Tel	+44 (0)1263 768909
Email	info@saracenshead-norfolk.co.uk
Web	www.saracenshead-norfolk.co.uk

The Fritton Arms

This is a small, chic, country-house inn on the Somerleyton estate – well worth the detour to this far-flung realm. And stately it is, 5,000 acres of green and pleasant land, with parkland behind running down to Fritton Lake. Inside, airy interiors mix original features with contemporary design. You'll find period colours, rugs on stripped floors, 16th-century sand-blasted beams, then beautifully upholstered armchairs in front of a lovely old fireplace. There are sofas in the sitting room, fresh flowers on the piano, a roaring fire in the well-stocked bar. Food is served here and there: at green leather booths in the Fish Room; in the low-ceilinged restaurant with original brick walls; or out on the gravelled terrace in summer. Try wood-fired pizzas, sizzling steaks, perhaps ham hock terrine, sea bass with chorizo, a plate of local cheeses. Attractive bedrooms have warm colours, smart fabrics, comfy beds, white robes and good bathrooms. Some in the eaves are open to the rafters, bigger rooms may have a sofa. Don't miss Somerleyton Hall, one of the finest in the land. The Broads are close. *Minimum stay: 2 nights at weekends. Pets by arrangement.*

Rooms	6 doubles, 3 twin/doubles: £110-£140. Singles from £95. Extra beds £25.
Meals	Lunch from £5.50. Dinner, 3 courses, £25-£30. Sunday lunch from £12.50.
Closed	Rarely.
Directions	From Beccles A143 north for Great Yarmouth. In Fritton, right, signed Fritton Lake. Hotel on right before lake.

Ewen Thompson
The Fritton Arms
Church Lane, Fritton,
Great Yarmouth, NR31 9HA

Tel +44 (0)1493 484008
Email info@frittonarms.co.uk
Web www.frittonarms.co.uk

The Collingwood Arms Hotel

The Collingwood is all things to all men, an elegant country house, a distinctly stylish pub, and a favourite of fishermen, who come to try their luck. Step inside and find a sofa in front of the fire in the hall, a beautiful sitting room with books and fresh flowers, then a welcoming bar with rugs on wood floors and the odd fishing rod on the walls. Fires burn, tales get told, the odd dram is taken. Lovely bedrooms have a smart country feel: airy, elegant, understated. Some are big with space for a sofa, a couple are smaller, but fine for a night, all have the same gentle style: warm colours, crisp linen, comfy beds, spotless bathrooms. Three overlook the garden, one has a claw-foot bath amid timber frames. Downstairs, a convivial restaurant has parquet floors, doors onto a well-kept garden and some excellent local food, perhaps wood pigeon with juniper, halibut with saffron and samphire, stem ginger panna cotta. You can fish the river from quirkily named beats: The Slap, Craw Point, Monument. Coast and castles wait, as do gardens, golf and beautiful walking. Hard to beat.

Rooms	10 doubles, 3 twin/doubles: £130-£170. 2 suites for 2: £200. Singles from £120. Extra beds £20.
Meals	Lunch from £4.50. Dinner: bar meals from £11.50; 3 courses in the restaurant £30-£40.
Closed	Never.
Directions	A697 north to Cornhill-on-Tweed. In town, left at roundabout & hotel on right after 150m.

Shona Wedderburn
The Collingwood Arms Hotel
Main Street,
Cornhill-on-Tweed, TD12 4UH

Tel +44 (0)1890 882424
Email enquiries@collingwoodarms.com
Web www.collingwoodarms.com

The Pheasant Inn

A super little inn lost in beautiful country, the kind you hope to chance upon. The Kershaws run it with great passion and an instinctive understanding of its traditions. The bars are wonderful. Brass beer taps glow, 100-year old photos of the local community hang on stone walls, the clock above the fire keeps perfect time. Fires burn, bowler hats and saddles pop up here and there, varnished ceilings shine. House ales are expertly kept, Timothy Taylor's and Wylam waiting for thirsty souls. Fruit and vegetables come from the garden, while Robin's lovely food hits the spot perfectly, perhaps twice-baked cheese soufflé, slow-roasted Northumberland lamb, brioche and marmalade bread and butter pudding; as for Sunday lunch, *The Observer* voted it 'Best in the North'. Bedrooms in the old hay barn are light and airy, cute and cosy, great value for money. You're in the Northumberland National Park – no traffic jams, not too much hurry. You can sail on the lake, cycle round it or take to the hills and walk. For £10 you can also gaze into the universe at the Kielder Observatory (best in winter). Brilliant. *Minimum stay: 2 nights at weekends.*

Rooms	4 doubles, 3 twins: £95-£100. 1 family room for 4: £95-£140. Singles £65-£70. Dinner, B&B £70-£75 p.p. Extra bed/sofabed £15 p.p.p.n.
Meals	Bar meals from £9.95. Dinner, 3 courses, £20-£30. Sunday lunch from £11.50.
Closed	Christmas.
Directions	From Bellingham follow signs west to Kielder Water & Falstone for 9 miles. On left, 1 mile short of Kielder Water.

Walter, Irene & Robin Kershaw
The Pheasant Inn
Stannersburn,
Hexham, NE48 1DD

Tel +44 (0)1434 240382
Email stay@thepheasantinn.com
Web www.thepheasantinn.com

Hart's Nottingham

A small enclave of good things. You're on the smart side of town at the end of a cul-de-sac, thus remarkably quiet. You're also at the top of the hill and close to the castle with views that sweep south for miles; at night, a carpet of light sparkles beneath you. Inside, cool lines and travertine marble greet you in reception. Smart bedrooms do the trick. They're not huge, but come with all the trimmings: wide-screen TVs, Bose sound systems, super little bathrooms, king-size beds wrapped in crisp white cotton. Those on the ground floor open onto the garden, each with a terrace where you can breakfast in good weather; rooms on higher floors have better views (six overlook the courtyard). There is a cool little bar, the hub of the hotel, but Hart's Restaurant across the courtyard serves breakfast and light bites, and offers excellent food: perhaps wild mushroom arancini, sea bream with lemon and hazelnut, quince soufflé with vanilla ice cream. There's lots to explore: the Lace Market, the city caves, Trent Bridge for the cricket (the England team stay here). There's a private car park for hotel guests, too.

Rooms	29 doubles: £134-£184. 2 suites for 2: £274. 1 family room for 4: £144-£202.
Meals	Continental breakfast £9; full English £14. Lunch from £14.95. Sunday lunch, 3 courses, £25. Dinner, 3 courses £30-£35.
Closed	Never.
Directions	M1 junc. 24, then follow signs for city centre & Nottingham Castle. Left into Park Row from Maid Marian Way. Hotel on left at top of hill. Parking £8.50 per night.

Adam Worthington
Hart's Nottingham
Standard Hill, Park Row,
Nottingham, NG1 6GN

Tel	+44 (0)115 988 1900
Email	reception@hartshotel.co.uk
Web	www.hartsnottingham.co.uk

Langar Hall

Langar Hall is one of the loveliest places in this book, reason enough to come to Nottinghamshire. It sits at the top of a hardly noticeable hill in glorious parkland, bang next door to the church. The Skirving family arrived 160 years ago, building on the site of Admiral Lord Howe's burned-down home. Much of what fills the house arrived then and it's easy to feel intoxicated by statues and busts in the pillared dining room, ancient tomes overflowing from bookshelves, an eclectic collection of art. Lila – Imogen's granddaughter – is now in charge, and very much following in her grandmother's footsteps; Langar remains a quirky country house with charming staff and a touch of bohemian flair. Bedrooms are lovely, some resplendent with antiques, others with beautiful wallpapers or a grand four-poster. As for dinner, it's a big treat, perhaps wild turbot with mussels and dill, Belvoir pheasant with cider and thyme, rhubarb soufflé with ginger beer sorbet. There's a cocktail bar, a conservatory, a flower-filled terrace for afternoon tea in summer, then beautiful gardens that delight. One of a kind.

Rooms	7 doubles, 2 twins, 1 four-poster: £100-£199. 1 suite for 2: £160-£225. 1 chalet for 2: £100-£125. Singles £100-£160. Extra bed/sofabed available £30 p.p.p.n.
Meals	Lunch £18.50-£23.50. Dinner £30-£50. Sunday lunch £39.50.
Closed	Never.
Directions	From Nottingham A52 towards Grantham. Right, for Cropwell Bishop, straight on for 5 miles. House next to church on edge of village, signed.

Lila Skirving
Langar Hall
Church Lane, Langar,
Nottingham, NG13 9HG

Tel +44 (0)1949 860559
Email info@langarhall.co.uk
Web www.langarhall.com

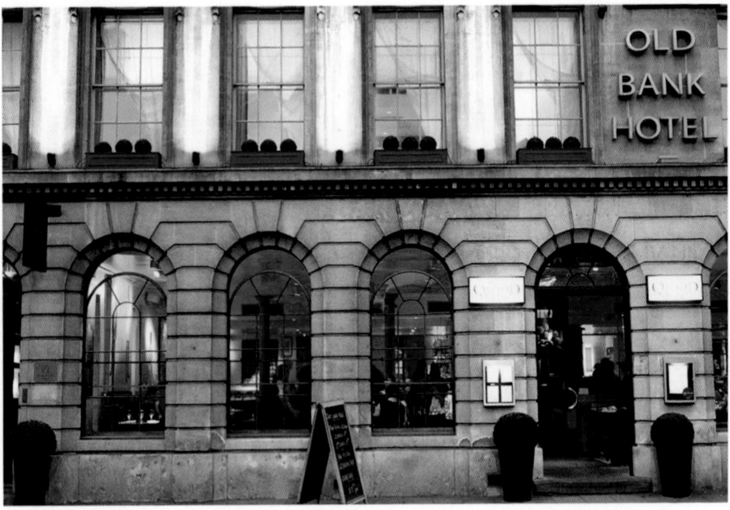

Old Bank Hotel

You're in the heart of old Oxford, with Merton College and Christ Church Meadow to the south, the Radcliffe Camera and the Bodleian Library to the north, and University College and the Botanic Gardens at Magdalen Bridge to the east. As for the Old Bank, its airy interiors are home to an exceptional collection of modern art and photography. The hub is the old tiller's hall, now a cocktail bar and brasserie, with six arched windows overlooking the high street. Food is on tap all day long, anything from a pizza or a steak to afternoon tea, with meat from the owner's farm and fish from the Channel Islands. Bedrooms are gorgeous: beautiful beds, pleated curtains, original art, robes in chic bathrooms. Some have sofas, others padded windows, you get flat-screen TVs and good WiFi throughout. There's a peaceful library bar for residents, a decked courtyard for breakfast in summer, then the rarest commodity in Oxford: free off-street parking. The University Church of St Mary stands opposite, so climb its tower for the best views of Oxford. The Ashmolean and Pitt Rivers Museums are close. *Minimum stay: 2 nights at weekends*

Rooms	26 doubles, 14 twin/doubles: £215-£485. 2 suites for 3: £395-£560.
Meals	Breakfast £5-£15. Lunch & dinner £5-£30. Afternoon tea from £6.95.
Closed	Never.
Directions	Cross Magdalen Bridge for city centre. Straight through 1st set of lights, then left into Merton St. Follow road right; 1st right into Magpie Lane. Car park 2nd right.

Rebecca Mofford
Old Bank Hotel
92-94 High Street,
Oxford, OX1 4BJ

Tel	+44 (0)1865 799599
Email	info@oldbank-hotel.co.uk
Web	www.oldbank-hotel.co.uk

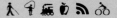

Old Parsonage Hotel

The Old Parsonage has been at the centre of Oxford life for over 350 years. It stands in the middle of town on land owned by University College and was once home to Oscar Wilde. It is one of the loveliest places to stay in town, its beautiful interiors touching every corner. Chief among its virtues are its shaded dining terrace, its exceptional art collection, and its first-floor library (curated by Philip Blackwell), which opens onto a small roof terrace. Inside, flames flicker in an ancient fireplace, newspapers wait by mullioned windows, fresh flowers scent the air. The restaurant doubles as an art gallery, its charcoal walls crammed with portraits, a theatrical setting for a good meal, perhaps Devon crab, blanquette de veau, lemon tart with crème fraîche. Bedrooms come in pale greys with the best beds, the crispest linen, pretty throws and padded bedheads. Bigger rooms have sofas, some overlook the back garden, all have robes and spoiling oils and in beautiful marble bathrooms. The 'city of dreaming spires' is on your doorstep, there are bikes to borrow on which to explore. *Minimum stay: 2 nights at weekends*

Rooms	22 doubles, 7 twins: £215-£485. 6 suites for 3: £395-£560.
Meals	Breakfast £5-£15. Lunch from £18. Dinner, 3 courses, £25-£45. Sunday lunch £25-£30. Afternoon tea £25.
Closed	Never.
Directions	From A40 ring road, south onto Banbury Road; through Summertown & hotel on right just before St Giles church.

Jeremy Mogford
Old Parsonage Hotel
1 Banbury Road,
Oxford, OX2 6NN

Tel	+44 (0)1865 310210
Email	reservations@oldparsonage-hotel.co.uk
Web	www.oldparsonage-hotel.co.uk

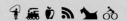

Turl Street Kitchen & Tower House Rooms

You land in the middle of Oxford at this quirky restaurant with rooms and find yourself surrounded by ancient colleges, with the Ashmolean Museum and the Bodleian Library both close. Interiors come in canteen style, with waitresses buzzing about, an open kitchen on display, a cool, shabby chic feel and happy chatter from people in for breakfast, lunch and dinner – this is a very popular community hub. Local food is sourced ethically and the menu changes twice a day, perhaps spiced carrot soup, steak and kidney pie, blood orange and vanilla cheesecake. There's WiFi throughout, the daily papers, a first-floor sitting room straight out of a student house. It's fun, easy going, a place for all. It's also a social enterprise, with profits going to charity, as they do 50 paces around the corner at Tower House Rooms, a terraced house with a difference: the old city wall runs through it with a 16th-century watch tower attached. Some rooms are small and share a bathroom, others are big, perhaps with a claw-foot bath. Expect good beds, smart colours, white linen, pretty throws. It's a peaceful spot, too.

Rooms	5 doubles; 3 doubles sharing 1 bathroom: £105-£170. Singles from £100. Cots available for children under 5 at no charge.
Meals	Lunch from £6.50. Dinner, 3 courses, £20-£25.
Closed	22 December to 2 January.
Directions	South from Broad Street on Turl Street. Right at Turl Street Kitchen onto Ship Street. On right after 50m.

Charis Sharpe
Turl Street Kitchen & Tower House Rooms
15 Ship Street,
Oxford, OX1 3DA

Tel +44 (0)1865 246828
Email info@towerhouseoxford.co.uk
Web www.towerhouseoxford.co.uk

The Feathers Hotel

Woodstock is the estate village to Blenheim Palace, one of Britain's finest houses, seat of the Dukes of Marlborough, birthplace of Winston Churchill. As for the hotel, it was once a draper's, then a butcher's, so it's no surprise it became a stylish hotel serving excellent food. In the morning you breakfast leisurely, then stroll up to the big house and spend the day dropping your jaw before coming home for afternoon tea in the courtyard. Inside, elegant, uncluttered interiors keep things simple: beautiful art, smouldering fires, a wall or two of original panelling, flowers everywhere. Ancient windows flood rooms with light, you find colourful rugs on wooden floors, then more gin than you can shake a stick at in the sitting-room bar (over 300 different bottles). Bedrooms have a contemporary feel with smart fabrics, lovely beds, mohair throws, delicate wallpapers. Some have sofas, all come with robes in fancy bathrooms. Back downstairs, delicious food waits in the restaurant, perhaps crab ravioli, loin of venison, treacle tart with blackberry sorbet. Bicester Village and Oxford are close. *Minimum stay: 2 nights at weekends in summer.*

Rooms	13 doubles, 3 twin/doubles: £99-£229. 5 suites for 2: £159-£319. Singles £99.
Meals	Lunch from £5. Bar meals from £10. Dinner £37.50-£45; 5-course tasting menu £55 (not Sunday eve). Sunday lunch from £14.
Closed	Never.
Directions	North from Oxford on A44. In Woodstock left after traffic lights & hotel on left.

Dominique Ghislane
The Feathers Hotel
Market Street,
Woodstock, OX20 1SX

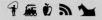

Tel +44 (0)1993 812291
Email enquiries@feathers.co.uk
Web www.feathers.co.uk

Artist Residence Oxfordshire

Justin and Charlie's ability to create beautiful small hotels at the speed of light is unprecedented. Their fourth – lost in the peace a few miles west of Oxford – is a reinvention of the country pub, though not as you might think. This isn't a stripped-back monument to contemporary design, rather a cool take on all things retro with quirky art and a little neon mixed in for good measure. You'll find vintage wallpapers, vivid colours, glass cabinets filled with curios, then a pink, up-cycled sofa in the cocktail bar. Country rugs cover flagstone floors, a fire burns on both sides in the bar, an original pine bench comes with plumped-up cushions. You eat in the restaurant amid ferns and flock wallpaper, perhaps Dorset crab with sorrel sauce, local venison with rainbow chard, gin and tonic panna cotta; there's a pie and a pint at the bar, too, and a dining terrace that overlooks the kitchen garden. Stunning bedrooms set the standard for others to follow: fat beds, exposed timbers, robes in flawless bathrooms, old tea chests for bedside tables. We've hardly scratched the surface. Exceptional. *Minimum stay: 2 nights at weekends.*

Rooms	1 double, 3 twin/doubles: £130-£295. 1 suite for 2: £240-£350. Extra beds £40 p.p.p.n. Under 12s £30.
Meals	Lunch from £6.50. Dinner, 3 courses, about £40; 5-course tasting menu, £60. Sunday lunch from £15.95.
Closed	Never.
Directions	West from Oxford on A40, exiting after 5 miles for Witney East. At bottom of slip road, left for South Leigh. In village on right.

Charlie & Justin Salisbury
Artist Residence Oxford
Station Road, South Leigh,
Witney, OX29 6XN

Tel +44 (0)1993 656220
Email oxford@artistresidence.co.uk
Web www.artistresidenceoxford.co.uk

The Shaven Crown

The Great Hall, with its spectacular roof, dates to 1368 – quite some sitting room. It was built by monks from Bruern Abbey, reborn as a royal hunting lodge after the Dissolution of the Monasteries, then gifted to the village as an inn. Phil and Evelyn rescued it from neglect, then spent a year restoring long-lost glories, no mean feat. Potter about and find parquet flooring in the airy bar, books and armchairs in the pretty snug, then mullioned windows in the restaurant, where you dig into some lovely local food, perhaps rabbit rillettes with pear purée, loin of venison with a port wine sauce, espresso mousse with rum ice cream. In summer you can decant into a gorgeous courtyard for afternoon tea in the sun. Bedrooms have an elegant simplicity: airy colours, chic fabrics, beautiful beds, sparkling bathrooms. One has a beamed roof, a couple are smaller, but have courtyard views. You're in the heart of the Cotswolds: Stratford for Shakespeare, Cheltenham for the races and Oxford for the spires all within easy reach. There's jazz in the hall once a month. Dogs are very welcome.

Rooms	4 doubles, 3 twin/doubles: £95-£135.
Meals	Lunch from £6.50. Dinner, 3 courses, £25-£35. Sunday lunch from £17.95.
Closed	Rarely.
Directions	North from Burford on A361 for 5 miles. In village, on left.

Phil & Evelyn Roberts
The Shaven Crown
High Street,
Shipton under Wychwood, OX7 6BA

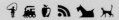

Tel +44 (0)1993 830500
Email relax@theshavencrown.co.uk
Web www.theshavencrown.co.uk

The Swan

Free-range bantams strut in the garden, a pint of Hooky waits at the bar. This lovely old pub sits on the river Windrush with the village cricket pitch waiting beyond. It started life as a water mill and stands on the Devonshire estate, hence the pictures of the Mitford sisters that hang on the walls. Outside, wisteria wanders across golden stone and creepers blush red in the autumn sun. Interiors hit the spot: low ceilings, open fires, beautiful windows, stone walls. Over the years thirsty feet on their way to the bar have worn grooves into ancient flagstones (including those of prime ministers and French presidents). As for the food, seasonal menus brim with local produce, offering delicious delights, perhaps game terrine with pear chutney, roast partridge with a red wine jus, rhubarb and apple crumble. Bedrooms in the old forge have 15th-century walls and 21st-century interior design; those in the cottage across the lane are yards from the river. Expect crisp linen, comfy beds, warm colours and good art. Several have claw-foot baths, one has a pink chaise longue. Burford is close.

Rooms	4 doubles, 5 twin/doubles, 1 twin: £125-£150. 1 suite for 2: £195. Singles from £70.
Meals	Lunch from £5. Dinner, 3 courses, about £30. Sunday lunch from £14.95.
Closed	Christmas Day & Boxing Day.
Directions	West from Oxford on A40 for Cheltenham/Burford. Past Witney & village signed right at 1st r'bout.

Archie & Nicola Orr-Ewing
The Swan
Swinbrook,
Burford, OX18 4DY

Tel +44 (0)1993 823339
Email info@theswanswinbrook.co.uk
Web www.theswanswinbrook.co.uk

The Kings Head Inn

A beautiful English inn, a 17th-century cider house made of ancient stone that sits on the green in a Cotswold village with free-range hens strutting their stuff and a family of ducks bathing in the pond. Inside, locals gather to chew the cud, scoff great food and wash it down with Cotswold ales. The fire burns all year, you get low ceilings, painted stone walls, the odd settle, country rugs on flagstone floors. Nicely priced bedrooms have lots of colour and style. Those in the main house have more character, those in the courtyard are bigger (and quieter). You'll find painted wood, pretty fabrics, rustic furniture, spotless bathrooms; most have great views, too. Breakfast and supper are taken in a pretty dining room (exposed stone walls, pale wood tables), while you can lunch by the fire in the bar on devilled kidneys, grilled mackerel, a plate of British cheeses. There are lovely unpompous touches like jugs of cow parsley in the loo. There's loads to do, too: antiques in Stow, golf at Burford, circular walks through gorgeous country. The front terrace teems with life in summer. *Minimum stay: 2 nights at weekends.*

Rooms	9 doubles, 3 twin/doubles: £100-£135. Singles £80-£100.
Meals	Lunch from £7.50. Dinner, 3 courses, about £30. Sunday lunch £15.
Closed	25-27 December.
Directions	East out of Stow-on-the-Wold on A436, then right onto B4450 for Bledington. Pub in village on green.

Archie & Nicola Orr-Ewing
The Kings Head Inn
The Green, Bledington,
Chipping Norton, OX7 6XQ

Tel +44 (0)1608 658365
Email info@kingsheadinn.net
Web www.kingsheadinn.net

The Feathered Nest Country Inn

The village is tiny, the view is fantastic, the bar is lively, the rooms are a treat. This 300-year-old malthouse sits in 55 acres of green and pleasant land and is utterly gorgeous inside and out. The view from the garden is one of the best in the Cotswolds – a five-mile sweep across quilted fields to a distant ridge. Interiors are just as good. A warm rustic style mixes beautifully with original timbers and old stone walls. A fire smoulders in the lovely bar, doors in the restaurant open onto the terrace, the garden room has tartan walls and the white wine cellar on display. Bedrooms delight. One is enormous, two have the view, beds are dressed in crisp linen; most have power showers, one has a claw-foot bath, all have robes. You get coffee machines and iPod docks, too. Delicious food waits downstairs, perhaps octopus with lemon and garlic, pollock with saffron and fennel, tarte tatin with vanilla ice cream. You eat on the terrace in summer looking out on the lake and distant farms. A couple of luxurious cabins are soon to be sprinkled across the grounds – Amanda and Tony do nothing by halves. Magical. *Minimum stay: 2 nights at weekends.*

Rooms	4 doubles: £245-£295. Dinner, B&B £180-£205 p.p.
Meals	Lunch, 2-3 courses, £29-£35. Dinner, 2-3 courses, £55-£68.
Closed	Rarely.
Directions	North from Burford on A424 for Stow-on-the-Wold. After 4 miles right for Nether Westcote. In village.

Tony & Amanda Timmer
The Feathered Nest Country Inn
Nether Westcote,
Chipping Norton, OX7 6SD

Tel +44 (0)1993 833030
Email reservations@thefeatherednestinn.co.uk
Web www.thefeatherednestinn.co.uk

The Olive Branch

A lovely pub in a sleepy Rutland village, where bridle paths lead out across peaceful fields. It dates to the 17th century and is built of Clipsham stone, as is York Minster. Inside, a warm, informal, rustic chic hits the spot perfectly with open fires, old beams, stone walls and choir stalls in the bar. But there's more here than cool design. This is a place to come and eat great food, the lovely, local seasonal stuff that's cooked with passion by Sean and his brigade, perhaps potted pork and stilton with apple jelly, haunch of venison with a juniper fondant, then a boozy rhubarb trifle. Bedrooms in Beech House across the lane are gorgeous. Three have terraces, one has a free-standing bath, all come with crisp linen, pretty beds, Roberts radios and real coffee. Super breakfasts – smoothies, boiled eggs and soldiers, the full cooked works – are served in a stone-walled barn with flames leaping in the wood-burner. The front garden fills in summer, the sloe gin comes from local berries, and Newark is close for the biggest antiques market in Europe. Picnic hampers can be arranged. A total gem.

Rooms	5 doubles: £115-£195. 1 family room for 4: £115-£195. Singles from £97.50. Extra beds £30.
Meals	Lunch from £8.50. Dinner, 3 courses, £28.50-£40. Sunday lunch from £24.50.
Closed	Rarely.
Directions	A1 5 miles north of Stamford, then exit onto B668. Right & right again for Clipsham. In village (Beech House across the road from The Olive Branch).

Ben Jones & Sean Hope
The Olive Branch
Main Street, Clipsham,
Oakham, LE15 7SH

Tel	+44 (0)1780 410355
Email	info@theolivebranchpub.com
Web	www.theolivebranchpub.com

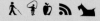

Hambleton Hall Hotel & Restaurant

Hambleton is matchless, one of the seven wonders of English country-house hotels. It sits on a tiny peninsular that juts into Rutland Water. You can sail on it, cycle round it, or watch terns and osprey commute across it. Back at the house the undisputed wonders of Hambleton wait: sofas by the fire in the panelled hall, a pillared bar in red for cocktails, a Michelin star in the elegant dining room. French windows in the sitting room – beautiful art, fresh flowers, the daily papers – open onto fine gardens. Expect clipped lawns and gravel paths, a formal parterre garden that bursts with summer colour and a walled swimming pool with views over parkland to the water. Bedrooms are flawless: hand-stitched Italian linen, mirrored armoires, Roberts radios and marble bathrooms. Stefa's eye for fabrics, some of which coat the walls, is impeccable; the Pavilion, a two-bedroom suite, has its own terrace. Polish the day off with ambrosial food, perhaps beetroot terrine with horseradish sorbet, fallow venison with Asian pear, passion fruit soufflé with banana sorbet. Barnsdale Gardens are close. *Minimum stay: 2 nights at weekends.*

Rooms	15 twin/doubles: £270-£725. 1 suite for 4: £290-£725. Singles £200. Dinner, B&B £210 p.p.
Meals	Lunch from £29. Dinner, 3 courses, £69; tasting menu £92. Sunday lunch £58.
Closed	Never.
Directions	From A1, A606 west towards Oakham for about 8 miles, then left, signed Hambleton. In village bear left and hotel signed right.

Tim & Stefa Hart
Hambleton Hall Hotel & Restaurant
Ketton Road, Hambleton,
Oakham, LE15 8TH

Tel	+44 (0)1572 756991
Email	hotel@hambletonhall.com
Web	www.hambletonhall.com

Old Downton Lodge

The last time anything really happened here was in 1067 when Edric the Wild got a bit shirty with invading Normans. Fast forward five hundred years and Old Downton is taking shape. It's a fine old building, a little like walking onto the set of Wolf Hall, with original timbers, mighty crossbeams and beautiful stone walls. It sits in pristine country. Pheasants strut, hills roll, woodlands sprawl along distant ridges; a stunning walk across it all takes you over to Ludlow. Back at the house Pippa and Willem look after you in great style. There's a lovely sitting room in the old dairy with a roaring fire and an honesty bar, then a dining room in an 11th-century barn that resembles a medieval banqueting hall. In summer, life moves into the courtyard (once used for cattle auctions), where you can eat, drink and make merry in good weather. Big bedrooms mix timber frames, stone walls, flagged floors and oak furniture, while bathrooms have robes and lashings of hot water. Back outside, follow the river Teme up to Downton Gorge for ferns, otters, Roman baths and bluebells in spring. Blissful.

Rooms	5 doubles, 2 twins, 2 four-posters: £145-£205. Dinner, B&B from £117.50 p.p.
Meals	Dinner, 6-9 courses, from £60.
Closed	Rarely.
Directions	North from Ludlow on A49, then west after 2 miles on A4113. 1st left (after 2 miles). Straight on for 4 miles; hotel on right.

Willem & Pippa Vlok
Old Downton Lodge
Downton-on-the-Rock,
Ludlow, SY8 2HU

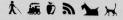

Tel +44 (0)1568 771826
Email bookings@olddowntonlodge.com
Web www.olddowntonlodge.com

The Castle Hotel

This thriving medieval market town sits amid some of the loveliest country in the land, a launch pad for walkers and cyclists alike, with Offa's Dyke, Long Mynd and the Kerry Ridgeway all close. After a day in the hills, roll back to this quirky hotel for a night of gentle carousing. You'll find heaps of country comforts: hearty food, impeccable ales, super rooms with honest prices. Downstairs, there's a coal fire in the pretty snug, oak panelling in the breakfast room, and Millie the short-haired dachshund who patrols the corridors with aplomb. Stylish bedrooms upstairs have all been refurbished. Expect good beds, warm colours, flat-screen TVs, an armchair if there's room. Some are up in the eaves, several have views of the Shropshire hills, two have baths in the room. Back downstairs you find the sort of food you'd want after a day in the hills, perhaps hot garlic prawns, beef and ale pie, sticky toffee pudding. Don't miss the hugely popular real ale festival in July, the beer drinker's equivalent of Glastonbury. The garden terrace, with long country views, is a fine spot for a sundowner.

Rooms	9 doubles, 1 twin: £95-£150. 2 family rooms for 4: £130-£155. Singles from £75. Dinner, B&B from £82.50 p.p. Extra beds for children £20.
Meals	Lunch from £4.50. Dinner, 3 courses, about £25.
Closed	Christmas Day & 10 days in January.
Directions	At top of hill in town, off A488.

Henry & Rebecca Hunter
The Castle Hotel
Bishops Castle, SY9 5BN
Tel +44 (0)1588 638403
Email stay@thecastlehotelbishopscastle.co.uk
Web www.thecastlehotelbishopscastle.co.uk

Pen-y-Dyffryn Country Hotel

In a blissful valley lost to the world, a small country house that sparkles on the side of a peaceful hill. This is one of those lovely places where guests return again and again, mostly due to Audrey and Miles, who run a very happy ship. Outside, fields tumble down to a stream that marks the border with Wales. Daffodils erupt in spring, the lawns are scattered with deckchairs in summer, paths lead into the hills for fine walking. Lovely interiors are just the ticket: Laura Ashley wallpaper and an open fire in the quirky bar; colourful art and super food in the pretty restaurant; the daily papers and the odd chaise longue in the sitting room. Bedrooms hit the spot. Most have the view, one has a French sleigh bed, a couple have jacuzzi baths for two. Four lovely rooms outside are dog-friendly and have their own patios. You get warm colours, crisp linen, pretty fabrics and sparkling bathrooms. After a day in the hills come back for a good dinner, perhaps wild mushroom risotto, pan-fried wood pigeon, hot chocolate fondant with vanilla ice-cream. Offa's Dyke and Powis Castle are close. *Minimum stay: 2 nights at weekends*

Rooms	8 doubles, 4 twins: £120-£190. Singles £90-£99. Dinner, B&B £99-£136 p.p. Extra bed/sofabed £35 p.p.p.n.
Meals	Light lunch for residents by arrangement. Dinner £30-£37.
Closed	Rarely.
Directions	Leave Oswestry on B4580, signed Llansilin. Hotel 3 miles up. Approach Rhydycroesau, left at town sign, first right.

Miles & Audrey Hunter
Pen-y-Dyffryn Country Hotel
Rhydycroesau, Oswestry, SY10 7JD
Tel +44 (0)1691 653700
Email stay@peny.co.uk
Web www.peny.co.uk

Sebastian's

This cute little restaurant with rooms occupies an old merchant's house that dates from 1640. Michelle and Mark have been at the helm for some 25 years cooking up a fine reputation – not only for their delicious food, but for the quirky, old-world interiors in which they serve it. Inside you find huge beams, timber frames, half panelling and stripped floors. Big warm colours sit on the walls, smartly clothed tables are lit by candles, deco posters of the Orient Express hang in every room (Mark supplies the train with canapés and desserts). Back in the restaurant, sofas wait in front of a fire that smoulders from morning to night in winter. Here you drool over the menu before digging into delicious food, perhaps scallop ravioli with lemon grass and ginger, short rib of beef in a red wine sauce, dark chocolate mousse with honey ice cream. Six nicely-priced rooms wait, two in the main house (timber frames, lots of colour), four off the attractive courtyard (comfy sofas, lovely bathrooms). Plans are afoot for a couple of suites. Welsh hills wait to the west, so bring your walking boots.

Rooms	4 doubles, 2 twin/doubles: £85. Singles £75.
Meals	Breakfast £6.95-£11.95. Dinner £28-£35 (Wed/Thurs). Dinner, 5 courses, £44 (Fri/Sat). No dinner Sun-Tues.
Closed	Rarely.
Directions	In middle of Oswestry on B4580.

Michelle & Mark Sebastian Fisher
Sebastian's
45 Willow Street, Oswestry, SY11 1AQ

Tel	+44 (0)1691 655444
Email	info@sebastians-hotel.com
Web	www.sebastians-hotel.co.uk

Meeson Hall

Sitting in eight acres of lawns and woodland with open country all around, this lovely country house dates back to 1640 and is a treasure trove of beautiful things – the Jacobean chimney piece in the dining room is one of the finest in the land. Guests have the run of the ground floor: a grandly panelled hall with a crackling fire, an airy drawing room for afternoon tea and a library filled with original art. You eat communally in the splendid dining room, merrily digging into Mark's lovely home cooking – perhaps pâté with redcurrant jelly, a Barnsley chop with a red wine jus, followed by bread and butter pudding. Bedrooms come in smart country-house style: warm colours, smartly dressed beds, antique furniture, fresh flowers. There are sofas, silver teapots, perhaps a chandelier, then robes and the odd claw-foot bath in wallpapered bathrooms. Outside, chickens provide eggs for breakfast and bluebells run riot in spring. All of which would be blossom in the wind without Adrian and Mark, who go out of their way to make your stay here special. Ironbridge, birthplace of the Industrial Revolution, is close. *Over 16s welcome.*

Rooms	4 doubles: £165-£215. 1 suite for 4: £180-£320. Singles from £145.
Meals	Lunch from £10. Dinner, 3 courses, £30. Sunday lunch £25. Afternoon tea from £10.
Closed	Rarely.
Directions	North from Telford on A41. Cross B5062, then right in Waters Upton. Through village, right at bridge after 1 mile for Meeson. Ignore 1st left, through village, left at house with red-brick wall. On left after 500m.

Adrian Jones & Mark Scarrott
Meeson Hall
Meeson, TF6 6PG

Tel +44 (0)1952 541262
Email enquiries@meesonhall.co.uk
Web www.meesonhall.co.uk

The Haughmond

This is one of those lovely places that sits in beautiful country, serves delicious food and looks after guests without the slightest hint of pomposity. It's an 18th-century inn that doubles as a hub for village life, and it comes with a small shop full of local produce. It ticks to its own beat, locals pop in to chat, cyclists and walkers drop in for coffee, dogs are very welcome. The big draw is Martin's food and the restaurant is busy for lunch and dinner most days, no mean feat for a country inn. Whatever can be is sourced locally and the seven-course tasting menu is a steal; highlights include mackerel with cucumber, beef with horseradish, a sinful pistachio soufflé. You can walk it all off from the front door; the place takes its name from a nearby hill, where big views wait at the top. Back at the inn, spotless rooms are both warmly stylish and nicely priced. A couple are bigger, all have comfy beds, crisp linen and good bathrooms. One has a Juliet balcony, those at the back have country views, all have fresh flowers, local art and smart TVs. Shrewsbury is close. An affordable treat.

Rooms	2 doubles, 3 twin/doubles: £90-£120. Singles from £80. Extra bed £10.
Meals	Lunch from £8 (Tues-Sat). Dinner, 3 courses, about £30. Tasting menu, 7 courses, £40 (Mon-Sat). Sunday lunch £16-£20.
Closed	Christmas & New Year.
Directions	M54, A5, then A49 north. Right at 1st r'bout, then first right signed Upton Magna. In village.

Martin & Mel Broad
The Haughmond
Upton Magna,
Shrewsbury, SY4 4TZ

Tel +44 (0)1743 709918
Email contact@thehaughmond.co.uk
Web www.thehaughmond.co.uk

The Talbot Inn at Mells

The Talbot is an absolute stunner, one of the loveliest inns in the land. It sits in a timeless village lost in a tangle of country lanes, a 15-century coaching inn reborn for the 21st-century. Sweep under the carriage arch and you enter a cobbled courtyard, where life gathers in good weather. There's a tithe-barn sitting room with big sofas and a Sunday cinema, then the Coach House Grill, where you eat at weekends under hanging beams. As for the main house, weave along ancient passageways and find stone walls, rugs on wood floors, crackling log fires and a low-ceilinged bar for a pint of Butcombe. The restaurant has colonised several cosy rooms and delicious food flies from the kitchen, perhaps white onion and cider soup, monkfish and mussel stew, chocolate and salted caramel sundae. Bedrooms are the best, some smaller, others huge with claw-foot baths, walk-in showers and modern four-posters. Add lovely staff to the mix and you have a slice of heaven. There's a colourful garden and great local walking, so bring your boots. The First World War poet, Siegfried Sassoon, is buried in the churchyard.

Rooms	8 doubles: £100-£160.
Meals	Lunch & dinner £5-£30. Sunday lunch from £15.
Closed	Rarely.
Directions	From Frome A362 for Radstock; left turn for Mells. At mini-roundabout take right to Mells. After 1 mile turn right to Mells.

Matt Greenlees
The Talbot Inn at Mells
Selwood Street, Mells,
Frome, BA11 3PN

Tel +44 (0)1373 812254
Email info@talbotinn.com
Web www.talbotinn.com

The Swan

The Swan is gorgeous, a contemporary take on a village local. It's part of a new wave of pubs that open all day and do so much more than serve a good pint. The locals love it. They come for breakfast, pop in to buy a loaf of bread, then return for afternoon tea and raid the cake stands. It's right on the bustling street, with a sprinkling of tables and chairs on the pavement in French-café style. Interiors mix old and new brilliantly. You get Farrow & Ball colours and cool lamps hanging above the bar, then lovely old rugs on boarded floors and a wood-burner to keep things toasty. Push inland to find an airy restaurant open to the rafters that overlooks the garden. Here you dig into Tom Blake's fabulous food (he's ex-River Cottage), anything from grilled Cornish herring to a three-course feast, maybe crispy Lyme Bay cuttlefish, slow cooked Quantock venison, chocolate and salted caramel tart. Bedrooms are lovely. Two have fancy baths in the room, you get vintage French furniture, iPod docks, colourful throws and walk-in power showers. Glastonbury is close, as are the Mendips.

Rooms	5 doubles, 2 twin/doubles: £75-£185. Extra bed £20. Cots available.
Meals	Lunch from £5. Dinner, 3 courses, about £25. Sunday lunch from £14. Bar meals only Sun night.
Closed	Rarely.
Directions	M5, junc. 22, then B3139 to Wedmore. In village.

Natalie Zvonek-Little
The Swan
Cheddar Road,
Wedmore, BS28 4EQ

Tel +44 (0)1934 710337
Email info@theswanwedmore.com
Web www.theswanwedmore.com

The White Hart

Cool inns with lovely rooms in interesting parts of the land are a big hit with lots of us – we like the easy style, the local food, the good prices and the happy staff. The White Hart is a case in point, a beautifully refurbished inn. It sits on Somerton's ancient market square, 16th-century bricks and mortar, 21st-century lipstick and pearls. Inside, old and new mix beautifully: stone walls and parquet flooring, lovely sofas in front of the fire, funky lamps hanging above the bar. You'll find soft colours, padded window seats, country rugs, antler chandeliers. There's a cute booth in a stone turret, then lovely food waits, perhaps a chargrilled steak, Cornish crab cakes or wood-roasted pork loin. In summer, you spill onto a smart courtyard or into the garden for views of open country. Upstairs, fabulous bedrooms await. You might find timber frames, a claw-foot bath, a wall of paper or stripped boards. All have super beds, flat-screen TVs, lovely bathrooms and a nice price. Beautiful Somerset is all around, don't miss it.

Rooms	8 doubles: £75-£165.
Meals	Lunch from £6. Dinner, 3 courses, £25-£30. Sunday lunch from £15.
Closed	Rarely.
Directions	South from Glastonbury on B3151. Right for Somerton, left into village and on left in square.

Kirsty Schmidt
The White Hart
Market Place,
Somerton, TA11 7LX

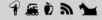

Tel +44 (0)1458 272273
Email info@whitehartsomerton.com
Web www.whitehartsomerton.com

The Pilgrims Restaurant with Rooms

Medieval pilgrims in search of King Arthur's tomb would stop here for sustenance before heading out across the marshes on their way to Glastonbury Abbey. These days, the food, the welcome and the rooms are all so lovely you're more likely to suffer a crisis of faith and stay put. Jools is to blame – his food is far too good to miss, good enough to alter the DNA of these walls – the Pilgrims is not an inn these days, but a restaurant with rooms. All the lovely old stuff survives – stone walls, timber frames, panelled walls and a couple of sofas in front of the fire. Tables in the restaurant are nicely spaced apart with subtle lighting and service that hits the spot. As for the food, expect local ingredients cooked to perfection, perhaps Lyme Bay scallops, rack of lamb, smooth dark chocolate pot with a hint of stem ginger. Five lovely bedrooms wait in the old skittle alley. Three have cathedral ceilings, all come with exposed stone walls, flat-screen TVs and crisp linen on good beds. As for the bathrooms, expect double-ended baths, separate power showers, fluffy robes. Wells and Glastonbury are close.

Rooms	4 doubles, 1 twin/double: £100-£130. Singles £80-£130.
Meals	Lunch from £8. Dinner, 3 courses, about £30. Sunday lunch £19. No food on Mondays.
Closed	Rarely.
Directions	On B3153 between Castle Cary & Somerton. In village by traffic lights.

Julian & Sally Mitchison
The Pilgrims Restaurant with Rooms
Lovington,
Castle Cary, BA7 7PT

Tel +44 (0)1963 240597
Email jools@pilgrimsrestaurant.co.uk
Web www.pilgrimsrestaurant.co.uk

The Devonshire Arms

What makes a great little inn these days? The Devonshire Arms has all the ingredients: lots of style, good prices, a community feel, some lovely rooms. It's in the right place, too, bang on the village green, with a terrace at the front, a garden at the back and a courtyard in between. Inside, is just as good. This isn't one of those places where every table is laid up for food; on the contrary, the best seats in the house are in the bar – a couple of armchairs in front of the fire. Step inside and find stylish interiors throughout. You get painted panelling in the restaurant – a sort of contemporary take on an 18th-century gentleman's club – then cool colours in the bar, where you can grab a pint of Butcombe, then spin outside to watch village life pass by. Lovely rooms have terrific prices. You'll find good beds, white linen, pretty furniture and excellent bathrooms; one has a free-standing bath. Elsewhere, red leather banquettes, fresh flowers, kind staff, the daily papers. As for the food, it's just the ticket: local partridge, fillet of bream, treacle tart with buttermilk ice cream.

Rooms	8 doubles, 1 twin/double: £95-£140. Singles from £85. Extra bed/sofabed £20 p.p.p.n.
Meals	Lunch from £5.95. Dinner, 3 courses, about £30. Sunday lunch from £12.95.
Closed	25-26 December.
Directions	A303, then north on B3165, through Martock to Long Sutton. On village green.

Philip & Sheila Mepham
The Devonshire Arms
Long Sutton,
Langport, TA10 9LP

Tel +44 (0)1458 241271
Email mail@thedevonshirearms.com
Web www.thedevonshirearms.com

Little Barwick House

A beautiful restaurant with rooms lost in peaceful lanes south of Yeovil. Tim and Emma rolled west 14 years ago and now have a legion of fans who come to feast on their ambrosial food. Their small Georgian country house stands privately in three acres of peace. Horses graze in the paddock below, afternoon tea is served in the garden to the sound of birdsong in summer. Inside, chic interiors flood with light thanks to fine windows that run along the front. There's an open fire in the bar, eclectic reading in the sitting room, then contemporary art in the high-ceilinged dining room. Gorgeous bedrooms have a country-house feel and come with warm colours, pretty fabrics, Roberts radios, a sofa if there's room. You'll find fresh garden flowers, antique furniture, and White Company oils in compact bathrooms. Dinner is the main event, heaven in three courses. Everything is homemade and cooked by Tim and Emma, an equal partnership in the kitchen – perhaps Lyme Bay scallops, saddle of wild venison, dark chocolate tort with armagnac ice-cream. Posh wines by the glass come courtesy of clever technology. *Children over 5 welcome.*

Rooms	4 doubles, 2 twins: £100-£170. Singles £75-£140. Dinner, B&B £105-£130 p.p. Extra bed/sofabed available £25 p.p.p.n.
Meals	Lunch, 2-3 courses, £25.95-£29.95 (not Tues). Dinner, 2-3 courses, £41.95-£47.95.
Closed	Sunday nights & Mondays.
Directions	From Yeovil A37 south for Dorchester; left at 1st r'bout. Down hill, past church, left in village and house on left after 200 yds.

Emma & Tim Ford
Little Barwick House
Rexes Hollow Lane, Barwick,
Yeovil, BA22 9TD

Tel +44 (0)1935 423902
Email info@littlebarwick.co.uk
Web www.littlebarwickhouse.co.uk

Lord Poulett Arms

An idyllic inn that's hard to beat. It's like stepping into the pages of a Jane Austen novel. A clipped country elegance runs throughout – old stone walls and period colours, then noble portraits on the walls and beautiful old settles to take the strain. There are drawbacks – sooner or later you will have to leave, probably with a touch of envy for the locals. Smart rusticity abounds. A fire burns on both sides in the dining room, where you eat under beams at antique tables. You'll find the daily papers, sofas in the locals' bar, a pile of logs at the back door, then an informal French garden with a piste for boules. Bedrooms upstairs have a lovely style with fancy flock wallpaper, pretty fabrics and fresh flowers, perhaps a small chandelier or a carved wooden bed. Two rooms have slipper baths in the room; two have claw-foot baths in bathrooms one step across the landing; the suite is enormous and has an open fire. The food is just as lovely, perhaps pea and ham soup, confit pork belly, praline fondant with coffee ice cream. Don't miss Sunday lunch or summer barbecues. An affordable treat.

Rooms	2 doubles; 2 doubles with separate bath: £85-£95. 1 suite for 3: £100-£150. Singles from £60.
Meals	Lunch from £5. Dinner, 3 courses, £20-£35. Sunday lunch £18-£21.
Closed	Never.
Directions	A303, then A356 south for Crewkerne. Right for West Chinnock. Through village, 1st left for Hinton St George. Pub on right in village.

Steve & Michelle Hill
Lord Poulett Arms
High Street,
Hinton St George, TA17 8SE

Tel	+44 (0)1460 73149
Email	reservations@lordpoulettarms.com
Web	www.lordpoulettarms.com

Swain House

Watchet is a sleepy town on the West Somerset coast, and while its day may have passed, its medieval harbour that once made it rich inspired Coleridge to write his famous poem *The Rime of The Ancient Mariner*. As for this stylish B&B, it makes a great little base for gentle explorations – you'll find excellent hill walking, beaches, the coastal path, even a music festival in August. Once an antiques shop, it sits on the colourful, main street in town with a big window looking out onto the world. Downstairs, there's a stylish dining room that doubles as a sitting room, with a sofa in front of a fire and hanging lamps at the breakfast table. Upstairs, lovely rooms wait, the sort you expect to find in a boutique inn. You get a huge noble portrait covering one wall, then pretty armchairs, smart fabrics, padded bedheads and old-style radiators. Excellent bathrooms have walk-in showers, free-standing baths, robes and REN oils – exactly what you want after a day in the hills. Pub grub waits in town, posher nosh is a little further afield. The nearby car park is nicely priced, too.

Rooms	4 doubles: £135. Singles from £115.
Meals	Restaurants in village.
Closed	Rarely.
Directions	M5, junc. 23, then A39 for Minehead. Right in Williton, then immediately left for Watchet. Approaching town, left over railway, then follow road into town. On right after 200m. Car park on right after 50m.

Jason & Annie Robinson
Swain House
48 Swain Street,
Watchet, TA23 0AG

Tel +44 (0)1984 631038
Email stay@swain-house.com
Web www.swain-house.com

Luttrell Arms

You get a triple whammy here: spectacular Dunster Castle, its beautiful estate village and this medieval coaching inn on the high street – the view from the terrace across to the castle is candy for your eyes. Inside, a recent refurbishment has brought in a warm style. You'll find a beautiful restaurant with papered walls, an attractive sitting room for afternoon tea, an open fire in the high-ceilinged bar, then a boot bar for sleeping dogs and a game of cribbage. There are a couple of terraces for lunch in the sun, sofas on a veranda that overlooks a tiny courtyard. Bedrooms are scattered about, some with village views, others overlooking the estate. Four are huge with grand four-posters, two sitting under a 500-year-old hammer beam roof. Others have period furniture, pretty wallpapers, perhaps a small private terrace; smaller rooms are simpler, but have good beds. Tasty food spans the spectrum, perhaps a posh burger in the bar to smoked haddock chowder, braised shin of beef and chocolate and raspberry tart in the restaurant. Cliff tops and wild moors wait for fabulous walking. *Minimum stay: 2 nights at weekends.*

Rooms	4 doubles, 20 twin/doubles, 4 four-posters: £110-£220. Singles £90-£100.
Meals	Lunch from £4.95. Bar meals from £10.95. Dinner, 3 courses, about £30. Sunday lunch from £15.95. Afternoon tea £12.95.
Closed	Rarely.
Directions	A39 towards Minehead, then south for Dunster on A396. On left on High Street.

Becca Way
Luttrell Arms
36 High Street,
Dunster, TA24 6SG

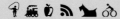

Tel +44 (0)1643 821555
Email enquiry@luttrellarms.co.uk
Web www.luttrellarms.co.uk

Cross Lane House

A medieval farmhouse in a National Trust village, where a 500-year-old bridge sweeps you across to ancient woodland. Outside, a cobbled courtyard leads up to a hay barn that's open on one side – not a bad spot for breakfast in good weather. Inside, original panelling survives, while Max and Andrew's flawless design gives a delicious country-house feel, making this an intimate bolthole in which to linger. You'll find a sitting room packed with beautiful things – books galore, original flagstones, sofas in front of a roaring fire. There's a spy hole in the panelling, some ancient graffiti, too, then a gorgeous dining room in period colours with wood floors, beautiful art and wonderful food, perhaps Devon crab cakes, boeuf Bourguignon, chocolate brownies with toffee popcorn and salted caramel ice cream. Bedrooms upstairs are deeply satisfying: lovely beds, bowls of fruit, timber frames, super bathrooms. One is smaller, two are bigger, the family suite has two bedrooms. You get binoculars, Roberts radios, Cowshed oils, even mini bars 'on the house'. Exmoor waits. The road passes quietly at night. *Minimum stay: 2 nights at weekends*

Rooms	3 doubles: £155-£200. 1 suite for 3: £185-£215. Dinner, B&B from £112 p.p.
Meals	Lunch from £6 (Wed-Sat, Easter-Sept). Dinner £27-£34. Sunday lunch £18-£24. Afternoon tea £19.95.
Closed	Rarely.
Directions	A39 west from Minehead. On right after 5 miles, 1 mile before Porlock.

Max Lawrence & Andrew Stinson
Cross Lane House
Allerford,
Minehead, TA24 8HW

Tel	+44 (0)1643 863276
Email	max@crosslanehouse.com
Web	www.crosslanehouse.com

The Anchor

The Anchor is one of those lovely places that has resisted the urge to be precious. This is a cool little seaside inn where relaxed informality reigns; kids are welcome, staff are friendly, dogs fall asleep in the bar. You're 500 yards from the sea with a terrace that fills with locals in summer and lawns that run off towards the water. Inside, beautiful simplicity abounds – Cape Cod meets English country local. You get books everywhere, beautiful art, roaring fires, a happy vibe. The big draw is Sophie's lovely food. Game and venison come from local estates, fish and seafood from nearby waters, samphire and sea kale are foraged along the coast. Bedrooms fit the mood perfectly. Those in the house are warm and homely; garden rooms are big and airy with sofas inside and terraces that overlook nearby dunes. Don't miss dinner, perhaps fish soup, game ravioli, chocolate fondant with caramel ice cream. You wash it all down with Mark's legendary collection of bottled beers and fancy wines. There are festivals by the score – don't miss Latitude or Folk East. Starry skies amaze. Unmissable. *Minimum stay: 2 nights at weekends & in high season.*

Rooms	10 doubles: £105-£165. Singles £85-£100. Extra bed/sofabed £20-£30 p.p.p.n.
Meals	Lunch from £5.25. Dinner, 3 courses, about £30. Sunday lunch, 2 courses, £20.
Closed	Rarely.
Directions	From A12 south of Southwold, B1387 to Walberswick.

Mark & Sophie Dorber
The Anchor
Main Street, Walberswick,
Southwold, IP18 6UA

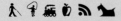

Tel +44 (0)1502 722112
Email info@anchoratwalberswick.com
Web www.anchoratwalberswick.com

Wentworth Hotel

The Wentworth has the loveliest position in town, the beach literally a pebble's throw from the garden, the sea rolling east under a vast sky. Inside, fires smoulder, clocks chime and seaside elegance abounds. It's all terrifically English, with vintage wallpapers, kind local staff and an elegant bar that opens onto a terrace garden. The restaurant looks out to sea, spilling onto a sunken terrace in summer for views of passing boats. Proper English fare is the order of the day: stilton soup, breast of guinea fowl, lemon posset with raspberries and shortbread. The hotel has been in the same family since 1920 and old-fashioned values mix harmoniously with interiors that are refreshed often to keep things sparkling. Airy bedrooms are deeply comfy, those at the front have sea views (and binoculars). Expect warm colours, smart fabrics, padded headboards and good beds; all have stylish bathrooms, too. You'll find sofas galore in the sitting rooms, but you may want to spurn them to walk by the sea. Joyce Grenfell was a regular. The Snape Maltings are close. *Minimum stay: 2 nights at weekends.*

Rooms	7 doubles, 24 twin/doubles: £140-£220. 4 singles: £85-£119. Dinner, B&B from £83 p.p.
Meals	Lunch from £5. Dinner, 2-3 courses, £21-£26.50.
Closed	Never.
Directions	A12 north from Ipswich, then A1094 for Aldeburgh. Past church, down hill, left at x-roads; hotel on right.

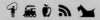

Michael Pritt
Wentworth Hotel
Wentworth Road,
Aldeburgh, IP15 5BD
Tel +44 (0)1728 452312
Email stay@wentworth-aldeburgh.com
Web www.wentworth-aldeburgh.com

The Crown & Castle

A great place to wash up for a few lazy days. Orford is hard to beat, a sleepy Suffolk village blissfully marooned at the end of the road. River, beach and forest wait, as does the Crown & Castle, a welcoming English hostelry where the art of hospitality is practised with unstinting flair. The inn stands in the shadow of Orford's 12th-century castle. Uncluttered interiors have a warm, airy feel with stripped floorboards, open fires, wonderful art and flickering candles at night. Chic bedrooms have Vi-Spring beds, fancy bathrooms, lovely fabrics, the odd armchair. Four in the main house have watery views, the suite is huge, the garden rooms big and light, the courtyard rooms a real delight. All have crisp white linen, TVs, DVDs and digital radios. Wellington boots wait at the back door, so pull on a pair and explore Rendlesham Forest or hop on a boat and chug over to Orford Ness. Ambrosial food awaits your return, perhaps potted brown shrimps, a faultless steak and kidney pie, crushed pistachio meringue with a chocolate ice-cream sundae. Sutton Hoo is close. Dogs are very welcome. *Minimum stay: 2 nights at weekends. Children over 8 welcome.*

Rooms	18 doubles, 2 twins: £130-£260. 1 suite for 2: £265-£335. Dinner, B&B from £95 p.p.
Meals	Lunch from £8.50. Dinner, à la carte, around £35.
Closed	Rarely.
Directions	A12 north from Ipswich, A1152 east to Woodbridge, then B1084 into Orford. Right in square for castle. On left.

David & Ruth Watson
The Crown & Castle
Orford,
Woodbridge, IP12 2LJ

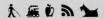

Tel +44 (0)1394 450205
Email info@crownandcastle.co.uk
Web www.crownandcastle.co.uk

Kesgrave Hall

This Georgian mansion sits in 38 acres of woodland and gardens, sound-proofing it from the outside world. It was home to US airmen during WWII, but the locals have reclaimed it as their own now and they come for the easy style, the excellent service, the delicious food and the informal vibe. The emphasis here is firmly on the food, so it's almost a restaurant with rooms, albeit quite a grand one. Inside, you find wellington boots in the entrance hall, high ceilings in the big sitting room, stripped boards in the humming bistro and doors that open onto a terrace in summer. Colourful bedrooms have lots of style. One is huge and comes with a free-standing bath and a faux leopard-skin sofa. The others might not be quite as wild, but they're lovely nonetheless, some cosy in the eaves, others in beautifully refurbished outbuildings. Expect warm colours, crisp linen, good lighting and fancy bathrooms. Back downstairs, tasty food flies from the kitchen, perhaps smoked haddock fishcakes, a char-grilled steak, a delicious coffee cheesecake with Tia Maria ice cream. Suffolk's magical coast waits.

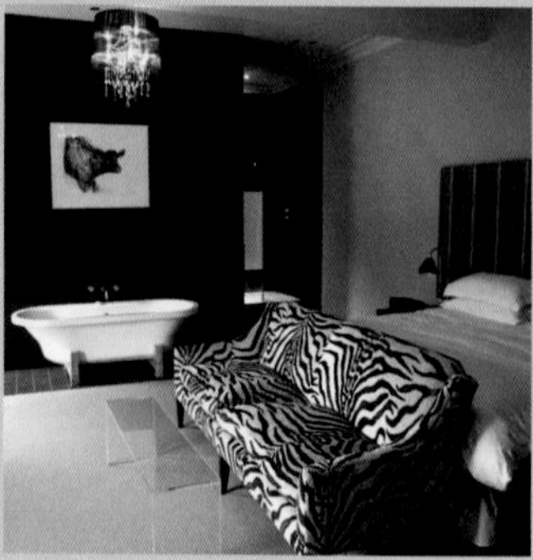

Rooms	10 doubles, 7 twin/doubles: £130-£230. 6 suites for 2: £275-£300.
Meals	Breakfast £10-£16. Lunch & dinner, 3 courses, £25-£30.
Closed	Never.
Directions	Skirt Ipswich to the south on A14, then head north on A12. Left at 4th r'bout; signed right after 0.25 miles.

Oliver Richards
Kesgrave Hall
Hall Road, Kesgrave,
Ipswich, IP5 2PU

Tel	+44 (0)1473 333741
Email	reception@kesgravehall.com
Web	www.milsomhotels.com

The Crown at Woodbridge

This cute little hotel in the middle of Woodbridge slopes downhill to the river, its rainbow of pastel colours making it a landmark in town. Inside, open-plan interiors flood with light courtesy of a glass ceiling. A Windermere skiff hangs above the bar, you find painted panelling, comfy sofas, slate floors and a wood-burner to keep things cosy. An airy restaurant comes in pale olive with leather banquettes, wooden floors and contemporary art, a fine spot for some tasty local food, perhaps seared scallops with Suffolk chorizo, slow braised pork with glazed carrots, white chocolate and passion fruit cheese cake. Breakfast is just as good; expect poached fruits, flagons of juice, smoked kippers, the best sausages in Suffolk. Bedrooms above vary in size, but all have the same feel: off-white colours, duck-down duvets, padded headboards, Hypnos beds. You'll find panels of entwined willow, pitchforks hanging on the wall, robes and power showers in sparkling bathrooms. Don't miss Sutton Hoo, the Aldeburgh food festival or Rendlesham Forest, the UK's equivalent of Area 51. *Minimum stay: 2 nights at weekends.*

Rooms	8 twin/doubles: £100-£180. 2 family rooms for 4: £140-£200. Extra beds/sofabeds £25 p.p.
Meals	Lunch & dinner £6-£30. Sunday lunch from £12.50.
Closed	Never.
Directions	A12 north from Ipswich, then B1438 into town. Pass station & left into Quay St. On right.

Laura Miles
The Crown at Woodbridge
Thoroughfare,
Woodbridge, IP12 1AD

Tel +44 (0)1394 384242
Email info@thecrownatwoodbridge.co.uk
Web www.thecrownatwoodbridge.co.uk

The Swan at Lavenham Hotel & Spa

This medieval inn has never looked better. It's a spectacular tangle of ancient timbers and sagging beams, with roaring fires, soaring ceilings and lovely staff, who weave through the throng, delivering sinful plates of afternoon tea or cocktails before supper. Potter about and find a minstrel's gallery in the vaulted dining room, a fabulous old bar that was a favourite haunt of WWII airmen, then a courtyard garden, where you can stop for a glass of Pimm's in summer. As if that wasn't enough, a beautiful new spa has recently appeared: you'll find six treatment rooms, a sauna and steam room, then sunbeds encircling a vitality pool on the terrace; sheer bliss. As for the stylish bedrooms, some are vast with four-posters and timber-frames, others more contemporary with cool colours and sofas. All have comfy beds, crisp white linen, robes in fancy bathrooms, while beds are turned down during dinner. There's an open-plan brasserie for lighter bites, then a 14th-century hall for weddings. As for Lavenham, it's one of the best preserved medieval towns in the land. Bury St Edmunds is close, too. *On-site parking available.*

Rooms	32 twin/doubles, 2 four-posters: £120-£280. 10 suites for 2: £230-£330. 1 single: £90. Dinner, B&B £245-£420 per room. Ask about special offers.
Meals	Lunch, 2 courses, from £16.95. Dinner, 3 courses £39.95. Brasserie, 2 courses, from £16.
Closed	Never.
Directions	In village.

Ingo Wiangke
The Swan at Lavenham Hotel & Spa
High Street,
Lavenham, CO10 9QA

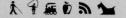

Tel +44 (0)1787 247477
Email info@theswanatlavenham.co.uk
Web www.theswanatlavenham.co.uk

The Great House

The ingredients here are simple. Take a medieval wool town trapped in aspic, add a 15th-century merchant's house that overlooks the square, then whisk up the best food in Suffolk and you have one of the loveliest restaurants with rooms in the land. It sits opposite the Guildhall, its Georgian façade giving way to original interiors, where timber frames and old beams mix beautifully with light colours and varnished wood floors. It is French to its core, with a cheese board to beat all others, and it's all the work of Régis and Martine, who have been at helm for over 30 years. You eat in the airy dining room with an ancient fireplace in one corner, perhaps foie gras terrine with a port jelly, steamed skate with capers, honey parfait with apple and Calvados mousse. Bedrooms are just as good: timber frames, wonky floors, beautiful beds, a sofa if there's room. You'll find decanters of sherry, coffee machines, flat-screen TVs, robes in chic bathrooms. Four are huge, one has a regal four-poster, another a 14th-century fireplace in its bathroom. There's a courtyard for breakfast in the sun, too. *Minimum stay: 2 nights at weekends.*

Rooms	4 doubles, 1 twin/double: £105-£239. Singles from £105. Dinner, B&B from £119 p.p. Extra bed/sofabed £15-£20 p.p.p.n.
Meals	Breakfast £12-£17. Lunch £25 (not Mon/Tue). Dinner £36.50 (not Sun/Mon). À la carte only Sat night.
Closed	January & 2 weeks in summer.
Directions	A1141 to Lavenham. At High Street 1st right after The Swan or up Lady Street into Market Place. On-site parking.

Régis & Martine Crépy
The Great House
Market Place,
Lavenham, CO10 9QZ

Tel +44 (0)1787 247431
Email info@greathouse.co.uk
Web www.greathouse.co.uk

The Bildeston Crown

Chris and Haley ran the Crown for ten years, upped sticks to head a few miles north, then got an offer they couldn't refuse and now the place is theirs. Their home is this beautifully preserved 15th-century inn. All the lovely old bits survive – timber frames, sagging beams, an ancient inglenook with a roaring fire – but interiors have an elegant, contemporary style with bold colours, stripped floorboards, comfy sofas and big art on the walls. Farmers drop in to chew the cud, walkers come to defrost in front of the fire while knocking back a pint of local ale, and the world and his wife come from near and far for Chris' delicious local food, perhaps truffled arancini with English asparagus, pheasant and foie gras Wellington, then an After Eight soufflé with chocolate ice cream. Stylish rooms have comfy beds, wonky floors, lots of colour and art. One has a fake Canaletto hanging above a claw-foot bath, another has a four-poster bed, all have robes in good bathrooms and flat-screen TVs. Don't miss Bury St Edmunds, a market town steeped in history. Medieval Lavenham is close, too. *Minimum stay: 2 nights at weekends.*

Rooms	11 doubles, 1 twin: £100-£175. Dinner, B&B from £87.50 p.p. Singles from £70.
Meals	Lunch from £6.50. Bar meals from £14. Dinner, 3 course, £30-£40. Sunday lunch from £17. Afternoon tea £15.
Closed	Never.
Directions	A12 junc. 31, then B1070 to Hadleigh. A1141 north, then B1115 into village & on right.

Hayley & Chris Lee
The Bildeston Crown
104 High Street,
Bildeston, IP7 7EB

Tel +44 (0)1449 740510
Email reception@thebildestoncrown.com
Web www.thebildestoncrown.com

The Crown

The Crown is all things to all men, a lovely country pub, a popular local restaurant, a small boutique hotel, a welcoming bolthole in Constable country. It sits in a pretty village with long views from its colourful terrace over the Box Valley, not a bad spot for a glass of Pimm's after a day exploring the area. It dates to 1560 and has old beams and timber frames, though interiors have youthful good looks: warm colours, tongue-and-groove panelling, terracotta-tiled floors, a fancy wine cellar behind a wall of glass. You'll find rugs and settles, the daily papers, leather armchairs in front of a wood-burner. Four ales wait at the bar, 30 wines come by the glass and there's seasonal food that will make you smile, perhaps confit duck leg ravioli, pan-roasted cod with chorizo and crayfish, popcorn panna cotta. Airy bedrooms are quietly hidden away at the bottom of the garden – excellent beds, lovely linen, a dash of colour and super bathrooms. All have armchairs or sofas, three have French windows that open onto private terraces with fine views. A great place to eat, sleep and potter.

Rooms	10 doubles: £145-£250. 1 suite for 2: £225-£295. Singles from £110. Extra bed/sofabed £20-£30 p.p.p.n.
Meals	Lunch & dinner £5-£30.
Closed	25-26 December.
Directions	North from Colchester on A134, then B1087 east into Stoke-by-Nayland. Right at T-junction; pub on left.

Richard Sunderland
The Crown
Park Street, Stoke-by-Nayland,
Colchester, CO6 4SE

Tel +44 (0)1206 262001
Email info@crowninn.net
Web www.crowninn.net

The Northgate

What do you want when you sneak off for a couple of days away? A small city steeped in history, beautiful country waiting beyond, a welcoming hotel with attractive bedrooms and excellent food? The Northgate – recently renovated from top to toe – offers all that and more. It's small and sits 500 metres from Abbey Gardens, the crown jewel of medieval Bury St Edmunds. Inside, the welcome is as warm as the water that pours from your power shower. Downstairs, the cocktail bar doubles as a sitting room, doors open onto a terrace for lunch in the sun, a well-kept garden waits beyond. Bedrooms above have a contemporary country-house feel: cool colours, smart wood furniture, pretty throws on beds that come with cool bedheads. Bathrooms are just as good: some have walk-in showers, two have freestanding baths in the room, all are excellent. As for the food, it's on tap all day: breakfast, elevenses, lunch, afternoon tea, then a delicious dinner, perhaps mackerel with apple and parsnip, rump of mutton with water chestnuts, an irresistible banana soufflé. Cambridge and Newmarket are close.

Rooms	7 doubles, 1 twin/double: £155-£225. 1 family room for 4: £280. Extra beds £15 p.p.p.n.
Meals	Lunch from £6. Dinner, 3 courses, about £35. Tasting menu, 9 courses, £75.
Closed	Never.
Directions	A14, junction 43, then south into Bury St Edmunds. Left at 1st r'bout onto Northgate Street. On right after 500m.

Steve Smith
The Northgate
13-14 Northgate Street,
Bury St Edmunds, IP33 1HP

Tel +44 (0)1284 339604
Email info@thenorthgate.com
Web www.thenorthgate.com

The Packhorse Inn

The rise of the cool country inn continues apace and the Packhorse is a prime example, a beautifully renovated country pub rescued from neglect. It's a small-scale pleasure dome – stylish interiors, ambrosial food, beautiful bedrooms and bathrooms – yet it remains a village local with a bar that welcomes all. The downstairs is open plan with a fire that burns on both sides and the odd armchair to take the strain. You'll find varnished floorboards, lots of art, lamps hanging above a cool bar. Chic bedrooms are scattered about. Coach house rooms have a warm rustic elegance, those in the house are a little fancier, a couple with baths in the room; all have fantastic bathrooms. Irresistible food waits below, maybe truffled goat's cheese with quince and figs, Suffolk venison and kidney pudding, plum tarte tatin with fruit-cake ice-cream. There's a terrace for good weather, then a private dining room that can turn into a meeting room. This is prime horse-racing country: Newmarket is three miles west, the peerless Frankel is at stud nearby. Cambridge and Bury St Edmunds are close.

Rooms	6 doubles, 2 twin/doubles: £100-£175. Singles from £85. Extra beds for children £10.
Meals	Lunch from £6. Dinner, 3 courses, about £35.
Closed	Rarely.
Directions	A14, junc. 38, then north onto A11. Take 1st exit east on B1085. Through Kentford and into Moulton. Left at green and on left.

Michael Box
The Packhorse Inn
Bridge Street, Moulton,
Newmarket, CB8 8SP

Tel +44 (0)1638 751818
Email info@thepackhorseinn.com
Web www.thepackhorseinn.com

Park House Hotel & Spa

This splendid country-house hotel sits in 10 acres of English gardens with quilted fields circling the grounds and the South Downs Way passing within a mile. Potter about outside and find a croquet lawn, two grass tennis courts and a six-hole golf course that slips into the country. Shrubberies burst with colour, there's a terrace for afternoon tea, wellington boots wait at the front door for long country walks. There's a beautiful spa, too. You can snooze on sunbeds while listening to birdsong on the terrace by the outdoor pool, or nip inside to the indoor pool and find treatment rooms, a sauna and a gym. The hotel is just as good, its country-house interiors filled with colour and style. You'll find an honesty bar that overlooks the garden, a sitting room for the daily papers, a conservatory that opens onto a terrace for scrumptious breakfasts. Smart rooms have heavenly beds, chic bathrooms, big country views, perhaps a terrace. Delicious food is the final delight, perhaps crab and ginger risotto, duck with honey-glazed parsnips, mint chocolate soufflé with passion fruit sorbet. Exceptional.

Rooms	6 doubles, 10 twin/doubles: £112-£370. 4 family rooms for 4: £196-£370. 1 cottage for 4: £250-£385.
Meals	Lunch from £23.95. Dinner from £30. Afternoon tea £19.95.
Closed	Never.
Directions	South from Midhurst on A286. At sharp left bend, right (straight ahead), signed Bepton. On left after 2 miles.

Sarah Stacey
Park House Hotel & Spa
Bepton,
Midhurst, GU29 0JB

Tel	+44 (0)1730 819020
Email	reservations@parkhousehotel.com
Web	www.parkhousehotel.com

Halfway Bridge Inn

This lovely country inn has exactly what lots of us want: warm and stylish interiors, local ales waiting in the bar, delicious food that draws a crowd, peaceful bedrooms for a good night's sleep. It sits back from the A272, with Goodwood to the south, Petworth to the east, and the South Downs all around for great walks and bike rides. Inside, you find a cosy world of original wood floors, whitewashed walls, smouldering fires, low beamed ceilings. It's all very cute, small but perfectly formed, with snug rooms giving a Dickensian feel. It dates to the mid-1700s and while a 21st-century makeover brought colour and style in equal measure, Sam made sure the inn lost none of its original charm. The airy bar has an open fire and 25 wines by the glass, board games, the daily papers and doors onto a terrace for lunch in the sun. Big bedrooms in a stone barn wait across the lane. Expect sleigh beds, good bathrooms, beams and panelled walls. As for the food, it's a cut above, perhaps devilled kidneys, roasted guinea fowl, lemon and lavender terrine. Chichester and Arundel Castle are both close. *Minimum stay: 2 nights at weekends.*

Rooms	6 doubles: £145-£190. 1 suite for 2: £210-£230. Singles £90-£155. Extra bed/sofabed £30 p.p.p.n.
Meals	Lunch from £6.50. Dinner, 3 courses, about £30. Sunday lunch from £16.50.
Closed	Never.
Directions	On A272 halfway between Midhurst & Petworth.

Sam Bakose
Halfway Bridge Inn
Halfway Bridge,
Petworth, GU28 9BP

Tel +44 (0)1798 861281
Email enquiries@halfwaybridge.co.uk
Web www.halfwaybridge.co.uk

The Crab & Lobster

This 17th-century whitewashed inn sits on Pangham Harbour, a tidal estuary that teems with preening birds. It's a peaceful stop, protected by a country lane mostly ignored by tourists. Inside, the restaurant/bar comes with a smouldering fire at one end and a wood-burner at the other. You'll find pretty art, fresh flowers and a chic alcove with banquette seating; in summer, life spills onto a terrace for lunch in the sun. Beautiful bedrooms come in duck-egg blue with crisp white linen, garden flowers, flat-screen TVs and chic bathrooms. Three have views across fields to the water, the other has a telescope with which to scan the high seas; the cottage has a well-equipped kitchen and a sitting room, too. By day you explore an area overflowing with history: Fishbourne Roman Palace: 11th-century Arundel Castle, and Bosham, where King Canute tried to turn back the waves;. Excellent food waits your return, perhaps Selsey crab and tiger prawn cocktail, filet of pork with burnt apple purée, peach tarte tatin with vanilla ice cream. The Witterings, for miles of beach and dunes, will help you walk it off. *Minimum stay: 2 nights at weekends.*

Rooms	4 doubles: £175-£205. 1 cottage for 4: £290-£360. Singles £100-£120. Extra bed/sofabed available £30 p.p.p.n.
Meals	Bar meals from £6.50. Lunch from £11.95. Dinner, 3 courses, £35. Sunday lunch, 2 courses, £26.
Closed	Never.
Directions	Mill Lane is off B2145 Chichester to Selsey road, just south of Sidlesham.

Sam Bakose
The Crab & Lobster
Mill Lane, Sidlesham,
Chichester, PO20 7NB

Tel +44 (0)1243 641233
Email enquiries@crab-lobster.co.uk
Web www.crab-lobster.co.uk

The Bull

This 16th-century inn on the South Downs has lots to offer – a cracking bar, four fancy bedrooms, tasty local food and an excellent array of ales and craft beers from across the globe. Step inside and it's like travelling back to Dickensian England. Light is rationed on aesthetic grounds, beams sag, fires roar and happy locals gather for a pint of Bedlam, the pub's own brew. You can eat wherever you want – meat from Sussex farms, game from local estates, fish from short-range boats – perhaps cider steamed mussels with pancetta, venison pie with chestnut mash, steamed ginger and treacle sponge. Upstairs, four stylish bedrooms have recently been refurbished (two larger, two above the bar), with four more coming soon. Expect Farrow & Ball colours, chic fabrics, old-style radiators and comfy beds. Bigger rooms have sofas, you might find timber frames, a cow-hide rug or a low beamed ceiling. All have digital radios, flat-screen TVs and smart little bathrooms. Bring walking boots and mountain bikes and scale the Ditchling Beacon for big views. Brighton and Gatwick are close. Don't miss Sunday lunch. *Minimum stay: 2 nights at weekends.*

Rooms	3 doubles, 1 twin/double: £100-£160.
Meals	Lunch & dinner from £12. Dinner, 3 courses, £25-£35. Sunday lunch from £15.
Closed	Never.
Directions	Leave A23 just north of Brighton for Pyecombe. North on A273, then west for Ditchling on B2112. In centre of village at crossroads.

Dominic Worrall
The Bull
2 High Street, Ditchling,
Hassocks, BN6 8TA

Tel +44 (0)1273 843147
Email info@thebullditchling.com
Web www.thebullditchling.com

The Griffin Inn

It's not often you end up discussing the death of Athenian democracy with a barman, but that sort of thing is quite common here. The Griffin is English to its core, a posh inn with a streak of scruffiness, a community local that draws a devoted crowd. They come for the lively bar, the attractive restaurant and the club room for racing on Saturdays. In summer, life spills onto a smart terrace for local food cooked in a wood-fired oven. There's a bar in the garden, weekend barbecues, deckchairs scattered across the lawns for ten-mile views over Pooh Bear's Ashdown forest to Sheffield Park. Quirky bedrooms are nicely-priced. Some have wonky floors, others a four-poster, you'll find timber frames, lovely old furniture, then robes and free-standing baths; those in the coach house are quieter. Seasonal menus offer tasty rustic food, perhaps rabbit gnocchi, local pheasant, dark chocolate torte with honey ice cream; excellent wines help you wash it all down. The pub has three cricket teams that travel the world in pursuit of glory – you may find them in the bar on a summer evening after a hot day in the field. *Minimum stay: 2 nights at bank holiday weekends.*

Rooms	6 doubles, 7 four-posters: £85-£150. Singles £70-£80 (Sun-Thur).
Meals	Bar meals from £6.50. Dinner, 3 courses, £30-£40.
Closed	Christmas Day.
Directions	From East Grinstead A22 south, right at Nutley for Fletching. On for 2 miles into village.

Nigel & James Pullan
The Griffin Inn
Fletching,
Uckfield, TN22 3SS

Tel +44 (0)1825 722890
Email info@thegriffininn.co.uk
Web www.thegriffininn.co.uk

Wingrove House

This beautiful hotel is proof positive that small hotels are infinitely lovelier than their big brothers. It stands at the end of a pretty village with an ancient church on one side and the South Downs Way passing on the other. You enter through a walled garden that leads up to a stone terrace, where wisteria hangs from the balcony and bamboo sways in the breeze, a lovely spot to linger in good weather. In winter you retreat to the sitting room, where wood floors, an open fire and painted panelling give a warm contemporary feel. Super bedrooms have cool colours, smart fabrics and robes in excellent bathrooms. Two open onto the veranda, the biggest at the back overlooks the churchyard, some have double-ended baths, others vast walk-in showers. The restaurant, recently refurbished, has a chic rustic feel. An open fire keeps things cosy on colder nights, a wall of glass opens onto a dining terrace in summer. Delicious food waits, perhaps locally smoked salmon, slow-braised venison, sticky toffee pudding with salted caramel ice cream. Walks start from the front door: Cuckmere Haven and Beachy Head wait.

Rooms	7 doubles: £100-£195. 1 cottage for 6: £750-£1,200.
Meals	Lunch, 2 courses from £18.95; 3 courses from £25 (Thur-Sun). Dinner £29-£35.
Closed	Never.
Directions	M23, A23, then A27 east from Brighton. Past Berwick, then south at r'bout for Alfriston. In village on left.

Ian Graham
Wingrove House
High Street, Alfriston,
Polegate, BN26 5TD

Tel +44 (0)1323 870276
Email info@wingrovehousealfriston.com
Web www.wingrovehousealfriston.com

Belle Tout Lighthouse

A fine old lighthouse atop a white cliff with stunning views in every direction. To your left, Beachy Head, to your right, Birling Gap – it's a magical position with the South Downs rolling down into the English Channel. As for the lighthouse, it dates to 1832. It was once moved 57 feet back to stop it crumbling into the sea and it featured prominently in the BBC's production of *The Life and Loves of a She-Devil*. It re-opened in 2010 after a splendid renovation as a lovely little B&B hotel. Bedrooms are rather wonderful: not huge, but all have windows that bring the outside in. You get white walls to soak up the light, fantastic views of rolling hills, pretty fabrics, lovely linen, the odd exposed brick wall; shower rooms are small but sweet, one room has a bath. Ian's legendary breakfasts are served on high with views of sea and cliff. There's a wood-burner in the sitting room, where guests gather each night before climbing up to explore the lantern. Good food waits in the village: a lovely pub and an excellent Thai restaurant. Magnificent walking waits. *Minimum stay: 2 nights. Over 15s welcome.*

Rooms	6 doubles: £145-£220. Singles from £101.50.
Meals	Pub/restaurant within 1 mile.
Closed	Christmas & New Year.
Directions	A259 to East Dean, then south for Beachy Head. Keep left at Birling Gap and on right above sea.

Ian Noall
Belle Tout Lighthouse
Beachy Head Road,
Beachy Head, Eastbourne, BN20 0AE

Tel +44 (0)1323 423185
Email info@belletout.co.uk
Web www.belletout.co.uk

The Old Rectory

This is one of those lovely places where everything hits the spot: friendly owners, beautiful interiors, delicious breakfasts, a great position at the top of the old town, with lanes winding down to the sea. As for this Georgian rectory, it sits in the shadow of its church and comes with a delightful garden, a great spot for drinks in summer. Interiors are pristine: hand-printed wallpapers, painted wood floors, busts and sculpture to add colour and flair. Rooms at the front flood with light, an open fire waits in the sitting room, as does an honesty bar. Much is the work of Lionel Copley, once design director for Katharine Hamnett. Bedrooms are hard to fault: crisp linen on smart beds, sumptuous fabrics and old style radiators, robes in beautiful bathrooms. A couple have claw-foot baths, one has a tromp l'oeil mural in its bathroom. Breakfast is a feast: home-baked bread, mixed fruit smoothies, house sausages and home-cured bacon. Cliff walks, sandy beaches and the excellent Jerwood Gallery wait as does a castle built by William the Conqueror. Excellent restaurants are on your doorstep. A treat. *Minimum stay: 2 nights at weekends.*

Rooms	6 doubles, 1 twin/double: £110-£165. 1 suite for 4: £190-£240. Singles from £90.
Meals	Restaurants nearby.
Closed	2 weeks in January, 1 week at Christmas.
Directions	In Hastings, leave sea behind you and take A259 east for Folkestone. After 800m hotel on right next to church.

Tracey-Anne Cook & Helen Styles
The Old Rectory
Harold Road,
Hastings, TN35 5ND
Tel +44 (0)1424 422410
Email info@theoldrectoryhastings.co.uk
Web www.theoldrectoryhastings.co.uk

Strand House

As you follow the Royal Military Canal down to miles of sandy beach, bear in mind that 600 years ago, you'd have been in the sea. This is reclaimed land and Strand House, built in 1425, originally stood on the harbour. Outside, you find wandering wisteria, colourful flowerbeds and a woodland walk that leads up to the village. Inside, medieval interiors have low ceilings, timber frames and mind-your-head beams. There are reds and yellows, sofas galore, a wood-burner in the sitting room and an honesty bar. It's a home-spun affair: Hugh cooks breakfast, Mary looks after guests in style. Quirky bedrooms sweep you back in time. One has an ancient four-poster, some have wonky floors, three open onto a terrace, all have good beds and robes for tiny shower rooms. As for the cottage, airy rooms have more space, and the suite, with its balcony and views across fields, is a treat. The house, once a work house, was painted by Turner and Millais. Local restaurants wait: Webbe's at The Fish Café, the Kings Head in Rye, top notch food at the Curlew in Bodiam. Dogs are very welcome.
Minimum stay: 2 nights at weekends & in high season. 3 dog-friendly rooms available.

Rooms	5 doubles, 1 twin/double, 5 triples; 1 double with separate bath: £80-£150. 1 suite for 4: £180. Singles from £60. Extra beds £25 p.p. Dogs £7.50.
Meals	Dinner for groups by arrangements (minimum 8 people).
Closed	Rarely.
Directions	A259 west from Rye for 2 miles. House on the left at foot of hill, opposite Bridge Inn pub.

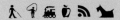

Mary Sullivan & Hugh Davie
Strand House
Tanyards Lane, Winchelsea,
Rye, TN36 4JT
Tel +44 (0)1797 226276
Email info@thestrandhouse.co.uk
Web www.thestrandhouse.co.uk

The George in Rye

Rye is beautiful, old England trapped in aspic. It was a Cinque Port, Henry James lived here and the oldest church clock in England chimes at the top of the hill. The George stands on its cobbled high street right in the thick of things. Built in 1575 from reclaimed ships' timbers, its exposed beams and panelled walls remain on display. Inside, old and new mix beautifully – expect Jane Austen in the 21st century. There's a roaring fire in the bar, screen prints of the Beatles on the walls in reception, a sun-trapping courtyard for lunch in summer. Beautiful bedrooms come in all shapes and sizes (a couple are small), but chic fabrics, Frette linen and Vi-Spring mattresses are standard, as are good books, fine bathrooms, white robes and cashmere covers on hot water bottles. Some are huge with zinc baths in the room, one has a round bed. You eat in the George Grill, an open kitchen on display, perhaps Provençal fish soup, grilled rib-eye with hand-cut chips, gooseberry soufflé with bay leaf ice cream. Walk it off by following the river down to the sea. *Mapp and Lucia* was filmed in the town.

Rooms	8 doubles, 21 twin/doubles: £135-£195. 5 suites for 2: £295-£325. Singles from £95.
Meals	Lunch from £6. Dinner, 3 courses, £30-£40. Afternoon tea £12.50.
Closed	Never.
Directions	Follow signs up hill into town centre. Through arch; hotel on left, below church. 24-hour parking 5 minutes down hill.

Alex & Katie Clarke
The George in Rye
98 High Street, Rye, TN31 7JT

Tel +44 (0)1797 222114
Email stay@thegeorgeinrye.com
Web www.thegeorgeinrye.com

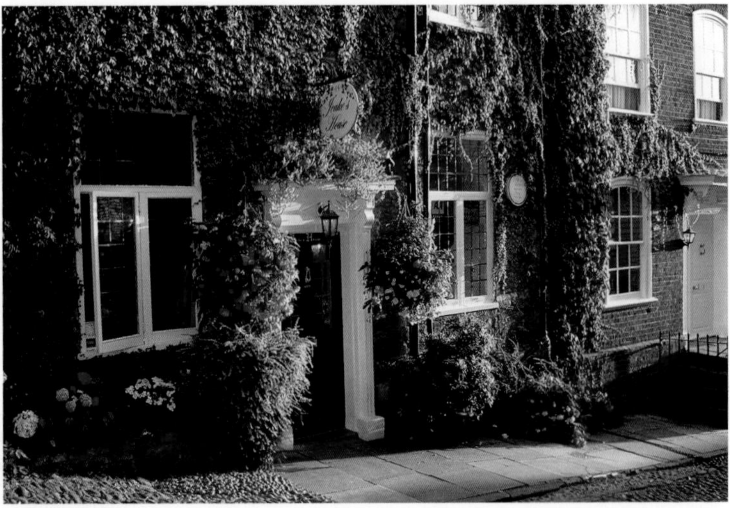

Jeake's House

Rye is gorgeous, one of those lovely English towns that's been around for centuries, but has never lost its looks. The same is true of Jeake's House, which sits in the old town on a pretty cobbled street away from the crowds. In its 300-year history it's been a wool store, a school and the home of American poet Conrad Potter Aiken. Inside, style abounds. The galleried dining room – once an old Baptist chapel – is now painted deep red and full of busts, books, clocks and mirrors, a fine setting for your bacon and eggs. There's a raffish bar, where a fire burns in winter, then a pretty sitting room with a Broadwood square piano. Potter about and find timber frames, ancient beams and some strikingly furnished bedrooms; several have four-posters, one has a telly concealed in the wood-burner, all are deeply comfortable and excellent value for money. As for Rye, art galleries, antiques shops, old churches and river walks wait; don't miss the Summer Exhibition in early September. All this would be blossom in the wind without Jenny, whose natural joie de vivre makes this a very special place. *Children over 8 welcome.*

Rooms	7 twin/doubles; 1 double with separate bath: £95-£128. 3 suites for 2: £130-£150.
Meals	Restaurants within walking distance.
Closed	Never.
Directions	From centre of Rye on A268, left off High St onto West St, then 1st right into Mermaid St. House on left. Private car park, £3 a day for guests.

Jenny Hadfield
Jeake's House
Mermaid Street,
Rye, TN31 7ET

Tel	+44 (0)1797 222828
Email	stay@jeakeshouse.com
Web	www.jeakeshouse.com

The Gallivant

This cool little hotel stands across the road from Camber Sands, where five miles of pristine beach are home to kite surfers, beach cricketers and sun worshipers alike. As for the Gallivant, a recent refurbishment has brought a stunning new look to every corner. Bedrooms, small and large, are now things of great beauty. Snug cabin rooms are clad in wood with brass lamps hanging from the ceiling; baby Hamptons have daybeds and marble bathrooms; deck rooms at the back come in cool whites with doors onto private terraces. Then come the garden rooms – heaven for hedonists – with double-ended baths in the room (and doors that slide for privacy), then small decks in the garden, where you'll also find a massage hut and deckchairs in summer. All have great storage, flawless bathrooms and crisp linen for Hypnos beds. As for the food, most is sourced within 10 miles and you eat in an airy restaurant that opens onto a terrace in summer, perhaps cod with lime and cucumber, salt marsh lamb with root veg, chocolate torte with Frangelico jelly. There's tea and cake 'on the house' every afternoon, too. *Minimum stay: 2 nights at weekends.*

Rooms	20 doubles, some with garden access and terraces: £95-£245. Singles £85-£240.
Meals	Lunch from £16. Dinner, 3 courses, from £35.
Closed	Rarely.
Directions	A259 east from Rye, then B2075 for Camber & Lydd. On left after 2 miles.

Elise Roberts
The Gallivant
New Lydd Road,
Camber, Rye, TN31 7RB

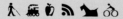

Tel +44 (0)1797 225057
Email enquiries@thegallivant.co.uk
Web www.thegallivant.co.uk

The Bell Alderminster

A lively inn on the Alscot estate with gardens that run down to a small river. There's a beautiful terrace, too, a popular spot for lunch in the sun, washed down by a pint of home-brewed ale. Inside, chic interiors mix of old and new to great effect – low beamed ceilings and exposed brick walls, then lots of colour and leather banquettes. You'll find candles everywhere, armchairs in front of the fire, black-and-white screen prints of estate life. Recent additions include an airy new restaurant with a wall of glass that opens onto the terrace, then a balcony above, where you can scoff afternoon tea while gazing out on open country. There's good food, too, with lamb and beef straight from the estate. You'll find sharing plates, soups and salads, perhaps seared tuna with chilli fritters, rump steak with a pepper sauce, banana sponge with toffee ice cream. Stylish bedrooms have smart fabrics, crisp linen, sofas or armchairs if there's room. Two are small, suites are enormous and have gorgeous bathrooms. A road passes to the front, quietly at night. Stratford waits up the road for all things Shakespeare.

Rooms	5 doubles, 2 twins: £100-£145. 2 suites for 2: £150-£170. Singles from £70 (Sun-Thur).
Meals	Bar meals from £7. Lunch, 2 courses, from £14.50. Dinner, 3 courses, from £18. Sunday lunch, 3 courses, £25.
Closed	Never.
Directions	On A3400 in Alderminster.

Sean Piernan
The Bell Alderminster
Shipston Road, Alderminster,
Stratford-upon-Avon, CV37 8NY

Tel +44 (0)1789 450414
Email info@thebellald.co.uk
Web www.thebellald.co.uk

The Howard Arms

The Howard stands on Ilmington Green, eight miles south of Stratford-upon-Avon. It was built at roughly the same time as Shakespeare wrote *King Lear* and little has changed since. It's a lovely country inn and comes with original fixtures and fittings: polished flagstones, heavy beams, mellow stone walls, a crackling fire. Outside, roses ramble on golden stone walls, while a pretty garden waits at the back. Good food comes as standard, perhaps ham hock terrine with homemade piccalilli, marinated duck breast with bok choy, apple tarte tatin with mascarpone cream; there's fish and chips and a good burger, too. Elsewhere, you find oils on walls, books on shelves, settles in alcoves, beautiful bay windows. A colourful dining room floods with light courtesy of fine arched windows that overlook the green. Bedrooms in the main house have a charming old-world feel, garden rooms are more contemporary with excellent bathrooms. You can walk across fields to Chipping Campden; Simon de Montfort once owned this land. The village church dates to the 11th century and has Thompson mice within.

Rooms	5 doubles, 3 twin/doubles: £110-£130. Singles £72-£104. Extra bed/sofabed £10 p.p.p.n.
Meals	Lunch from £4.50. Bar meals from £9.50. Dinner, 3 courses, £25-£30.
Closed	Never.
Directions	From south take A429 Fosse Way through Moreton-in-Marsh. After 5 miles left to Ilmington.

Robert Jeal
The Howard Arms
Lower Green,
Ilmington, CV36 4LT

Tel +44 (0)1608 682226
Email info@howardarms.com
Web www.howardarms.com

The Rectory Hotel

This Georgian rectory dates to 1780 and sits in two acres of sublime English gardens, with the church tower peeping up above fine tress. From the outside, little seems to have changed in a hundred years, but step inside and find a newly refurbished house that sparkles at every turn. There's a chic sitting room with sofas in front of a roaring fire, then a restaurant that starts in a panelled dining room and flows into a conservatory, where doors open onto the garden for breakfast on the lawn in summer. Rooms above are just as good – super beds, stylish fabrics, perhaps a claw-foot bath in your room or ceilings open to the rafters. Light floods in, bigger rooms have sofas, all have contemporary elegance in spades. You get smart TVs (and movies to stream), super-fast WiFi, then robes in magical bathrooms. Back downstairs, the bar has the feel of a gentleman's club and opens onto the garden for Pimm's in the sun; keep going and find sunbeds circling the swimming pool. Glorious food rounds off your day, perhaps octopus carpaccio, roast veal, Florentine doughnuts with Chantilly cream. *No minimum stay.*

Rooms	15 doubles: £150-£230. Extra beds for children £10.
Meals	Lunch from £6.50. Dinner, 3 courses, about £35. Sunday lunch £25.
Closed	Never.
Directions	M4, junc. 17, then north for 8 miles on A429. Signed right in village.

Neil Fincham Dukes
The Rectory Hotel
Crudwell,
Malmesbury, SN16 9EP

Tel +44 (0)1666 577194
Email info@therectoryhotel.com
Web www.therectoryhotel.com

The Methuen Arms

The Methuen has changed with the times. It started life as a 14th-century nunnery, turned into a coaching inn in 1608, then had a Georgian facelift in the late 1700s. In 2010 it was reborn as a chic boutique hotel – cosy and stylish with great food and delicious Butcombe ales. It sits on the edge of the village, with an avenue of trees around the corner that lead up to Corsham Court, an Elizabethan pile. As for the hotel, there's a sun-trapping courtyard where you can eat in summer, a restaurant that opens onto the garden, a locals' bar where the main currency is gossip, then a sitting-room bar where you can sink into an armchair in front of the wood-burner. It's all very pretty, an easy style runs throughout. You'll find shuttered windows, the odd beam, the daily papers, rugs on wood floors. Gorgeous bedrooms have warm colours, padded bedheads, good art, Roberts radios. There are robes in fine bathrooms, four of which have claw-foot baths, one of which is in the bedroom. Super food waits, perhaps cream of shallot soup, venison with heritage carrots, Wiltshire honey crème caramel. Bath is close.

Rooms	11 doubles, 2 twin/doubles: £140-£175. 1 family room for 4: £150-£220. Singles from £90.
Meals	Lunch from £5.95. Dinner, 3 courses, about £30. Sunday lunch from £18.50.
Closed	Never.
Directions	M4 junc. 17, then A350 south & A4 west. B3353 south into Corsham. On left.

Ashley Harlow & Abigail Vince
The Methuen Arms
2 High Street,
Corsham, SN13 0HB

Tel +44 (0)1249 717060
Email info@themethuenarms.com
Web www.themethuenarms.com

Timbrell's Yard

Those lovely people at the Draco Pub Co. have been doing what they do so well – opening another of their small-scale pleasuredomes. Their latest inn stands close to the bridge in Bradford-on-Avon with beautiful views across the river to the churchyard. Outside, a terrace at the front catches the sun, with this 18th-century listed building standing grandly behind. It's a lovely spot, good enough for Samuel Spode to paint; a copy of his work hangs in the restaurant, the real thing waits in the town's museum. Inside, you get that winning combination of stylish rooms, lovely food and well-kept ales, with cakes and coffee available all day. You'll find stripped floors, hanging lamps, exposed stone walls, then sofas in front of an open fire. Helpful staff weave about, delivering food that makes you smile, perhaps Dorset crab on toast, pork belly with sea salt crackling, vanilla panna cotta with rhubarb jelly. Bedrooms are beautiful. Fourteen have river views, two have baths in the room, mezzanine rooms have window seats where you can watch the river pass. Bathrooms are predictably divine.

Rooms	17 doubles: £85-£195. Extra beds for children £20.
Meals	Lunch & dinner £5-£35.
Closed	Rarely.
Directions	A363 south into Bradford-on-Avon. Over bridge and 1st right.

Henry Gray
Timbrell's Yard
49 St Margaret's Street,
Bradford-on-Avon, BA15 1DE

Tel +44 (0)1225 869492
Email info@timbrellsyard.com
Web www.timbrellsyard.com

Littleton Lodge

This chic B&B sits in a village ten miles north of Stonehenge. You're close to Salisbury for its medieval cathedral, which holds a copy of the Magna Carta, while the house backs onto the a'Beckett vineyard, and tours and tastings can be arranged. Inside, contemporary design has been beautifully considered – nothing here is skin deep. Downstairs, there's a library with books and charcoal panelling, then a drawing room, where a wardrobe opens to reveal an honesty bar. Fires smoulder, doors open into a conservatory, then out to a gravelled garden. Uncluttered rooms have much to admire: contemporary four-posters, beautiful chandeliers, colourful throws, smart grey armchairs. White marble bathrooms are just the ticket: two have walk-in showers, two have baths as well, all have Bramley lotions. You'll find smart TVs, coffee machines and James's delicious homemade shortbread. Breakfast is a local treat – juice from garden apples, honey from the vineyard, bacon and sausage from the village butcher. There's a plentiful supply of pubs and good local restaurants within five miles. Bath is close, too.

Rooms	1 double, 3 four-posters: £120-£150.
Meals	Good pub in village; good restaurants within 5 miles.
Closed	Christmas & New Year.
Directions	South from Devizes on A360 for 4 miles. On left in village.

James Bell & Sean Purslow
Littleton Lodge
High Street, Littleton Panell,
Devizes, SN10 4ES

Tel +44 (0)1380 813494
Email info@littletonlodge.com
Web www.littletonlodge.com

The Lamb at Hindon

The Lamb has been serving ale on Hindon's high street for 800 years. It's a yard of England's finest cloth, a place where shooting parties come to eat and farmers meet to chew the cud. Inside you find oak settles, roaring fires and painted panelling. A clipped Georgian elegance lingers; you almost expect Mr Darcy to walk in, give a tormented sigh, then turn on his heels and vanish. You'll find flagstone floors, stripped boards, window seats and gilded mirrors, then a pine booth, where officials sat collecting tolls from passing travellers. At night, candles come out, as do some excellent wines, and you dig into lovely food: perhaps ham hock with piccalilli, roast quail with parsnips, bread and butter pudding. Refurbished rooms have pretty colours, crisp linen, smart bathrooms and Bakelite phones. Some even have their own private gardens. Expect padded headboards, lovely art, a huge lampshade or a claw-foot bath. Three suites in converted outhouses have an elegant contemporary style with vintage luggage, the odd chandelier and lovely bathrooms. Stourhead and Stonehenge are close. *Minimum stay: 2 nights at weekends May-September.*

Rooms	9 doubles, 3 twins: £99-£149. 3 suites for 2: £129-£179. Extra bed/sofabed £15 p.p.p.n. Dogs £20.
Meals	Lunch & dinner £5-£35.
Closed	Never.
Directions	M3, A303 & signed left at bottom of steep hill 2 miles east of junction with A350.

Bernice Gallagher
The Lamb at Hindon
High Street, Hindon,
Salisbury, SP3 6DP

Tel	+44 (0)1747 820573
Email	lambhindon@youngs.co.uk
Web	www.lambhindon.co.uk

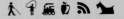

The Beckford Arms

A country-house inn on the Fonthill estate. You sweep in under the Triumphal Arch, which seems appropriate – this is one of the loveliest inns in the land. Outside, in the garden, you find hammocks in the trees and parasols on the terrace, then a church spire soaring beyond. Georgian interiors are no less lovely, a mix of original features and 21st-century style. There's a drawing room with facing sofas in front of a roaring fire; a restaurant with a wall of glass that opens onto the terrace; a bar with parquet flooring for an excellent local pint. Potter about and chance upon the odd chandelier, roaming wisteria and a rather grand mahogany table in the private dining room. Bedrooms are small but perfectly formed with prices to match: white walls, the best linen, sisal matting, good bathrooms. If you want something bigger try the pavilions on the estate; former guests include Byron and Nelson, though we doubt they had it so good. As for the food, it's lovely stuff, perhaps Brixham clam chowder, whole lemon sole, chocolate and Cointreau delice with blood orange sorbet. One of the best.

Rooms	7 doubles, 1 twin/double: £95-£120. 2 pavilions for 2: £175-£195.
Meals	Dinner about £30.
Closed	Never.
Directions	On the road between Tisbury & Hindon, 3 miles south of A303 (Fonthill exit).

Charlie Luxton
The Beckford Arms
Fonthill Gifford, Tisbury,
Salisbury, SP3 6PX

Tel +44 (0)1747 870385
Email info@beckfordarms.com
Web www.beckfordarms.com

Howard's House

This ancient village is a dream, a wormhole back in time, a fitting stage for this Grade-II listed house that dates to 1623. Outside, fine gardens sweep uphill to a ridge of old oak, where views stretch out across the valley. Inside, warm country-house interiors come with the odd beam, fine arched windows and original flagstones in the hall. You'll find smart sofas, fresh flowers and the morning papers in the cosy sitting room, where a fire crackles on colder days. In summer, doors open onto a pretty terrace, where you can breakfast in good weather. Elegant bedrooms are deeply comfortable with pretty fabrics, mullioned windows and super-comfy beds. You get bowls of fruit, a sofa if there's room, then robes in spotless bathrooms. Spin downstairs for some lovely country food, perhaps wood pigeon with garlic, lemon sole with crab bisque, passion fruit soufflé with mango sorbet; climb back up afterwards to find your bed turned down. Uplifting walks start from the front door, the renovated coach house is perfect for small parties. Salisbury, Stonehenge and the gardens at Stourhead are close.

Rooms	6 doubles, 2 twin/doubles, 1 four-poster: £190-£225. Singles from £120.
Meals	Lunch from £22.50. Dinner: seasonal menu £28-£33.50; à la carte £37-£46.50; 6-course tasting menu £65.
Closed	5 days over Christmas.
Directions	A30 from Salisbury, B3089 west to Teffont. There, left at sharp right-hand bend following brown hotel sign. Entrance on right after 0.5 miles.

Simon Greenwood
Howard's House
Teffont Evias,
Salisbury, SP3 5RJ

Tel +44 (0)1722 716392
Email enq@howardshousehotel.co.uk
Web www.howardshousehotel.co.uk

The Fish Hotel

Come for Scandi chic on a smart estate with some perfectly well-priced rooms. It's like summer camp, only for adults – a place designed for fun. Expect a striking simplicity with airy colours, white linen, padded bedheads, robes in sparkling bathrooms. Rooms are scattered about in pretty buildings on the hill, the suites altogether fancier with claw-foot baths in the room, huge beds, maybe a sofa or a wood-burner, too. They spiral around a central lodge, where you eat, drink and make merry. If the style is coolly contemporary, then the feel is cosy and informal, with lovely staff on hand to help. The big bar is the hub: sofas galore, cool colours, walls of glass that open onto a terrace, a funky wood-burner for winter nights. There's a games room for pool and table football, but much more waits outside: tennis, archery, quad biking, even segways. Deer roam the hill, there's a nature trail and maps for joggers. As for the food, you can eat in the bar, the restaurant, or out on the terrace in good weather; try crab on toast or lobster hotdog, and finish off with apple crumble and vanilla ice cream.

Rooms	10 doubles, 33 twin/doubles: £99-£155. 4 suites for 2: £175-£225. Dinner, B&B from £82.50 p.p.
Meals	Lunch from £5. Dinner, 3 courses, £25-£35.
Closed	Never.
Directions	A44 east from Broadway for two miles. Turn left halfway up Fish Hill. Keep left at folk and follow signs to the hotel.

Zena Carter
The Fish Hotel
Farncombe Estate,
Broadway, WR12 7LJ

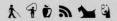

Tel +44 (0)1386 858000
Email reservations@thefishhotel.co.uk
Web www.thefishhotel.co.uk

Brocco on the Park

Sheffield is a friendly city, an arty hub that's full of surprises, a fact ably demonstrated by this stunning small hotel. It sits amid leafy streets, with a smart park to the front, then hills beyond that ripple over to the Peak District. Picasso stayed here when he attended the World Peace Congress in 1950, though things have changed a little since – a recent refit has turned this into a small-scale pleasure dome. Downstairs, there's a Scandi feel in the café/kitchen, with joggers and dog walkers swapping the park for delicious smoothies or a slice of cake. Bedrooms are divine, as good as they look. Expect the best white linen, smart neutral colours, the coolest bathrooms with robes and organic oils. A vast window in one room opens to frame the view; another has a free-standing bath; all are named after birds, their colours reflected in the fabrics. Back downstairs, tasty food waits at night, perhaps cauliflower and pistachio fritters, rib-eye steak with wild mushrooms, spiced plum crumble with vanilla ice cream. Don't miss the Millennium Gallery, the Winter Garden or the cool streets around you.

Rooms	6 doubles, 2 twin/doubles: £85-£220. Extra bed/sofabed £35 p.p.p.n.
Meals	Breakfast & lunch from £7. Dinner from £12. Sunday lunch from £16.
Closed	Rarely.
Directions	Leave ring road to southwest at Waitrose, signed Castleton A625. After 1.5 miles, at 1st r'bout, take last exit. Hotel on left.

Tiina Carr
Brocco on the Park
92 Brocco Bank,
Sheffield, S11 8RS

Tel +44 (0)114 266 1233
Email hello@brocco.co.uk
Web www.brocco.co.uk

The Parisi Hotel

This lovely small hotel makes a great base for a night or two in glorious York. It stands within the Roman wall, opposite St Denys Church, which lost its spire to cannon fire in the Civil War. It's all the work of two sisters, Sophie and Maria, who renovated from top to toe, bringing a chic, colourful style to this Victorian rectory. Inside, you'll find original art on every wall in the airy breakfast room, sofas in front of the wood-burner in the beautiful library, then a door that leads out to a gravelled courtyard, where you can sink into wicker armchairs when the sun shines. Bedrooms are just as good: cool colours, smart fabrics, excellent beds, '60s retro furniture. You get lots of art, coffee machines, iPhone docks, flat-screen TVs. Some rooms are smaller, all have sparkling bathrooms, one has a free-standing bath in the room. Cross the river, weave through lanes, arrive at York Minster, one of the largest Gothic cathedrals in Europe. Back at the hotel, five excellent restaurants wait within 200 metres. Northern Soul nights take place locally, too. You won't want to leave. *Minimum stay: 2 nights at weekends.*

Rooms	10 doubles: £99-£189. 1 suite for 2: £179-£229.
Meals	Restaurants 200m.
Closed	3 weeks in January.
Directions	A64, then A1079 west (the only way into Walmgate). Through arch into old town, left after 500 metres (one way). On left.

Maria & Sophie Scott
The Parisi Hotel
51 St Denys Road,
York, YO1 9QD

Tel +44 (0)1904 658815
Email info@theparisi.com
Web www.theparisi.com

West Park Hotel

Harrogate made its name in Georgian England as a spa town for the gentry. These days it holds the title of 'happiest place to live in Britain.' It's also one of the prettiest, with grand houses, leafy streets and the Stray, 200 acres of park and gardens that unfurls itself directly opposite this stylish hotel. Outside, you can sit at tables and watch the world go by. Inside, the bar and restaurant come as one, a lively spot that draws a crowd and comes with leather booths, chic bar stools, lots of colour and style. Cocktails, locals ales, wines from around the world all wait, as does some excellent bistro food, perhaps moules marinières, rack of lamb, apple and caramel tart. Bedrooms are lovely: crisp linen, the best mattresses, smart TVs and cool bathrooms. Bigger rooms at the front overlook the Stray, smaller ones at the back share the same style. Stay on a Sunday night and you can 'eat your bill;' whatever you spend on dinner will be removed from the cost of your room! Don't miss the Turkish baths or the gardens at Harlow Carr. The Tour de Yorkshire passes at the end of the road in April.

Rooms	11 doubles, 6 twin/doubles: £125-£245. 6 suites for 2, 2 suites for 4: £205-£365. Singles from £110. Extra bed £10.
Meals	Breakfast from £3.95. Lunch from £6.50. Dinner, 3 courses, £25-£40. Afternoon tea from £12.95. Sunday lunch from £14.95.
Closed	Never.
Directions	On the A61 in centre of town, 300m for junction with A59.

Nathan George
West Park Hotel
19 West Park Road,
Harrogate, HG1 1BJ

Tel +44 (0)1423 524471
Email enquiries@thewestparkhotel.com
Web thewestparkhotel.com

The White Bear Hotel

At five o'clock on Friday evenings there's only one place to be in Masham: the tap room at the White Bear, home of Theakston's beer. The great and the good gather to mark the end of the week, the odd pint is sunk, the air is thick with gossip. Interior design is 1920s trapped in aspic: red leather, polished brass, a crackling fire. But there's only half the story. Slip next door and discover this welcoming inn. There's an smart dining room, stripped boards in the bar, a flower-filled terrace for lunch in the sun. Stylish rooms occupy the old Lightfoot brewery and come in contemporary style, with warm colours, comfy beds, chic new bathrooms and attractive prices. Some have views across town, the penthouse is vast and open to the rafters. There's a courtyard for guests, a sitting room, too; staff will bring drinks if you want privacy and peace. Good food waits in the restaurant, perhaps king scallops, duck with red cabbage, treacle sponge pudding. Tours of the brewery are easily arranged, with a pint of your choice at the end. Don't miss the beer festival in June or the Sheep Fair in September.

Rooms	12 twin/doubles: £125. 1 suite for 2: £200. 2 family rooms for 4: £125-£155.
Meals	Lunch from £5. Bar meals from £11.95. Dinner, 3 courses, about £30.
Closed	Never.
Directions	North from Ripon on A6108. In Masham up hill (for Leyburn). Right at crest of hill. Signed.

Sue Thomas
The White Bear Hotel
Wellgarth, Masham,
Ripon, HG4 4EN

Tel +44 (0)1765 689319
Email sue@whitebearmasham.co.uk
Web www.thewhitebearhotel.co.uk

The Angel Inn

The old drovers' inn remains staunchly, reassuringly traditional – but offers wines that have come, over the years, to rival the hand-pumped Yorkshire ales. There's even a 'cave' for functions and private-party tastings. Expect nooks, crannies, beams and crackling fires, and a stylish restaurant. Thought has gone into every detail, from the antique furniture in the timbered rooms (one with a marvellous oak-panelled bar) to the fabrics and the colours. Menus change with each season and include dishes ranging from filo 'moneybags' of seafood in lobster sauce – the fish comes fresh from Fleetwood – to their own Yorkshire twist on tapas ('Yapas'!). Vegetarians are looked after and the sticky toffee pudding is legendary. Exquisite bedrooms, split between the converted barn and adjacent Sycamore House, are all different; perhaps a French armoire, a brass bed, a claw-foot bath, a private garden. All have top-quality fabrics, pretty colours, cosy bathrooms, and, in the newer rooms, a contemporary feel. The glorious up-hill-and-down-dale drive to get here is part of the charm.

Rooms	9 doubles: £150-£175. 5 suites for 2: £175-£200. Singles from £125. Extra beds £25.
Meals	Lunch from £7.50. Bar meals from £15.95. Dinner, 3 courses, £35-£55. Sunday lunch £24.50.
Closed	Christmas Day & 1 week in January.
Directions	North from Skipton on B6265. Left at Rylstone for Hetton. In village.

Juliet Watkins
The Angel Inn
Hetton,
Skipton, BD23 6LT

Tel +44 (0)1756 730263
Email info@angelhetton.co.uk
Web www.angelhetton.co.uk

The Traddock

A northern outpost of country-house charm, beautiful inside and out. It's a family affair and those looking for a friendly base from which to explore the Dales will find it here. You enter through the drawing room – crackling fire, pretty art, the daily papers, cavernous sofas. Potter about and find polished wood in the dining room, panelled walls in the breakfast room, then William Morris wallpaper in the sitting room bar, where you can sip a pint of Skipton ale while playing Scrabble. Bedrooms are gorgeous, some coolly contemporary, others warmly traditional. The star of the show is the new suite – sand-blasted timbers, a lovely big sofa, a stunning free-standing bath – but all are charming, with chic fabrics, warm colours, comfy beds and the odd claw-foot bath. Downstairs, a white-washed sitting room opens onto the garden for afternoon tea, while delicious food waits in the restaurant, perhaps seafood chowder, braised lamb shank, apple and calvados mousse. Walks start at the front door, there are cycle tracks, even caves to explore (one is bigger than St Paul's). Unbeatable. *Minimum stay: 2 nights at weekends March-November.*

Rooms	8 doubles, 1 twin/double: £95-£165. 2 suites for 2: £180-£235. 2 family rooms for 4: £95-£175. Dinner, B&B from £80. Extra beds £15 p.p.p.n.
Meals	Lunch from £9.50. Dinner, 3 courses, around £30. Picnics from £7.50. Afternoon tea from £15.95.
Closed	Never.
Directions	0.75 miles off the A65, midway between Kirkby Lonsdale & Skipton, 4 miles northwest of Settle.

Paul Reynolds
The Traddock
Austwick,
Settle, LA2 8BY

Tel +44 (0)15242 51224
Email info@thetraddock.co.uk
Web www.thetraddock.co.uk

The Burgoyne Hotel

Reeth is one of those English throwbacks, a beautiful village in the Dales that's hardly changed in 200 years. It was mentioned in the Domesday Book, has the finest grouse moors in the land and its sweeping views over Swaledale stretch for miles. The Burgoyne looks out over it all – afternoon tea in the garden on a sunny day is hard to beat. Inside, an elegant past lives on: a smart drawing room with a crackling fire where you gather for drinks before dinner; a restaurant in racing green where you feast on delicious Yorkshire food; country-house bedrooms full of comfort, with warm colours, good beds, white linen, a sofa if there's room. You'll find pine shutters, cushioned window seats, a four-poster in the old snooker room; all but one has the view. The food is old-school, but utterly delicious, perhaps pheasant and venison terrine, Dover sole with brown shrimps, lemon tart with raspberry sorbet. Best of all are Julia and Mo, who run the place with unstinting kindness. There are maps for walkers, fishing can be arranged, a market passes on Fridays. Richmond is close, too. A delight.

Rooms	4 doubles, 1 twin, 1 four-poster; 2 doubles with separate bathroom, 1 twin with separate bathroom: £130–£190. 1 suite for 2: £210. Singles from £112.50. Extra beds for children under 13: £25. Dogs: £10 a night.
Meals	Dinner, 2 courses, £27; 4 courses, £40.
Closed	Monday to Thursday in January.
Directions	From Richmond A6108, then B6270 to Reeth. On north side of village green.

Julia & Mo Usman
The Burgoyne Hotel
Reeth, Richmond, DL11 6SN
Tel +44 (0)1748 884292
Email enquiries@theburgoyne.co.uk
Web www.theburgoyne.co.uk

The Coach House at Middleton Lodge

You'll think you've washed up in Tuscany or Provence. These gorgeous stone barns were crumbling a few years ago, now they're home to one of the loveliest hotels in the north. In summer, life spills onto the courtyard for lunch in the sun, but step through the arched glass doors and find a spectacular restaurant open to the rafters, where contemporary design mixes with rustic bricks and mortar. There's a funky bar, an open fire, a sitting room for guests that opens onto a terrace. Rooms are just as good, with chic fabrics, Roberts radios, super-comfy beds and robes in cool bathrooms. Five open onto a terrace, most have claw-foot baths, all have a sofas or a chaise longue. New for 2017 are ten stunning rooms in the renovated farmhouse, a swimming pool with a bar in the pool house, and a two-acre kitchen garden where you can get married. Good food waits, some home-grown, much from Yorkshire, perhaps cured sea trout with horseradish, slow cooked lamb with onion broth, chocolate with caramel and banana ice cream. The Dales wait to the west, the Moors to the east, but you may well choose to stay put.

Rooms	14 doubles: £140-£210. 1 family room for 4: £190-£310. Cot available. Singles from £135.
Meals	Lunch from £5.50. Sunday lunch from £12.50. Dinner, 3 courses, £30-£35. Not Mon or Tue mid-Oct to mid-March.
Closed	Rarely.
Directions	Leave A1 at Scotch Corner and head east for Middleton Tyas. Left in village onto Kneeton road. Right after one mile; left after 300 yards. Hotel signed on right.

James & Rebecca Allison
The Coach House at Middleton Lodge
Middleton Tyas, Richmond, DL10 6NJ

Tel +44 (0)1325 377977
Email info@middletonlodge.co.uk
Web www.middletonlodge.co.uk/coach-house

Estbek House

A cute little find on the Whitby coast, a friendly restaurant with rooms ten paces from the beach at Sandsend. It's small, intimate and very welcoming. Tim cooks brilliantly, David talks you through his excellent wine list and passes on the local news. Cliffs rise to the north, the beach runs away to the south, ducks on the river occasionally waddle across the road. There's a terrace at the front for drinks in summer and a small bar on the lower ground, where you can watch Tim at work in his kitchen. Upstairs, two dining rooms swim in coastal light and come with stripped floors and white tablecloths. People come from miles around for the seafood – the lobster thermidor is a big draw – but carnivores are well looked after, so try home-smoked salmon with a gin and tonic jelly, stuffed pork tenderloin or Whitby crab, strawberry and champagne trifle. Bedrooms – smallish on the first floor, tiny on the second! – have crisp linen and shuttered windows. Breakfast is delicious, David's mum makes the marmalade. Cliff walks and the moors wait, and you can follow the river up to Mulgrave Castle.

Rooms	5 doubles: £200-£255. Price includes dinner for 2.
Meals	Dinner included; non-residents, 3 courses, about £35.
Closed	2 January to 12 February.
Directions	North from Whitby on A174 to Sandsend. On left in village by bridge.

David Cross & Tim Lawrence
Estbek House
East Row, Sandsend,
Whitby, YO21 3SU

Tel	+44 (0)1947 893424
Email	info@estbekhouse.co.uk
Web	www.estbekhouse.co.uk

Broom House at Egton Bridge

As lovely a place to stay on the moors as you could hope for. You wind your way in – up dale, down hill – with a carpet of purple heather in late summer and a golden fleece of bracken in autumn. As for this attractive house, it sits on the edge of a pretty village, with fine views of Esk Dale from the garden terrace. Inside, airy interiors are stylish and comfortable, the perfect tonic after a day in the hills. Downstairs, there's a sitting room with garden views, then a dining room for Michael's delicious breakfasts – Whitby kippers, Glaisdale bacon, smoothies from garden strawberries. In summer, you decant onto the terrace for birdsong with your bacon and eggs. Stylish rooms have warm colours, comfy beds, white cotton, perhaps a sofa or doors onto the terrace. All have fine bathrooms, one with a free-standing bath. By day you explore the moors, spin over to Whitby or try a leg of the coast-to-coast path, which passes outside. At night you follow the river into the village for dinner at one of its pubs. You couldn't be in better hands – Michael and Georgina look after you in style. Pure bliss.

Rooms	6 doubles: £89-£137. 1 twin: £116-£125. 1 suites for 2: £139-£145. 1 suite for 2-4: £140-£200.
Meals	Two good pubs in village.
Closed	1 December – 28 February.
Directions	Leave A171 for Egton. Through village to Egton Bridge, under bridge, then right into Broom House Lane. Under bridge and on right.

Georgina & Michael Curnow
Broom House at Egton Bridge
Broom House Lane, Egton Bridge,
Whitby, YO21 1XD

Tel +44 (0)1947 895279
Email mail@broom-house.co.uk
Web www.broom-house.co.uk

The Talbot Hotel

A 17th-century hunting lodge on the Fitzwilliam estate, not far from Castle Howard. It stands on the edge of town with Malton's streets on one side and country views on the other. Outside, there's a croquet lawn, a terrace for lunch, and paths that lead down to the river. Inside, an easy elegance abounds. A fire burns in the drawing room, you find fresh flowers, lovely art, the daily papers and cavernous sofas. Bedrooms have chic fabrics, warm colours and botanical prints on the walls. Several have the view, all have robes in gorgeous bathrooms. Now to the serious stuff – delicious local food. Malton, an ancient market town, is the food capital of Yorkshire, with a festival every May that was started by the estate. No surprise then to discover the hotel has two restaurants serving the best Yorkshire produce. They also run a cookery school and have food trails to follow – to pie shops, vineyards, local farms and breweries. Dinner, predictably, is a treat, perhaps pressed Yorkshire duck, local lamb with an olive jus, coffee crème brûlée. There's a farmers' market every other Saturday, too. *Minimum stay: 2 nights at weekends.*

Rooms	23 doubles: £110-£190. 2 suites for 4, 1 suite for 2: £270-£320. Dinner, B&B from £100 p.p.
Meals	Lunch from £4.95. Bar meals from £10.95. Dinner, 3 courses, about £35. Sunday lunch from £20. Afternoon tea from £19.50.
Closed	Rarely.
Directions	A64 north from York, then B2148 into Malton. Keep right in town and on right after half a mile.

David Macdonald
The Talbot Hotel
45-47 Yorkersgate, Malton, YO17 7AJ

Tel	+44 (0)1653 639096
Email	reservations@talbotmalton.co.uk
Web	www.talbotmalton.co.uk

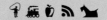

Channel Islands

Photo: White House Hotel,
entry 213

The Georgian House

Alderney is pristine – miles of sandy beaches, ancient coastal forts, cliff-top walks and nature trails, wild flowers and migrating birds. It's a slice of heaven and where else to stay than this quirky island bolthole, part village inn, part restaurant with rooms, part friendly chic hotel. After 30 years holidaying here, Holly's family bought one of their favourite places, whipped it into shape and now it's the beating heart of the island, a magnet for locals and visitors alike. It sits on St Anne's cobbled high street, opposite the art-house cinema; filmgoers sneak over for drinks in the interval. Downstairs, the bar comes with wooden floors, an open fire and lots of gossip. An airy restaurant spills onto a sun-trapping courtyard in summer, a fine spot for the freshest seafood, delicious steaks, island ice creams. Bedrooms – some in the hotel, others across the road in Victoria House – are just the ticket: not huge, but deeply comfy, with lovely beds, the odd stone wall and cute bathrooms. Hire bikes, grab a picnic, laze about on the beach. Night skies amaze. A perfect island adventure.

Rooms	2 doubles, 2 twin/doubles: £70-£95. Singles from £45.
Meals	Light lunch from £6. Dinner, 3 courses, £25-£30.
Closed	Mid-January to mid-March.
Directions	Sent on booking. Airport pick-ups.

Holly Fisher
The Georgian House
Victoria Street, St Anne, GY9 3UF
Tel +44 (0)1481 822471
Email info@georgianalderney.com
Web www.georgianalderney.com

White House Hotel

Herm is unique, a tiny island run benignly by the 40 souls lucky enough to live on it. They keep things blissfully simple: no cars, no TVs, just a magical world of sea and sky, a perfect place to escape the city. A coastal path rings the island; high cliffs rise to the south, sandy beaches laze in the north, cattle graze the hills between. You get fabulous views at every turn – shimmering islands, pristine waters, yachts and ferries zipping about. There's a beach café, succulent gardens, an ancient church, even a tavern for excellent ales. Kids love it, so do parents, and the self-catering cottages are extremely popular. As for the hotel, it's a delightful base from which to explore the island. You'll find open fires, four-course dinners, a tennis court, then a pool in the garden to keep you cool. Spotless bedrooms are scattered about, some in the village's colour-washed cottages, others with balconies in the hotel. Most come in contemporary style, a few are warmly traditional, all have sunny colours, watery views, padded headboards and sparkling bathrooms. Hard to beat.

Rooms	28 twin/doubles: £138-£208. 5 family rooms for 2, 5 family rooms for 4: £128-£208. 2 singles: £64-£84. 20 cottages for 6: £273-£1,288 per week.
Meals	Lunch from £5. Dinner, 4 courses, £28.50.
Closed	November to Easter.
Directions	Via Guernsey. Trident ferries leave from the harbour at St Peter Port 8 times a day in summer (£11 return).

Siôn Dobson Jones
White House Hotel
Herm Island, GY1 3HR

Tel +44 (0)1481 750075
Email hotel@herm.com
Web www.herm.com

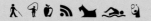

Hotel Ziggurat

This quirky small hotel has big views of islands and sea and a very pretty terrace from which to drink them in. It sits high on the hill, halfway up Constitution Steps, an ascent that removes all need of membership to a fitness club. But the climb is worth it – you find a warm welcome, a lovely style, some tasty food and excellent cocktails. Interiors have colour in spades. Step inside and you come face to face with Ishtar (well, her statue), the Mesopotamian goddess of love and war. Potter about and find a cute bar with shisha pipes, an airy restaurant where framed Moroccan textiles hang on walls, then doors onto the garden, where three smart, garden huts double as restaurant tables in good weather. Cute bedrooms are scattered about, most with semi-private terraces. You'll find comfy beds (three are cabin-like with one side against a wall), then padded heads, crisp linen and smart, new bathrooms with power showers; a couple have baths, too. Don't miss the food: Persian mezze, lamb shank tagine, Amaretto cheesecake. Ferries for day trips to Herm and Sark are easily arranged.

Rooms	12 doubles, 1 twin: £100-£160. 1 single: £70-£90.
Meals	Dinner, 3 courses, about £25 (not Sunday or Monday). Sunday brunch from £9.95.
Closed	Never.
Directions	Sent on booking.

Paul Hanson
Hotel Ziggurat
No. 5, Constitution Steps,
St Peter Port, GY1 2PN
Tel +44 (0)1481 723008
Email stay@hotelziggurat.com
Web www.hotelziggurat.com

The Old Court House

This lovely hotel sits on St Aubin's harbour with views across the bay to St Helier and beyond. Outside, there's a sun-trapping terrace where you can watch sailing boats come and go. Inside, you find the star of the show, this beautiful house that mostly dates to 1610, but comes with a 13th-century granite staircase, too. Downstairs, there's an airy bar, then a restaurant split between two rooms. One has the feel of a galleon's dining quarters and featured as Diamond Lil's bar in the TV series *Bergerac*. The other, the old courthouse itself, has ancient walls of golden stone, then hanging lamps, painted beams and the original fireplace. Both are a delight, as is the food: lots of fresh seafood, delicious duck, sticky toffee pudding; a bistro below is popular with locals. Cute rooms have a soft, chic style: a wall of beautiful paper, white linen for Hypnos mattresses, super little bathrooms with big power showers. Two have slipper baths, one has a hot tub on a private terrace. As for Jersey, expect sandy beaches, gardens and galleries, castles and cliff-top walks. You can surf, sail and kayak, too. *No minimum stay.*

Rooms	7 twin/doubles, 1 four-poster: £100-£300. 2 singles: £50-£75.
Meals	Lunch from £4.95. Restaurant: dinner, 3 courses, about £35. Bistro: mains from £10.95. Sunday lunch from £14.95.
Closed	Never.
Directions	On harbour in St Aubin. No. 15 bus from airport (10 minutes).

Darren Lyons
The Old Court House
Le Boulevard, St Aubin,
St Brélade, JE3 8AB

Tel +44 (0)1534 746433
Email info@oldcourthousejersey.com
Web www.oldcourthousejersey.com

Scotland

Photo: Cringletie House, entry 251

The Creggans Inn

If you're looking for a small hotel in a great position with lovely rooms and excellent food, you'll find it here. There's a little history, too – the inn was once owned by the real James Bond. Sir Fitzroy Maclean was one of a cast of characters on whom Ian Fleming based his hero; the fact the Royal Navy send their big ships into Loch Fyne is purely coincidental. These days, life at the inn is decidedly restful. Views from the front stretch for miles, the loch eventually giving way to the distant peaks of the Kintyre peninsular. Inside, an airy elegance abounds. There's a first-floor sitting room with big views; a locals' bar which doubles as the clubhouse for the shinty team; then picture windows in the smart restaurant, where you dig into super food while watching the sun set, perhaps Ramsay haggis with whisky sauce, pot roast chicken with a thyme jus, bread and butter pudding with honey glazed figs. Comfy bedrooms have lots of style: warm colours, pretty fabrics, delicate wallpapers, robes in sparkling bathrooms; most have loch views. Castles and gardens, golf and boat trips wait.

Rooms	4 doubles, 9 twin/doubles: £120-£180. 1 suite for 2: £160-£220. Singles from £85. Dinner, B&B from £80 p.p.
Meals	Lunch from £4.25. Bar meals from £10.95. Dinner, 3 courses, about £30.
Closed	Never.
Directions	From Glasgow, A82 to Tarbert, A83 towards Inverary for 13 miles, then left on A815 to Strachur (10 miles). Hotel on left before village.

Archie & Gillian MacLellan
The Creggans Inn
Loch Fyne, Strachur,
Cairndow, PA27 8BX

Tel	+44 (0)1369 860279
Email	info@creggans-inn.co.uk
Web	www.creggans-inn.co.uk

The Manor House

A 1780 dower house for the Dukes of Argyll – their cottage by the sea. Built of local stone, it sits high on the hill with long views over Oban harbour to the Isle of Mull. It's a lovely small hotel with a stylish old-school feel: a roaring fire in the drawing room, beautiful tiles in the entrance hall, an elegant bay window in the bar, then a half-panelled dining room for excellent food. Attractive bedrooms have warm colours, fresh flowers, crisp linen, bowls of fruit and the odd antique. A couple are smaller, those with sea views have binoculars with which to scan the seven seas. Bathrooms are spotless, one has claw-foot bath. Dinner is a five-course feast, perhaps west coast sea bass, pea and ham soup, elderflower sorbet, saddle of lamb, sticky apple cake with vanilla ice cream; there's excellent home baking and Loch Fyne kippers for breakfast. Ferries leave for the islands from the bottom of the hill; watch them sail while digging into afternoon tea on the terrace. There's a computer for guests to use and you can climb up to McCaig's Tower to watch the sun set over the Hebrides. *Over 12s welcome.*

Rooms	9 doubles, 2 twins: £120-£260. Dinner, B&B from £87.50 p.p.
Meals	Lunch from £6. Dinner, 5 courses, £44.
Closed	Christmas.
Directions	In Oban follow signs to ferry. Hotel on right 0.5 miles after ferry turn-off, signed.

Gregor MacKinnon
The Manor House
Gallanach Road,
Oban, PA34 4LS

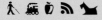

Tel +44 (0)1631 562087
Email info@manorhouseoban.com
Web www.manorhouseoban.com

The Pierhouse

The position here is unbeatable. You're at the end of the road, on the shores of Loch Linnhe, with views across to Lismore and rising mountains beyond. As for the Pierhouse – well, shipwrecked sailors would refuse rescue. Outside, there's a sun-trapping terrace from which to watch the odd boat chug past while digging into langoustines fresh from the waters around you. Interiors are just as good. Glass walls frame the view, there's a smart bar for a wee dram, a white-washed snug with sofas in front of a wood-burner, then, a restaurant for some of the best seafood on the west coast. Chic rooms have a wing to themselves, so expect deep peace. Those at the front have the view, all have an uncluttered Scandi feel with warm colours, padded bedheads, smart fabrics and robes in sparkling bathrooms. You get bowls of fruit, a sofa if there's room, crisp linen on comfy beds. There's lots to do: the ferry across to Lismore for fine walking, Ben Nevis, magical Ardnamurchan. As for the food, come back for oysters, scallops, lobster Thermidor or a rib-eye steak; the seafood platters are out of this world.

Rooms	4 doubles, 4 twin/doubles: £95-£215. 2 suites for 2: £145-£255. Extra beds: children 2-12 £30; 12+ £40.
Meals	Lunch from £4.95. Bar meals from £12.50. Dinner à la carte £30-£50.
Closed	Christmas & Boxing Day.
Directions	A82 north for Fort William, then A828 south for Oban. Right for Port Appin after 12 miles. At end of road.

Nick & Nikki Horne
The Pierhouse
Port Appin,
Appin, PA38 4DE

Tel +44 (0)1631 730302
Email reservations@pierhousehotel.co.uk
Web www.pierhousehotel.co.uk

The Airds Hotel & Restaurant

This chic country-house hotel on the Appin peninsular stands above Loch Linnhe with views across the water to the Morvern Mountains. It came to life in 1750, an inn for passengers taking the paddle steamers up to the Caledonian canal. These days, it's one of the loveliest places to stay on the West Coast. Its whitewashed exterior gives no hint of the wonders within. You enter through a small conservatory, then find yourself in a world of smouldering fires, freshly cut flowers, beautiful wallpapers and soft sofas. Bedrooms are divine: beautiful fabrics, warm colours, Frette linen on Vi-Spring beds, sparkling marble bathrooms with robes; in short, the best of everything. Those at the front have the view, bigger rooms have sofas, some at the back have terraces, all spoil you rotten. Best of all is the exceptional food, perhaps West Coast langoustines with pea purée, sea bass with clams and a lemongrass cream, apple terrine with salted caramel and cinnamon doughnuts. There's a garden for croquet and afternoon tea with views to the water. Worth every penny.

Rooms	8 twin/doubles: £180-£325. 3 suites for 4, with sofabed: £365-£410. 1 cottage for 5: £595-£940 per week. Dinner, B&B from £145 p.p. Extra bed/sofabed £25 p.p.p.n.
Meals	Lunch from £7. Dinner, 5 courses, £56. Tasting menu £77. Sunday lunch £21.45.
Closed	Monday & Tuesday November – January.
Directions	A82 north for Fort William, then A828 south for Oban. Right for Port Appin after 12 miles. On left after 2 miles.

Shaun & Jenny McKivragan
The Airds Hotel & Restaurant
Port Appin,
Appin, PA38 4DF

Tel +44 (0)1631 730236
Email airds@airds-hotel.com
Web www.airds-hotel.com

Tiroran House

The setting is magnificent – 17 acres of gardens rolling down to Loch Scridian. Otters and dolphins pass through, buzzards and eagles glide above, red deer visit the garden. As for this 1850 shooting lodge, you'll be hard pressed to find a more comfortable island base, so it's no surprise to discover it was recently voted 'Best Country House Hotel in Scotland' for the second year in a row. There are fires in the drawing rooms, fresh flowers everywhere, games to be played, books to be read. Airy bedrooms hit the spot: crisp linen, beautiful fabrics, the odd chaise longue; some have watery views, all have silence guaranteed. You eat in a smart dining room with much of the delicious food from the island or waters around it, perhaps mussel and oyster broth, saddle of lamb with carrot purée, chocolate torte with vanilla ice cream. You're bang in the middle of Mull with lots to do: Tobermory, the prettiest town in the Hebrides; Calgary and its magical beach; day trips to Iona and its famous monastery; cruises to Staffa and Fingal's Cave. Come back for afternoon tea – it's as good as the Ritz.

Rooms	5 doubles, 5 twin/doubles: £175-£220.
Meals	Dinner, 4 courses, £48.
Closed	Rarely.
Directions	From Craignure or Fishnish car ferries, A849 for Bunessan & Iona car ferry. Right onto B8035 for Gruline. After 4 miles left at converted church. House 1 mile further.

Laurence & Katie Mackay
Tiroran House
Tiroran,
Isle of Mull, PA69 6ES

Tel +44 (0)1681 705232
Email info@tiroran.com
Web www.tiroran.com

The Colonsay

Another fabulous Hebridean island, a perfect place to escape the world. Wander at will and find wild flowers in the machair, a golf course tended by sheep and huge sandy beaches across which cows roam. Wildlife is ever present, from a small colony of wild goats to a rich migratory bird population; the odd golden eagle soars overhead, too. At low tide the sands of the south give access to Oronsay. The island's 14th-century priory was one of Scotland's finest and amid impressive ruins its ornate stone cross still stands. As for the hotel, it brims with an easy style – airy interiors, stripped floors, fires everywhere, friendly staff. There's a locals' bar for a pint (and a brewery on the island), a pretty sitting room packed with books, a dining room for super food, a decked terrace for drinks in the sun. Bedrooms have local art, warm colours, lovely fabrics and the best beds; some have sea views, all have good bathrooms. Spin around on bikes, search for standing stones, lie in the sun and stare at the sky. There's a festival in May for all things Colonsay. Wonderful.

Rooms	4 doubles, 3 twins: £85-£150. 1 family room for 4: £105-£140. 1 single: £75-£80.
Meals	Lunch from £4.50. Packed lunch £7. Bar meals from £11.50. Dinner, 3 courses, about £25.
Closed	November, January/February.
Directions	Calmac ferries from Oban or Kennacraig (not Tue) or Hebridean Airways (Tue & Thur). Hotel on right, half a mile up road from jetty.

Jane Howard
The Colonsay
Scalasaig,
Isle of Colonsay, PA61 7YP

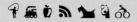

Tel +44 (0)1951 200316
Email hotel@colonsayestate.co.uk
Web www.colonsayestate.co.uk

Glenisle Hotel

The Glenisle has a great tradition in hospitality – it was once the village jail! These days, it's the best place to stay on Arran – stylish and friendly with views across Lamlash Bay to Holy Island. Outside, there's a pretty terrace for lunch in the sun. Inside, you find stone walls, roaring fires, then books and games in a stylish sitting room. It's quirky, too – part of the bar was rescued from an old paddle steamer, and the hotel holds a Christmas festival at the end of November. There are two restaurants – one overlooking the garden, the other with mirrors on one wall – and the food hits the spot nicely: perhaps fish chowder with home-smoked mussels, coffee-crusted haunch of Arran venison; dark chocolate delice with walnut ice cream. Smart, airy rooms have comfy beds, colourful throws and robes in cute bathrooms. Two at the front look out to sea, the suite has a claw-foot bath overlooking the bay. As for Arran, it's a small-scale version of Scotland: mountains to the north, lush farmland to the south, then sandy beaches and the odd castle waiting on the coast. A perfect island base.

Rooms	5 doubles, 5 twin/doubles: £129-£195. 1 suite for 2: £208-£228. 2 singles: £95-£98.
Meals	Lunch & dinner £6-£38.
Closed	Never.
Directions	South from Broddick for three miles to Lamlash. In village on right.

Geoffrey Dallamore & Timothy Billings
Glenisle Hotel
Lamlash, Isle of Arran, KA27 8LY

Tel +44 (0)1770 600559
Email enquiries@glenislehotel.com
Web www.glenislehotel.com

Cavens

This small patch of heaven is a delight. You leave the world behind you, take the road south from Dumfries, and soon you're rolling through stunning country with hardly a soul in sight. Sunlight plays in the trees, ridges run down to lush fields, then suddenly you turn a corner and the Solway Firth is sparkling before your eyes. All you need now is somewhere wonderful to stay, somewhere small and beautiful, with kind owners on hand to usher you though to a chic sitting room before pouring you a gin and tonic, dishing up some wonderful food and showing you to your delightful quarters. Which is exactly what you find at Cavens, a small country house hotel, where Jane and Angus look after guests in style. Two sitting rooms have open fires, period art and lots of books, then doors onto a garden where only birdsong will disturb you. As for the rooms, three are huge, one has the feel of a library, all have smart fabrics, super beds and garden views. Finally, dinner, an absolute delight, perhaps scallops with lime and Vermouth, venison with a port jus, a thin apple tart. Gardens, beaches and golf wait. Perfect.

Rooms	4 doubles, 1 twin: £200-£300. Price includes dinner for 2.
Meals	Lunch from £6. Dinner, 3-course à la carte, included; non-residents £35. Afternoon tea 'on the house.'
Closed	Rarely.
Directions	From Dumfries A710 to Kirkbean (12 miles). Signed in village on left.

Jane & Angus Fordyce
Cavens
Kirkbean,
Dumfries, DG2 8AA

Tel +44 (0)1387 880234
Email enquiries@cavens.com
Web www.cavens.com

Knockinaam Lodge

Lawns run down to the Irish sea, roe deer come to eat the roses, sunsets turn the sky red. This beautiful hunting lodge is one of the loveliest country-house hotels in the land. There's a Michelin star in the dining room, 150 malts in the panelled bar and a level of service you rarely find in such far-flung corners of the realm. There's history, too. Churchill once stayed and you can sleep in his room, then climb into the deepest of baths and read his books. Immaculate interiors abound: gorgeous bedrooms, faultless bathrooms, a morning room where the scent of fresh flowers mingles with wood smoke. You'll find beautiful art, the daily papers, games and books galore. Outside, cliff walks lead over to Portpatrick, peregrine falcons circle on high, bluebells carpet the hills in spring. When it's stormy, waves crash all around. There's golf on the coast at Portpatrick, then Luce Bay for miles of sand. John Buchan knew the house and described it in *The Thirty-Nine Steps* as the house to which Hannay fled. Remote, beguiling, utterly spoiling – grand old Knockinaam is simply unmissable.

Rooms	4 doubles, 5 twin/doubles: £290-£440. 1 family room for 4: £350-£420. Price includes dinner for 2.
Meals	Lunch, by arrangement, £32.50-£40. Dinner, 5 courses, included; non-residents £67.50.
Closed	Never.
Directions	From A77 or A75 pick up signs to Portpatrick. West from Lochans on A77, then left after 2 miles, signed. Follow signs for 3 miles to hotel.

David & Sian Ibbotson
Knockinaam Lodge
Portpatrick, Stranraer, DG9 9AD

Tel	+44 (0)1776 810471
Email	reservations@knockinaamlodge.com
Web	www.knockinaamlodge.com

Trigony House Hotel

A welcoming family-run hotel with good food and nicely priced rooms. There's a small spa in the garden, too, with rather good views from the hot tub. The house dates to 1700 and comes with Japanese oak panelling in the hall, a wood-burner in the sitting room and an open fire in the dining room, where doors open onto the terrace for dinner in summer. Adam cooks lovely rustic fare, perhaps prawns with coconut and coriander, saddle of roe venison, rhubarb and hazelnut crumble; a small, organic kitchen garden provides for the table in summer. Bedrooms – some big, some smaller – have warm colours, crisp linen, good beds and spotless bathrooms. A couple are dog-friendly, those at the back have the view, the suite opens onto a private garden. As for the spa, there's a treatment room, a sauna and a hot tub, so plenty of scope to recuperate after a day walking the Southern Upland Way or discovering the spectacular country between Moniaive and the Galloway Forest, a lost world of huge beauty you'll have to yourself. Don't miss Drumlanrig Castle for its gardens, walking trails and mountain bike tracks.

Rooms	4 doubles, 4 twin/doubles: £120-£140. 1 suite for 2: £165. Singles from £90. Extra beds £15.
Meals	Lunch from £7.50. Dinner £25-£35. Afternoon tea £15.
Closed	24-26 December.
Directions	North from Dumfries on A76; through Closeburn; signed left after 1 mile.

Adam & Jan Moore
Trigony House Hotel
Closeburn, Thornhill, DG3 5EZ

Tel +44 (0)1848 331211
Email trigonyhotel@gmail.com
Web www.trigonyhotel.co.uk

Letham House

Why stay in the big smoke when you can live the life of Riley at this baronial mansion that dates to 1645? It stands at the end of a tree-lined drive in 12 acres of woodland and gardens, with birdsong, strutting chickens and carpets of flowers to greet you. As for the house, it's a bona fide jaw-dropper. There's a wood-burner in the downstairs snug, then a crackling fire in a regal first-floor sitting room. You gather here for drinks before dinner (BYO), then spin down to the dining room, where you eat at one table in country-house style, feasting on delicious food, perhaps smoked haddock, chicken with tarragon, a chilled lemon mousse. After which you retire to delightful rooms and find huge beds, smart fabrics, antique furniture and garden flowers. Robes wait in fine bathrooms, three of which have claw-foot baths that overlook the garden. You're five miles from links golf at Gullane and North Berwick, ten miles from Edinburgh, with a bus that stops at the end of the drive. All of which would be blossom in the wind without Chris and Barbara, the undisputed stars of the show. Don't miss it. *Minimum stay: 2 nights at weekends July-August.*

Rooms	5 twin/doubles: £130-£195. Extra beds: children free; adults £20.
Meals	Dinner, 3 courses, £35. BYO.
Closed	Never.
Directions	A1 to Oak Tree Junction, 1 mile west of Haddington, then B6471 for Haddington. Right, up drive, immediately after 40mph sign.

Barbara & Chris Sharman
Letham House
East Lothian,
Haddington, EH41 3SS

Tel +44 (0)1620 820055
Email stay@lethamhouse.com
Web www.lethamhouse.com

23 Mayfield

A great base for all things Edinburgh. This attractive villa which stands in the shadow of Arthur's Seat was built in 1868 for a coffee merchant. Outside, much prized, off-street parking waits. Inside, Victorian splendour at every turn: original fireplaces, ornate ceilings and a stained-glass window on the landing. The sitting room comes in dark period colours with newspapers on poles, gilt-framed pictures that hang on chains, and you can grab a drink from the honesty bar, then sink into a chesterfield sofa and watch an old movie or listen to trad jazz. Breakfast is even better. In winter you eat by candlelight, a candelabra on each table, and it's a feast of Scottish produce: porridge with honey, Arbroath smokies, rare breed sausages, marshmallow pancakes. Bedrooms have style and comfort in spades: white linen, excellent beds, fancy bathrooms, maybe wood floors or a brass chandelier. One has panelled walls, all have good art, iPod docks and smart TVs; the family room has a Nintendo Wii. You can jump on a bus and whizz into town, excellent restaurants wait nearby. A very friendly place. *Minimum stay: 2 nights at weekends May-September*

Rooms	4 twin/doubles, 2 four-posters: £110-£185. 1 family room for 4: £130-£200. Singles from £90.
Meals	Restaurants within half a mile.
Closed	24-26 December.
Directions	A720 bypass, then north onto A722 for Edinburgh. Right onto A721 at T-junction with traffic lights. Over x-roads with main flow, under railway bridge, on right.

Ross Birnie
23 Mayfield
23 Mayfield Gardens,
Edinburgh, EH9 2BX

Tel +44 (0)131 667 5806
Email info@23mayfield.co.uk
Web www.23mayfield.co.uk

94DR

Close to Holyrood and Arthur's Seat, this super-friendly designer B&B is not only popular for its contemporary style, but for Paul and John, who treat guests like friends and make sure you see the best of their city. A traditional Victorian exterior gives no hint of the chic interiors that wait within. You'll find original floor tiles and ornate ceilings, but other than that it's a clean sweep of modern splendour: deep charcoal downstairs; pure white above. There's a sitting room with iPads in case you want to book a restaurant, then an honesty bar, an espresso machine and lots of handy guide books. Upstairs, stylish, well-priced bedrooms wait. Some are big with claw-foot baths, others smaller with walk-in power showers. All come with comfy beds, bathrobes, beautiful linen and fine contemporary art. The family suite (two rooms) has bunk beds and a PlayStation for kids. Delicious breakfasts are served in a conservatory overlooking the back garden, a memorable feast orchestrated by Paul, with lively conversation that travels the world. Majestic Edinburgh is yours to explore. *Minimum stay: 2 nights at weekends*

Rooms	3 doubles: £100-£145. 2 suites for 2: £125-£200. 1 family suite for 4: £125-£190. Singles from £80.
Meals	Restaurants within 0.5 miles.
Closed	2-15 January.
Directions	Leave A720 (ring road) at Sheriff Hall roundabout for A7 north into Edinburgh. Straight ahead for 3 miles and on left.

John MacEwan & Paul Lightfoot
94DR
94 Dalkeith Road,
Edinburgh, EH16 5AF

Tel	+44 (0)131 662 9265
Email	stay@94dr.com
Web	www.94dr.com

21212

A chic restaurant with rooms in Edinburgh's East End, with Holyrood Palace and the Botanic Gardens both close. Paul left his Michelin star down south, bought this Georgian townhouse, spent a fortune turning it into a 21st-century pleasure dome, then opened for business and won back his star. The house stands at the top of a hill with long views north towards the Firth of Forth. Inside, contemporary splendour waits. High ceilings and vast windows come as standard, but wander at will and find a cool first-floor drawing room, cherubs on the walls, busts and statues all over the place, even a private dining pod made of white leather. Stunning bedrooms have enormous beds, cool colours, fat sofas and iPod docks. Those at the front have the view, all have robes in magnificent bathrooms. As for the restaurant, the kitchen is on display behind a wall of glass and the food it produces is heavenly stuff, perhaps crab with caviar and scallops, chicken with pecan and pimiento, black cherry rice with cucumber and mint syrup. If that's not enough head up to Leith for afternoon tea on Royal Yacht Britannia. *Minimum stay: 3 days at New Year.*

Rooms	4 doubles: £95-£295.
Meals	Lunch from £22. Dinner, 3 courses, £70; 5-course tasting menu £85. Not Sunday or Monday.
Closed	Rarely.
Directions	A720 ring road, then A702/A7 into town. Right at T-junc. at Balmoral Hotel, then immediately left with flow. Right at second r'bout and 1st right. On right.

Paul Kitching & Katie O'Brien
21212
3 Royal Terrace,
Edinburgh, EH7 5AB
Tel +44 (0)131 523 1030
Email reservations@21212restaurant.co.uk
Web www.21212restaurant.co.uk

Six Brunton Place

You step inside to find Doric columns and five-foot candelabra in the reception hall and that's just the start of it. This is a quirky, designer B&B in the centre of town, with Leith Walk to the north, Edinburgh Castle to the west and Arthur's Seat over the hill to the south. Hilary looks after her guests in great style, spills local secrets and offers a glass of wine 'on the house' every evening. The sitting room doubles as the breakfast room and comes with a bust in front of the wood burner, a long sofa that encourages idleness, then Chinese wood carvings and beautiful art. Bedrooms are scattered about, all filled with beautiful things. The garden suite is huge, a great base for families; the cute snug is perfect for those who travel light; one sweeps you back to a graceful past with dark walls and flamboyant curtains that fall from on high. All have coffee machines, flat-screen TVs and robes in excellent bathrooms. Breakfast is a treat: strong coffee, freshly squeezed orange juice, porridge, the full cooked works. Excellent restaurants wait on your doorstep. Parking on London Road is £4 a day.

Rooms	3 doubles: £139-£179. 1 suite for 4: £179-£239. Singles from £89.
Meals	Restaurants 2-minute walk.
Closed	23-28 December.
Directions	A1/A199 north for Leith, then west onto A1140/A1/London Road into Edinburgh. On right with park on left.

Hilary Scott
Six Brunton Place
6 Brunton Place,
Edinburgh, EH7 5EG

Tel +44 (0)131 623 6405
Email contact@sixbruntonplace.com
Web www.sixbruntonplace.com

The Bridge Inn at Ratho

This lovely inn sits in a small village directly above the Union Canal. Footpaths head west into the country, you can hire bikes and follow the tow path into Edinburgh, or jump on the pub's canal boat for a Sunday lunch cruise. If all that sounds too strenuous, then plonk yourself down on the terrace and watch the odd boat chug past while sipping a pint of good ale. Inside, the view is weather-proofed by big windows in the dining room. An easy style runs throughout. You'll find wood-burners, smart colours, a whisky bar, the odd sofa. In summer, there are barbecues on Friday nights, an ice cream shed in the garden, even a small festival in May with live bands and lots of beer. Rooms aren't huge, but hit the spot. They're stylish and comfy with smart beds and crisp linen. All but one has the view, three have walk-in power showers, one has a claw-foot bath. The airport is ten minutes away, but you're not on the flight path, so peace reigns. Finally, don't miss nearby Jupiter Artland in summer, a wonderland of beautiful things. Children are very welcome.

Rooms	3 doubles, 1 twin/double: £80-£120. Singles from £65.
Meals	Lunch & dinner, £5-£35. Sunday lunch from £12.95.
Closed	Christmas Day.
Directions	West from A720 (ring road) on A71. Right at x-roads after 3 miles, signed Ratho. Right in village and inn on left above canal.

Graham & Rachel Bucknall
The Bridge Inn at Ratho
27 Baird Road,
Ratho, EH28 8RA

Tel +44 (0)131 333 1320
Email info@bridgeinn.com
Web www.bridgeinn.com

The Ship Inn

There are few inns where you can sit on the terrace and watch a game of cricket on the beach below. But it's not beach cricket as you know it. This is serious stuff, played at low tide, and Mark Waugh, Viv Richards and Wasim Akram have all tried their hand. As for this cute little boutique inn, it's as good as any in the land, and it doubles as the pavilion… and the venue for post-match celebrations, no doubt. On sunny days, you decant onto the terrace for lunch in the sun and gaze across the Firth of Forth to Edinburgh's hills. Inside, contemporary rustic design mixes with roaring fires and the odd stone wall. Sofas and armchairs are scattered about, staff weave through the throng delivering delicious food – fish and seafood from local waters, lamb and beef from nearby farms, sinful puddings you can't resist; there are regular barbecues on the terrace, too. Smart rooms have seaside colours, crisp linen, coffee machines, fancy bathrooms with walk-in showers; those at the front have sea views, too. St Andrews waits for a round of golf, the Fife coastal path for excellent walks. A perfect place.

Rooms	5 twin/doubles, 1 twin/double: £110-£160. Extra beds £15. Cots free.
Meals	Lunch & dinner £5-£35. Sunday lunch from £12.95.
Closed	Christmas Day & 2 weeks in January.
Directions	A917 east into Elie. In village, right after small green, onto Stenton Row. Straight ahead and on left.

Graham & Rachel Bucknall
The Ship Inn
The Toft, Elie, KY9 1DT

Tel	+44 (0)1333 330246
Email	info@shipinn.scot
Web	www.shipinn.scot

15 Glasgow

This is a smart Glasgow address – bang in the middle of town, yet beautifully insulated from it. The house, grand Victorian, stands on an attractive square with communal gardens guests can enjoy. Inside, the feel is distinctly contemporary, despite a couple of Corinthian pillars in the entrance hall. It's all been beautifully renovated, and while technically you're in a B&B, the interiors here are a match for any boutique hotel. Downstairs, a vast sitting room has a couple of sofas in front of a fire. Bedrooms upstairs are no less generous. Those at the back are large, the suites at the front are huge. All come with king-size beds, crisp white linen, handmade bedheads and robes in gorgeous bathrooms. Suites have a few added extras: big sofas, beautiful windows, one has a double-ended bath overlooking the square. Breakfast is brought to you whenever you want. As for dinner, you'll find good restaurants nearby: the Finnieston for seafood and gin cocktails; the Gannet for a flat-iron steak; Ben Nevis for a wee dram and live folk music most nights. Don't miss the excellent Burrell Collection. *On-site parking.*

Rooms	3 doubles: £120–£145. 2 suites for 2: £150–£175. Extra beds £20.
Meals	Restaurants on your doorstep.
Closed	Never.
Directions	West into Glasgow on M8. Exit at junc. 18 for Charing X (outside lane), then double back at lights. 1st left, 1st left, 1st left (really). Follow square round to house.

Lorraine Gibson
15 Glasgow
15 Woodside Place, Glasgow, G3 7QL
Tel +44 (0)141 332 1263
Email rooms@15glasgow.com
Web www.15glasgow.com

Mackay's Rooms

This is the north-west corner of Britain and it's utterly magical: huge skies, sandy beaches, aquamarine seas, cliffs and caves. You drive – or cycle – for mile upon mile with mountains soaring into the heavens and ridges sliding into the sea. If you like big, remote landscapes, you'll love it here; what's more, you'll pretty much have it to yourself. Mackay's – they have the shop, the bunkhouse and the garage, too – is the only place to stay in town, its earthy colours mixing with stone walls, open fires and stripped floors to great effect. Bedrooms (some big, others smaller) are extremely comfy. They come with big wooden beds and crisp white linen, while Fiona, a textiles graduate, has a fine eye for fabrics and upholstery. You also get excellent bathrooms, iPod docks, flat-screen TVs and DVD players. Breakfast sets you up for the day – grilled grapefruit, whisky porridge, venison sausages, local eggs – so head east to the beach, west for great golf or catch the ferry across to Cape Wrath and scan the sea for whales. There's surfing for the brave and the beautiful.

Rooms	6 doubles, 1 twin: £125-£165. 4 cottages for 6: £800-£1,600 per week. Singles from £110.
Meals	Restaurants in village.
Closed	October to May. Cottages open all year.
Directions	A838 north from Rhiconich. After 19 miles enter Durness village. Mackay's is on right-hand side opposite memorial.

Fiona Mackay
Mackay's Rooms
Durine, Durness,
Lairg, IV27 4PN

Tel +44 (0)1971 511202
Email stay@visitdurness.com
Web www.visitdurness.com

Scourie Hotel

This famous old fishing hotel is a treat from top to toe. It's a quirky place run with great panache by the Campbells, who bought it recently, refurbished in style and now it shines. It's supremely comfy – smart without being swanky, very much a country hotel. You'll find golden wallpapers, antique furniture, beautifully upholstered armchairs, then an open fire in the sitting room. It's a remarkably friendly place. Fishermen tend to come for the same week each year, re-booking when they leave, so everyone knows everyone and they all go out of their way to welcome interlopers into the fold. There's great tradition, too; a board master allocates fishing beats each morning, a gong announces dinner. Stylish rooms have comfy beds, pretty fabrics, beautiful new bathrooms and no TVs; bliss. Dinner is a treat, perhaps ham hock terrine, fresh local salmon, profiteroles with chocolate sauce. There are two bars, a pretty garden, paths that lead down to the sea. This is a wildly beautiful corner of Scotland: spectacular walking, wildlife tours and golf all wait. You're on the North Coast 500, too.

Rooms	6 doubles, 6 twins: £135. 2 family rooms for 3: £145-£160. 6 singles: £85. 1 chalet for 4: £200-£250. Dinner, B&B £97 p.p. Extra bed £25 p.p.
Meals	Lunch from £4.95. Bar meals from £10. Dinner, 3 courses, £32.
Closed	7 October to 1 April.
Directions	North from Ullapool on A835, then A837. In village on left.

Richard, Fiona & Charlotte Campbell
Scourie Hotel
Scourie,
Lairg, IV27 4SX

Tel +44 (0)1971 502396
Email stay@scouriehotel.com
Web www.scouriehotel.com

Nicely priced

The Torridon

Scotland's west coast is full of wonder and this grand old house is no exception. It sits cradled by mountains in 58 acres of woodland and gardens with lawns that roll down to the shores of Upper Loch Torridon. Red deer roam, eagles soar, highland cattle graze in fields. Inside, sparkling interiors thrill: a roaring fire in the panelled hall, a zodiac ceiling in the chic drawing room and 365 whiskies in the bar, one for each day of the year. Big windows pull in the view, canny walkers pour off the hills to recover in style. Bedrooms are hard to fault, some big, others bigger, all overflowing with contemporary delight. Expect bold colours, padded headboards, exquisite linen, magnificent bathrooms; one room has a shower in a turret. Outside, a stunning two-acre kitchen garden provides much for the table. You feast on ambrosial food in a beautiful dining room, perhaps west coast scallops, home-bred pork, Valrhona chocolate with pistachio and salted caramel. Dan and Rohaise also have the village inn with simpler food and good rooms from £130. Sea kayaking, guided walks, abseiling and mountain biking are all on tap.

Rooms	10 doubles, 2 twins, 2 four-posters: £230-£465. 4 suites for 2: £465-£485. 1 house for 4: £925-£1,425. Extra bed £40 p.p.p.n.
Meals	Lunch from £5.95. Dinner £50-£60. Tasting menu £75.
Closed	January.
Directions	A9 to Inverness, A835 to Garve, A832 to Kinlochewe, A896 to Annat (not Torridon). Signed on south shore.

Daniel & Rohaise Rose-Bristow
The Torridon
Annat,
By Achnasheen, IV22 2EY

Tel +44 (0)1445 791242
Email info@thetorridon.com
Web www.thetorridon.com

Doune Knoydart

There is nowhere quite like Doune. You arrive by boat – there's no road in – a ferry across to Knoydart, the last great wilderness in Britain. You'll find mountain, sea and sky – a thrilling landscape of boundless peace and ever-changing light. It's a haven for wildlife – killer whales, Golden eagles, red grouse, otters and badgers – 120 species live here. As for Doune, it sits on the Sound of Sleat with views across to Skye. It's a tiny community of happily shipwrecked souls and Martin, Jane and Liz look after you with great generosity. The dining room is the hub, pine-clad from top to toe, with a stove to keep you warm and games in case it rains. The food is delicious – crab from the bay, roast lamb from the hill, chocolate tart with homemade ice-cream. Bedrooms along the veranda are delightfully simple; pine-clad cabins with mezzanine bunks for children, hooks for clothes, sparkling showers, armchairs for watching the weather. The walking is magnificent, boat trips can be arranged, the night sky astounds. There's a lodge for groups, too. A very special place, miss it at your peril. *Minimum stay: 3 nights.*

Rooms	2 doubles, 1 twin, each with mezzanine bed for children: £90. 1 single with separate shower: £33. Dinner, B&B £78–£88 p.p. (includes packed lunch).
Meals	Dinner £35.
Closed	October – March.
Directions	Park in Mallaig; the boat will collect you at an agreed time.

Martin & Jane Davies
Doune Knoydart
Knoydart,
Mallaig, PH41 4PL

Tel +44 (0)1687 462667
Email martin@doune-knoydart.co.uk
Web www.doune-knoydart.co.uk

Kilcamb Lodge Hotel & Restaurant

Another stunning West Coast setting with Loch Sunart at the end of the garden and Glas Bheinn rising beyond. Kilcamb – a barracks during the Jacobite uprising – is a perfect base. There's a smart drawing room with an open fire, an elegant dining room for super food, a cool little brasserie for a spot of lunch, then a handful of deeply indulging rooms. A 12-acre garden rolls down to the water, where you might spot otters and seals. Ducks and geese fly overhead, if you're lucky you'll see eagles. Back inside, you'll find a whisky bar that also does a good line in gin, then driftwood lamps, fresh flowers, good books and local art. You can eat in the restaurant or the brasserie, either a five-course tasting menu or something simpler, perhaps hand-dived scallops, Highland lamb, raspberry bavarois with champagne sorbet. Bedrooms have a country-house feel, some with a contemporary twist. You'll find warm colours, smart fabrics and excellent beds. One has a balcony, most have the view, all have spotless bathrooms, some with separate showers. Don't miss Ardnamurchan or Senna Bay at the end of the road.

Rooms	2 doubles, 6 twin/doubles: £220-£380. 2 suites for 2: £300-£435. 1 family room for 4: £390-£435. Price includes dinner for 2.
Meals	Lunch from £7.50. Dinner, 3 courses, included; non-residents £50. Tasting menu £75. Sunday lunch £25. Afternoon tea £14.
Closed	January & first 2 weeks in December. Limited opening November & February.
Directions	From Fort William A82 south for 10 miles to Corran for ferry to Ardgour, A861 to Strontian. West of village on left.

David & Sally Ruthven-Fox
Kilcamb Lodge Hotel & Restaurant
Strontian,
Acharacle, PH36 4HY

Tel +44 (0)1967 402257
Email enquiries@kilcamblodge.co.uk
Web www.kilcamblodge.co.uk

Coruisk House

You follow the road for 15 miles through magnificent landscapes – down the glen, around the loch and over the mountain to Elgol. Your reward is this chic little restaurant with rooms waiting at the end of the track. A cool, rustic style has conquered every corner, ambrosial food flies from the kitchen, a glass of prosecco is yours on arrival. The breakfast room runs along the front of the house with a string of windows that frame the view. You'll find hanging lamps, up-cycled furniture, lime-washed walls and a painted settle. Airy rooms have big beds, mohair throws, white linen, robes in quirky bathrooms. New rooms in the cottage next door have the same delicious style and the odd claw-foot bath. As for Iain's glorious food, you eat in the restaurant, where a wood-burner keeps things cosy, perhaps crab brûlée with lobster bisque, Highland beef with braised oxtail, ginger steamed pudding with Drambuie ice cream. Drop down to Elgol harbour, where Bonnie Prince Charlie fled for his life, and gaze upon the mighty Cuillin rising from the sea. Stags roam the hills, boat trips can be arranged. Heaven.

Rooms	3 doubles: £140-£220. 1 suite for 4: £320-£400.
Meals	Dinner £40-£45.
Closed	31 October to 1 March (open for New Year).
Directions	West from Broadford on B8083 15 miles over to Algol. Over cattle grid at start of village and on right.

Iain Roden & Clare Winskill
Coruisk House
26 Elgol, Elgol,
Isle of Skye, IV49 9BL

Tel +44 (0)1471 866330
Email info@coruiskhouse.com
Web coruiskhouse.com

Viewfield House Hotel

It's a family affair, more like the Waltons than Hamlet, and the recent succession from father to daughter passed without a sword being drawn. Iona is now at the helm, but as Hugh is the only person on Skye who understands the plumbing system, he has been retained as a vital asset, and rightly so. As for their ancestral pile, it stands high above Portree Bay with long views across the Sound of Raasay. Twenty acres of gardens and woodland wrap around you; there's croquet on the lawn and a hill to climb for 360° views of peak and sea. Inside, aristocratic fixtures and fittings come as standard: hunting trophies, cases filled with curios, a grand piano and open fire in the drawing room. Bedrooms have a country-house feel: colourful fabrics, crisp linen, pretty furniture, sea views from those at the front; bathrooms do the job nicely and are in the throes of refurbishment. Majestic Skye waits: mountains, sea lochs and beaches, wildlife, castles and distilleries. Dinner is available by arrangement, but there are good restaurants in Portree, too. Highland porridge for breakfast is a treat. An old-school, island delight.

Rooms	4 doubles, 4 twin/doubles, 1 twin: £136-£170. 2 singles: £65-£85. Dinner, B&B £93-£110 p.p.
Meals	Dinner, 3 courses, £25-£30, price dependent on pre-booking. Packed lunch £9.
Closed	Mid-October to Easter.
Directions	On A87, coming from south, driveway entrance on left just before the Portree filling station.

Iona Macdonald & Jasper Buxton
Viewfield House Hotel
Viewfield Road,
Portree, Isle of Skye, IV51 9EU

Tel +44 (0)1478 612217
Email info@viewfieldhouse.com
Web www.viewfieldhouse.com

Culdearn House

Grantown is a great base for Highland flings. You can fish the Spey, jump on the whisky trail, check out a raft of castles, even ski in Aviemore. Loch Ness is close, as is Royal Deeside, there's golf everywhere and the walking is divine; in short, expect to be busy. As for Culdearn, it stands in a row of five identical houses that were built in 1860 by Lord Seafield, one for each of his daughters. These days it's a lovely small hotel where William and Sonia look after guests with unstinting kindness. There's an open fire and facing sofas in the smart sitting room, panelled windows and a marble fireplace in the dining room, then stylish bedrooms that offer the sort of comfort you hope for after a day in the hills. You get the comfiest beds, the crispest linen, decanters of sherry, fresh flowers and robes for spotless bathrooms. Back downstairs, William looks after a tempting wine list and 60 malts, while Sonia whisks up delicious four-course dinners, perhaps West Coast scallops, bramble sorbet, fillet of beef, a walnut and maple syrup parfait. Don't miss the ospreys at Boat of Garten. *Children over 10 welcome.*

Rooms 4 doubles, 1 twin/double, 1 twin: £150-£170. Singles from £75. Dinner, B&B from £100 p.p.

Meals Dinner, 4 courses, £45

Closed Rarely.

Directions North into Grantown from A95. Left at 30 mph sign & house directly ahead.

Sonia & William Marshall
Culdearn House
Woodlands Terrace,
Grantown on Spey, PH26 3JU
Tel +44 (0)1479 872106
Email enquiries@culdearn.com
Web www.culdearn.com

Barley Bree

A small bastion of good things a couple of miles north of Gleneagles. It's a family affair. Fabrice is French and cooks sublimely, Alison, a Scot, looks after the wine. It's a great little place – stylish, welcoming, not a hint of pomposity. It draws a crowd from near and far, ravenous diners in search of ambrosial food. And that's what you get, the best local produce cooked to perfection, perhaps hand-diver scallops with crayfish tails, saddle of lamb with white cabbage and pancetta, an irresistible tarte tatin. There's a fire in the sitting-room bar, where cocktails, cake and games are all on tap, then a chicly rustic restaurant with exposed stone, fine art and a wood-burner that burns on both sides; in summer you decant onto a terrace for lunch in the sun. Six comfy rooms have an easy style with crisp linen, good beds and robes for compact shower rooms. The big room, with a claw-foot bath, is worth splashing out on. As for Barley Bree – whisky soup to you and me – it's a phrase plucked from a Robert Burns poem. Don't miss Innerpeffray Library or the gardens at Drummond Castle. A treat.

Rooms	1 double, 5 twin/doubles: £95-£160. Singles from £75.
Meals	Lunch from £6.50. Dinner, 3 courses, about £40 (not Mon or Tue). Sunday lunch from £13.95.
Closed	One week in July & Christmas.
Directions	A9 north from Dunblane, then A822 for Muthill. In village on left before church.

Fabrice & Alison Bouteloup
Barley Bree
6 Willoughby Street,
Muthill, PH5 2AB

Tel	+44 (0)1764 681451
Email	info@barleybree.com
Web	www.barleybree.com

Mhor 84

The entirely benevolent expansion of the Mhor empire has mastered the Midas touch, turning this old roadside inn into the coolest motel in the land. Outside, the glen shoots down to Loch Voil, with mountains to climb and bike tracks to follow. Inside, chic white minimalism mixes with warm Scottish tradition, a perfect blend of relaxed 21st-century living. There's style and humour in equal measure – boarded floors, tractor seat bar stools, curios hanging on the walls, the odd sofa for afternoon tea. Fires roar, cake stands bulge, happy staff weave through the throng delivering fabulous food that you eat at old school tables – porridge with honey for breakfast, sourdough and hummus for lunch, Scotch rarebit, Tyree lobster and plum crumble for dinner. There's live folk music every Thursday – Ewan MacPherson of Shooglenifty often plays – and a fine selection of malts if you fancy a dram. Simple bedrooms have white walls, contemporary art, small armchairs and honest prices; spotless bathrooms are 1980s originals, all part of the fun. There's a games room, too, with a juke box and pool table.

Rooms	2 doubles, 4 twin/doubles: £70-£80. 1 family room for 4: £80-£110.
Meals	Breakfast from £4.50. Lunch from £3.90. Dinner, 3 courses, £25-£35.
Closed	Christmas Day.
Directions	A84 north from Callander. Through Strathyre, then right after three miles for Kingshouse. In village.

Dugald McGarry
Mhor 84
Balquhidder,
Lochearnhead, FK19 8NY

Tel +44 (0)1877 384646
Email motel@mhor.net
Web mhor.net/mhor-84-motel/

Monachyle Mhor

Monachyle is unique – a designer hotel on a remote hill farm that started life as a B&B. Today it's one of the hippest places to stay in Scotland and it's still run by the same family with the children at the helm. Dick farms, Melanie designs the magical rooms, Tom cooks some of the best food in Scotland. It sits in 2,000 acres of blissful silence at the end of the track with the Trossachs circling around you and Loch Voil shimming below. Sheep graze, buzzards swoop, the odd fisherman tries his luck. Inside, there's a cool little bar, a fire in the sitting room, then a slim restaurant that drinks in the view. Bedrooms ooze 21st-century chic: big beds, cool colours, fabulous design, hi-tech gadgets. Bathrooms are equally good, perhaps a deluge shower in a granite steam room or claw-foot baths with views down the glen. Loft-house suites are enormous, but the smaller rooms are lovely, too. Dinner is a five-course feast with beef, lamb, pork and venison all off the farm. Rob Roy lived in the glen, you can visit his grave. The hotel holds a festival in May – fabulous food and cool Scottish tunes.

Rooms	9 twin/doubles: £195-£215. 5 suites for 2: £265. 1 family room for 4: £195-£265.
Meals	Lunch from £5.50. Dinner, 5 courses, £50. Sunday lunch £32.
Closed	Two weeks in January.
Directions	M9, junc. 11, then B824 and A84 north. Right for Balquhidder 6 miles north of Callander. 5 miles west along road & Loch Voil. Hotel on right, signed.

Tom Lewis
Monachyle Mhor
Balquhidder,
Lochearnhead, FK19 8PQ

Tel	+44 (0)1877 384622
Email	monachyle@mhor.net
Web	mhor.net/monachyle-mhor-hotel/

Ardeonaig Hotel

This magical small hotel sits on the quiet side of Loch Tay with gardens that run down to the water and mountains that rise beyond. Silence and mother nature are the chief ingredients. You weave along a single-track lane, leaving the world behind, then find whitewashed walls adorned with hanging baskets and you've arrived. Inside, there's an elegant sitting room with a peat fire, a snug bar for a wee dram, a pretty restaurant that overlooks the burn. Outside, there's a courtyard garden for afternoon tea in the sun. Bedrooms are a delight, some smaller, others bigger, all with big beds, crisp linen, a sofa if there's room. White walls soak up the light, several have the view, one has a wood-burner, garden suites are huge; all have robes in spotless bathrooms. There's lots to do: you can kayak, bag a couple of munros, zoom down mountain-bike trails or just take to the hills and find ancient burial grounds, Rob Roy's hideouts and a ruined medieval castle. Dinner is a treat, perhaps home-smoked salmon, Perthshire lamb, peaches with whisky and heather. There's a music festival in Killin in June.

Rooms	8 doubles, 3 twin/doubles: £120-£200. 7 suites for 2: £175-£250. Dinne, B&B from £95 p.p. Singles from £110. Extra bed available.
Meals	Lunch from £6. Dinner, £31-£37.50. Sunday lunch from £16. Afternoon tea £6.50.
Closed	Never.
Directions	A9, then A827 for Kenmore via Aberfeldy. In Kenmore, take south side road along loch Tay for 10 miles. On right.

Ian Hitchens
Ardeonaig Hotel
South Loch Tay Side,
Near Killin, FK21 8SU

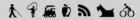

Tel +44 (0)1567 820351
Email info@ardeonaighotel.com
Web www.ardeonaighotel.co.uk

Dunalastair Hotel Suites

Rannoch Moor is one of those magical places where the hand of man has hardly touched the landscape. You're encircled by hills, with a couple of lochs thrown in for good measure. As for the road, it peters out at the station 20 miles west, where the London train stops and passengers disembark, bicycle in hand. Some, very sensibly, spin down to this chic hotel and check in for a night or two of luxury. It was built in 1860 and now a recent renovation has added 21st-century comfort and style. You'll find a roaring fire in the hall, a dram or two in the wee bar, colourful art in the big sitting room, then delicious food in the restaurant, perhaps Scottish scallops, loin of roe deer, apple parfait with rosemary and sage. In summer you decant into the courtyard for breakfast, lunch and dinner. Chic suites offer more than most: the best beds, sofas and smart TVs, well-stocked kitchenettes, then dining tables for room service. Swish bathrooms have walk-in showers, some have baths, too. Kind staff are the best, nothing is too much trouble. You can kayak, fish, hire bikes or bag a munro. *Minimum stay: 2 nights between July-August.*

Rooms	16 suites for 2, 14 suites for 4, 2 suites for 6: £169-£299.
Meals	Lunch from £6. Mains from £7.95. Dinner, 3 courses, £35. Afternoon tea £18. Food available all day.
Closed	Never.
Directions	A9 north to Pitlochry, then west for Dunalastair on B8019. In village, on right, past church.

Richard Deak
Dunalastair Hotel Suites
1 The Square,
Kinloch Rannoch, PH16 5PW

Tel	+44 (0)1882 580444
Email	bookings@dunalastairhotel.com
Web	www.dunalastairhotel.com

The Inn at Loch Tummel

You weave through the forest, then arrive at this 200-year-old inn to find views of field, hill, loch and sky. It's a magical spot, with a small garden to the front that drinks it all in. As for the inn, Alice and Jade rescued it from neglect, poured in love and money and now it shines. Interiors mix contemporary flair with Highland charm, the very definition of rustic chic. You'll find a cool little bar, painted beams and a wood-burner in the restaurant, then a first-floor sitting room with fat sofas, books and games, goatskin rugs and Jade's guitar. Bedrooms are a treat: chic fabrics, beautiful beds, cool colours, woollen throws. Some are big, none are small, one is dog friendly, most have the view. All have good art, decanters of whisky and spotless bathrooms, some with walk-in showers. By day you explore the hills, whizz down mountain bike trails or climb Schielhallion, the local munro. At night you return for delicious food, perhaps calamari with chilli and lemon, rack of local lamb, an espresso brownie with beetroot meringue. Queen's View, up the road, has one of the best views in Scotland. *Children over 5 welcome. Closed for check in on Sunday & Monday.*

Rooms	2 doubles, 4 twin/doubles: £105-£155.
Meals	Dinner with wine £27.
Closed	Christmas & January.
Directions	From Perth, A9 north, then turn off after Pitlochry, signed Killiecrankie. Left over Garry Bridge onto B8019. Inn 8 miles on right.

Alice & Jade Calliva
The Inn at Loch Tummel
Queens View,
Strathtummel, PH16 5RP

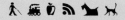

Tel +44 (0)1882 634317
Email info@theinnatlochtummel.com
Web www.theinnatlochtummel.com

Craigatin House & Courtyard

Craigatin is one of those lovely places where beautiful rooms have attractive prices and hands-on owners go out of their way to make your stay special. It stands peacefully in two acres of manicured gardens on the northern shores of town; good restaurants are a short stroll. Smart stone exteriors give way to warmly contemporary interiors, where beautiful windows flood rooms with light. There are shutters in the breakfast room, which overflows into an enormous conservatory where sofas wait in front of a wood-burner and walls of glass open onto the garden. Big uncluttered bedrooms – some in the main house, others in converted stables – are super value for money. Expect Farrow & Ball colours, comfy beds, crisp white linen, padded bedheads and pretty shower rooms. Breakfast offers the full cooked works and tempting alternatives, perhaps smoked haddock omelettes or apple pancakes with grilled bacon and maple syrup. As for Pitlochry – gateway to the Highlands – it's a vibrant town with lots to do: castles and mountains, lochs and forests, its famous Festival Theatre. You're on the whisky trail, too. *Minimum stay: 2 nights at weekends*

Rooms	11 doubles, 2 twins: £109-£118. 1 suite for 2: £136. Singles £99-£126.
Meals	Restaurants within walking distance.
Closed	Christmas.
Directions	A9 north to Pitlochry. Take 1st turn-off for town, up main street, past shops and signed on left.

Martin & Andrea Anderson
Craigatin House & Courtyard
165 Atholl Road,
Pitlochry, PH16 5QL

Tel	+44 (0)1796 472478
Email	enquiries@craigatinhouse.co.uk
Web	www.craigatinhouse.co.uk

Knockendarroch Hotel & Restaurant

This grand old house on a hill was built in 1880, then sold in 1910 for £100! It is also the birthplace of the Pitlochry Festival Theatre, the plays originally performed in the garden. These days it's simply a lovely place to stay with views from the front that shoot across the valley to forested hills. Inside, you find original tiles in the hall, a double sitting room with two fires, a whisky bar for a wee dram, a wallpapered restaurant with views of Ben Vrackie and plenty of original contemporary art. Good paths lead up through forest and moorland for big Highland views, not a bad way to work up an appetite for some very good food, perhaps fillet of hake with chilli and lemongrass, Perthshire lamb with parsnip purée, elderflower panna cotta with pear sorbet. Bedrooms are lovely, it really doesn't matter which you choose, though the big ones at the front do have exceptional views. You'll find comfy beds, smart fabrics, tartan throws and padded headboards, perhaps a cushioned window seat or a sofa if there's room. Two have balconies, most have binoculars to scan the hills. There's a drying room for wet gear, too. *Minimum stay: 2 nights at weekends. Children over 10 welcome.*

Rooms	12 twin/doubles: £140-£195. Dinner, B&B from £85 p.p.
Meals	Lunch from £5. Dinner, 3 courses, £25; £42 non-residents.
Closed	20 December to 6 February.
Directions	A9 north to Pitlochry. Up high street, right into Bonnethill Road. Right again into Toberargan Road and on right.

Struan & Louise Lothian
Knockendarroch Hotel & Restaurant
Higher Oakfield,
Pitlochry, PH16 5HT
Tel +44 (0)1796 473473
Email info@knockendarroch.co.uk
Web www.knockendarroch.co.uk

Killiecrankie House Hotel

No Highland fling would be complete without a night at Killiecrankie. Henrietta runs the place with great charm and has spent the last ten years pouring in love and money; now it shines. Outside, gardens galore: one for roses, another for vegetables, and a fine herbaceous border. Further afield, you'll find much to please: Loch Tummel, Rannoch Moor and magnificent Glenshee, over which you tumble for the Highland Games at Braemar. Return to the indisputable comforts of a smart country hotel: tartan in the dining room, 52 malts at the bar, views at breakfast of red squirrels climbing garden trees. There's a snug sitting room where a fire burns in winter; in summer doors open onto the garden. Delightful bedrooms come in different shapes and sizes. All are smart with pretty linen, warm colours, chic fabrics and lovely views. Dinner is predictably delicious, perhaps pea and mint soup, Highland venison, sticky toffee pudding. There's porridge with cream and brown sugar for breakfast. Castles, hills and distilleries wait. A great wee place with staff who care. *Minimum stay: 2 nights at weekends.*

Rooms	3 doubles, 5 twin/doubles: £250-£320. 2 singles: £150-£160. Price includes dinner for 2.
Meals	Lunch from £4.50. Dinner included; non-residents £42.
Closed	3 January to 18 March; Christmas.
Directions	A9 north of Pitlochry, then B8079, signed Killiecrankie. Straight ahead for 2 miles. Hotel on right, signed.

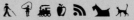

Henrietta Fergusson
Killiecrankie House Hotel
Killiecrankie,
Pitlochry, PH16 5LG
Tel +44 (0)1796 473220
Email enquiries@killiecrankiehotel.co.uk
Web www.killiecrankiehotel.co.uk

Cringletie House

Cringletie's splendours are hard to miss. You're wrapped up in 65 acres of beautiful grounds with daffodils that erupt in spring, cows that graze in lush fields and a peaceful walled garden for a game of boules. Pheasants strut, buzzards circle, views roll over nearby hills. As for the house, it dates to 1860, its playful turrets giving it a soft grandeur. Inside, you get the full works: an open fire in the hall, then a fine old staircase that sweeps you up to a striking first-floor dining room that has the feel of an 18th-century gentleman's club; expect panelled walls, vintage wallpapers and a spectacular muralled ceiling. There's a sitting room up here, too – equally grand, with fat sofas in front of the fire. Bedrooms are scattered about. Some downstairs open onto the garden, those at the top have the best views. It doesn't matter which you go for, they're all lovely, with warm colours, crisp linen, comfy beds and excellent bathrooms. Take to the hills, follow the Tweed or scoot up to Edinburgh; it's less than an hour by car.

Rooms	12 twin/doubles: £135-£245. 1 suite for 2: £235-£265. 1 cottage for 6: £235-£465.
Meals	Lunch from £9.50. Dinner, 3 courses, £37.50. Sunday lunch £22.50. Afternoon tea from £18.50.
Closed	3-25 January.
Directions	North from Peebles on A703. Hotel signed left after 2 miles.

Jeremy Osbourne
Cringletie House
Edinburgh Road,
Peebles, EH45 8PL

Tel	+44 (0)1721 725750
Email	enquiries@cringletie.com
Web	www.cringletie.com

Windlestraw

A small country house with lovely interiors and beautiful views down the Tweed Valley. Hills rise, deer roam, osprey glide through the afternoon sky. John and Sylvia came back from Dubai to do their own thing and have been hard at work presiding over a chic refurbishment. Fires roar, a grand piano waits to be played, there's a sun-trapping terrace for afternoon tea. You find a conservatory sitting room filled with books and curios, a panelled dining room for super food, then binoculars with which to scan the valley – sunsets turn the hills orange. Country-house bedrooms have a warm contemporary style: smart colours, comfy beds, sofas in the bigger rooms, fine views from those at the front. Spotless bathrooms do the trick: one has a claw-foot bath, bigger rooms have robes. Good food waits downstairs, perhaps scallops from Eyemouth, local lamb, an irresistible tarte tatin. There's lots to do: walking, fishing, mountain biking, even kayaking on the Tweed; if you try your hand on Pebbles golf course, the views may well be better than your game! There's a literary festival at Traquair House in August, too.

Rooms	5 doubles, 1 twin: £160-£200. Singles £105-£125. Dinner, B&B £120-£145 p.p. Extra bed/sofabed available: adults £25; children £15. Cots free.
Meals	Dinner, 5 courses, £40.
Closed	Christmas, January & February.
Directions	East from Peebles on A72. Into Walkerburn; house signed left on western flank of town.

John & Sylvia Matthews
Windlestraw
Galashiels Road,
Walkerburn, EH43 6AA

Tel +44 (0)1896 870636
Email stay@windlestraw.co.uk
Web www.windlestraw.co.uk

The Allanton Inn

Allanton, population 100. Welcome to the sleepy back of beyond, an untouched corner of the rural idyll that most people skip on their rush north. Well, there's no rush here, just patchwork fields, rolling hills and the river Tweed pottering off to the coast. As for this cute little inn, it's a great base from which to explore. The style is charming, the locals friendly, the prices lovely, the food a treat. It sits on the only street in town with a garden that backs onto open country; in summer you can have lunch in the sun while watching the farmer plough his fields. Inside, home-spun interiors have colour and style. There's an open-plan feel, the airy bar flowing into a half-panelled restaurant. You'll find a smouldering fire, fresh flowers, good art, local ales. Rooms have an easy style: padded bedheads, good bathrooms, Farrow & Ball colours. A couple are big, those at the back have the view. Super local food waits downstairs, perhaps an Eyemouth fish platter, rump of local lamb, lavender and raspberry brûlée. There's local honeycomb at breakfast, too. You can fish, walk, play a bit of golf. Perfect.

Rooms	3 doubles, 2 twin/doubles: £75-£95. 1 family room for 4: £100-£130. Singles from £70.
Meals	Lunch from £6.75. Dinner, 3 courses, £25-£35. Sunday lunch from £12.50.
Closed	Christmas.
Directions	West from Berwick on A6105, then left in Churnside onto B6437. On left in village.

William & Katerina Reynolds
The Allanton Inn
Allanton,
By Duns, TD11 3JZ

Tel +44 (0)1890 818260
Email info@allantoninn.co.uk
Web www.allantoninn.co.uk

Scarista House

All you need to know is this: Harris is one of the most beautiful places in the world. Beaches of white sand that stretch for a mile or two are not uncommon. If you bump into another soul, it will be a delightful coincidence, but you shouldn't count on it. The water is turquoise, coconuts sometimes wash up on the shore. The view from Scarista is simple and magnificent: field, ridge, beach, water, sky. Patricia and Tim are the kindest people. Their home is island heaven: peat fires, rugs on painted floors, books everywhere, a first-floor drawing room that floods with Harris light. Country-house bedrooms have warm colours and stylish bathrooms. There are walking sticks and wellington boots to help you up the odd hill, then a set of golf clubs by the front door in case you wish to play (the view from the first tee is one of the best in the game). Kind staff may speak Gaelic. The food is exceptional, perhaps quail with an armagnac mousse, Harris langoustine with garlic and butter, tarte tatin with cinnamon ice cream. Don't miss Uig Sands or the standing stones at Callanish. A perfect place.

Rooms	2 doubles, 1 twin: £207-£245. 2 suites for 2; 1 family room for 4: £233-£245. Singles £153.
Meals	Dinner, 3 courses, £44. Packed lunch from £7.50.
Closed	Christmas, 1 January to 28 February.
Directions	From Tarbert A859 south, signed Rodel. Scarista 15 miles on left after golf course. W10 bus stops at gate.

Patricia & Tim Martin
Scarista House
Scarista, Isle of Harris, HS3 3HX
Tel +44 (0)1859 550238
Email timandpatricia@scaristahouse.com
Web www.scaristahouse.com

Photo: Alec Studerus

Wales

Photo: Llys Meddyg, entry 276

The Dolaucothi Arms

Tucked away in the heart of the Carmarthenshire countryside, this gem of a pub shines bright. Lovely Esther and Dave have brought the Dolaucothi back to life – notice little touches like handsome floral reupholstering on the mix-and-match dining chairs, and clutches of blooms in jugs and antique bottles on tables and sills. Dave's gorgeous gardens flank the walk up the little path; as you come in, there's a happy buzz in the air and the tempting scent of fresh home cooking; nearly everything is lovingly cooked from scratch! The dining room and bar are all in warm neutrals, with terracotta tiles and wood-burners. Sink into the velvety green chesterfield in the snug with a bottle of local brew or a glass of wine – Esther and Dave can advise. Food wise, try lamb reared by Dolaucothi farmer Gary, or the homemade pies; both are local and delicious. Hop up the little staircase, and you'll find three quiet bedrooms with garden views in soft tones of olive or wild rose. Snuggle up with wool duvets and pillows topped with colourful Welsh blankets, and enjoy the peace. There's even a little tipple on the chest of drawers for a nightcap.

Rooms	3 doubles: £75-£90. Singles £65-£70. Extra bed/sofabed £20 p.p.p.n.
Meals	Lunch from £5. Dinner, 3 courses, £20-£25. Sunday lunch from £9.
Closed	Rarely.
Directions	A40 toward Llandovery then right turn onto A482 to Lampeter. After 8 miles, you'll see a Pumpsaint sign as you enter the village. Pub is on your left.

David Joy & Esther Hubert
The Dolaucothi Arms
Pumpsaint, Llanwrda, SA19 8UW

Tel	+44 (0)1558 650237
Email	info@thedolaucothiarms.co.uk
Web	www.thedolaucothiarms.co.uk

Ty Mawr Country Hotel

Pretty rooms, attractive prices and delicious food make this welcoming country house hard to resist. It sits in a very peaceful spot. You drive over hills, drop into the village, then wash up at this 16th-century stone house that comes in soft yellow. Outside, a sun-trapping terrace laps against a trim lawn, which in turn drops into a passing river. Gentle eccentricities abound: croquet hoops take odd diversions, logs are piled high like giant beehives, a seat has been chiselled into a tree trunk. Inside, original stone walls and low beamed ceilings give a warm country feel. There are fires everywhere – one in the attractive sitting room that overlooks the garden, another in the dining room that burns on both sides. Excellent bedrooms are all big. You get big beds, warm colours, crisp linen, good bathrooms. Some have sofas, all are dog-friendly, three overlook the garden. Back downstairs, the bar doubles as reception, while Welsh art on the walls is for sale. Steve's cooking is the final treat, perhaps Cardigan Bay scallops, organic Welsh beef, calvados and cinnamon rice pudding. Top stuff. *Children over 10 welcome.*

Rooms	3 doubles, 3 twin/doubles: £115-£130. Singles £80.
Meals	Dinner £25-£30.
Closed	Rarely.
Directions	M4 west onto A48, then B4310 exit, for National Botanic Gardens. 6 miles north to Brechfa. In village centre.

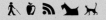

Annabel & Steve Thomas
Ty Mawr Country Hotel
Brechfa, SA32 7RA
Tel +44 (0)1267 202332
Email info@wales-country-hotel.co.uk
Web www.wales-country-hotel.co.uk

Wright's Food Emporium

This is one of those wonderful places you come across once every ten years, the sort that makes no effort to conform and so brings to life a quirky style that's delightful and authentic. It's a temple to local food – a café, a restaurant, a deli, and a wine shop, though it's not often you can sit in a wine shop, stick on a Bob Dylan LP and dig into glorious food washed down by organic wines. Its legion of fans come from near and far, with staff weaving through the throng to deliver manna from heaven. One room leads to another, all designed to please. You'll find tables crammed with delicious cakes; soups simmering away on the range; a fire and original flagstones in the back room; then a swish lean-to stuffed with curios and pot plants that opens onto a terrace. As for the deli, 'we sell the food we like' says Maryann of her culinary Aladdin's Cave. It's all fresh and local – breads, meat, eggs, vegetables, chutneys, jams, even chocolate. Two rustic-chic cottages are a steal for those wise enough to linger. Both come with kitchens you probably won't use. Don't think, just come, happiness waits.

Rooms	1 cottage for 4: £110-£280; £700-£875 per week. 1 cottage for 6: £110-£280; £760-£1250 per week.
Meals	Lunch from £6. Dinner, 3 courses, £25-£30. Last orders for food: Sun-Thur 7pm. Fri & Sat 9pm.
Closed	Tuesdays.
Directions	West on M4, A48, then north onto B4310. Right at B4300. First building on left in village.

Joel, Simon & Maryann Wright
Wright's Food Emporium
The Golden Grove Arms,
Llanarthne, SA32 8JU

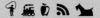

Tel +44 (0)1558 668929
Email maryann@wrightsfood.co.uk
Web www.wrightsfood.co.uk

The Cors

A bohemian bolthole, one of the best. Nick is a cook, an artist and a gardener, his two lush acres a beautiful retreat in summer. Gunnera, bamboo and tree ferns flourish while the river Coran potters past – not a bad spot for tea in summer. Inside, a small, personal world of French inspiration: a bar that sweeps you back to 1950s Paris, then doors that open onto a Victorian veranda where roses and clematis ramble. As for the food, you eat accompanied by cool tunes, with busts and paintings all around – perhaps at the front with garden views, or wrapped up behind in claret reds. At weekends the restaurant is open to all with ambrosial delights on the menu, perhaps smoked haddock crème brûlée, roasted rack of salt marsh lamb, a zesty lemon tart. In the week, delicious comfort food is on tap by arrangement: homemade soups, shepherd's pie, a plate of local cheeses. Simple rooms with a chic style wait at the top of a beautiful staircase: rugs on bare boards, vintage William Morris wallpapers, bold colours, the odd armoire – perfect for the price. Don't miss Laugharne for all things Dylan Thomas. *Minimum stay: 2 nights at weekends.*

Rooms	3 doubles: £80. Singles from £50.
Meals	Dinner, 3 courses, from £35 (Thur-Sat only). Sunday lunch from £17.
Closed	2 weeks in November.
Directions	A4066 south from St Clears for Laugharne. In village right at pub. Over bridge and on right.

Nick Priestland
The Cors
Newbridge Road,
Laugharne, SA33 4SH

Tel +44 (0)1994 427219
Email nick@thecors.co.uk
Web www.thecors.co.uk

Penbontbren

You're lost in lovely hills, yet only three miles from the sea. Not that you're going to stray far. These gorgeous suites don't just have wonderful prices, they're heaped with comforts, too – this is a great spot to come and do nothing at all. Richard and Huw have thought it all through. You get crockery and cutlery, kettles and fridges, then you're encouraged to bring your own wine or to buy provisions from the farm shop for lunch. As for the suites, expect big beds, super bathrooms, sofas and armchairs in pretty sitting areas, then doors onto semi-private terraces – perfect for lunch in summer. You get iPod docks, flat-screen TVs, robes and White Company lotions, too. The new garden room is a little smaller than the others, but has a big terrace to compensate. Breakfast is served in the main house – the full Welsh works. Beautiful hills, sandy beaches, Cardigan and magical St Davids all wait. Good local restaurants are on hand: lobster from the sea, lamb from the hills. Don't miss The Shed in Porthgain for excellent fish and chips. A great place to unwind with discounts for longer stays. *Minimum stay: 2 nights in high season.*

Rooms	6 suites for 2: £99-£125. 1 cottage for 7: £700-£1,150 per week. Singles £85-£99.
Meals	Restaurants within 3 miles.
Closed	Christmas.
Directions	North from Cardigan on A487. Through Tangroes, past sign for Tresaith and Penbryn, then 1st right, signed Penbontbren. On left after 1 mile.

Richard Morgan-Price & Huw Thomas
Penbontbren
Glynarthen,
Llandysul, SA44 6PE

Tel	+44 (0)1239 810248
Email	contact@penbontbren.com
Web	www.penbontbren.com

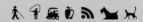

Nanteos Mansion

A grand old manor house lost at the end of a one-mile drive, with a small lake, a walled garden and 25 acres of ancient woodland. Views at the front stretch across fields to nearby hills, four pillars stand at the front door, sofas wait by a wood-burner in the hall. The house dates to 1731, but stands on medieval foundations. It is most famous for the Nanteos Cup – the Holy Grail to you and me – which legend says was carried here by monks from Glastonbury Abbey. A grand renovation recently brought the house back to life – electric-shock therapy performed by interior designers. Downstairs, there's a morning room, a sitting-room bar and an elegant restaurant where you dig into delicious food, perhaps chilli salt squid, roast partridge stuffed with chorizo, chilled chocolate fondant. Stylish rooms wait – big suites are grand and gracious, some panelled, others with fine wallpaper – but all rooms have lots of colour, original art and robes in chic bathrooms. There's lots to do: rivers to fish, mountains to climb, coastal paths to follow. Don't miss the music room (Wagner visited).

Rooms	9 doubles: £120-£160. 5 suites for 2: £170-£300. 1 single: £75-£95. 5 family rooms for 4: £125-£270. Extra bed/sofabed £15-£45 p.p.p.n.
Meals	Lunch from £7.50. Dinner £33.95-£39.50. Sunday lunch from £22.
Closed	Rarely.
Directions	Leaving Aberystwyth to the south, take A4120 Devil's Bridge Road, then immediately right onto B4340. House signed left after 1 mile.

Nigel Jones
Nanteos Mansion
Rhydyfelin,
Aberystwyth, SY23 4LU

Tel +44 (0)1970 600522
Email info@nanteos.com
Web www.nanteos.com

Escape Boutique B&B

A designer B&B with lovely rooms, attractive prices and some seriously fancy bathrooms. The house stands high on the hill, away from the crowds, a short stroll from the buzz of town and its two-mile beach. This is a 19th-century mill owner's villa and its fine old windows, sparkling wood floors and carved fireplace bear testament to its Victorian roots. Other than that it's a clean sweep of funky interiors. Sam and Gaenor scoured Europe for their eclectic collection of colourful retro furniture that fills the rooms – orange swivel chairs, iconic G-plan sofas, beautiful beds wrapped in crisp white linen. You'll find cow-hide rugs, funky wallpapers, big views from rooms at the front. All come with flat-screen TVs, Blu-ray DVD players and iPod docks. Bathrooms are excellent: one room has a shower for two, another has a copper bath in the room. Downstairs, there's an honesty bar in the sitting room, while delicious breakfasts are served in an attractive dining room. Good food waits in town – the Seahorse for fish, Mamma Rosa for Italian. Great Orme waits above for big views of the bay. *Minimum stay: 2 nights at weekends.*

Rooms	8 doubles, 1 twin/double: £95-£149. Singles from £80.
Meals	Restaurants within walking distance.
Closed	Christmas.
Directions	A55 junc. 19, then A470 for Llandudno. On promenade, head west hugging the coast, then left at Belmont Hotel and house on right.

Sam Nayar & Gaenor Loftus
Escape Boutique B&B
48 Church Walks,
Llandudno, LL30 2HL

Tel +44 (0)1492 877776
Email info@escapebandb.co.uk
Web www.escapebandb.co.uk

Osborne House

Osborne House – originally the summer residence of a Cheshire brewer – dates to 1850, and was one of the first houses to be built on the promenade. It fell into the hands of Elyse's parents in the mid-1980s, who refurbished from top to toe, turning 23 small rooms into seven enormous suites. They didn't hold back – expect a grand Victorian feel with a dash of Belle Époque. You'll find Corinthian columns, crystal chandeliers, noble portraits on the walls, comfy sofas in front of the fire. Downstairs, there's a sitting room at the front with views of the bay, a bar in the middle for the daily papers, then curtains that open theatrically onto a muralled dining room at the back. Suites are huge – big sitting rooms, brass beds, claw-foot baths and walk-in showers. You'll find rugs on wood floors, ornate marble fireplaces, armchairs and sofas to take the strain; all but one have sea views. Bistro food waits downstairs, perhaps seared scallops, a rib-eye steak, baked toffee and chocolate sponge. There's off-road parking, too, and you can use the pool at the Empire, Osborne House's sister hotel. *Minimum stay: 2 nights at weekends.*

Rooms	7 suites for 2: £135-£185. Dinner, B&B from £82.50 p.p.
Meals	Lunch from £5. Dinner from £10.95. Afternoon tea from £8.50.
Closed	1 week over Christmas
Directions	A55, junc. 19, then A470 into Llandudno. At sea, turn left, then right at r'bout onto North Parade. On left.

Elyse Waddy
Osborne House
Promenade,17 North Parade,
Llandudno, LL30 2LP

Tel +44 (0)1492 860330
Email sales@osbornehouse.co.uk
Web www.osbornehouse.co.uk

The Hand at Llanarmon

The Hand sits in glorious country – vast skies, rolling hills, country lanes that deliver you into the middle of nowhere. It's a popular spot with walkers, mountain bikers and wildlife spotters, who spend their days having fun in the hills before rolling down to this 16th-century drovers' inn for the pleasures of a country local. A coal fire burns on the range in reception, a wood fire crackles in the front bar, a wood-burner keeps things cosy in the restaurant. Expect stone walls, low beamed ceilings, old pine settles and candles on the mantelpiece. There's a locals' bar for darts and pool, then a quiet sitting room for maps and books, which doubles as a treatment room. Delicious food draws a crowd, so grab a table and dig into excellent country fare, perhaps Welsh Cheddar brûlée, roast rump of local lamb, sticky toffee pudding with caramel sauce. Airy rooms, all recently refurbished, have a contemporary feel with Welsh woollen throws on good beds and views of village and hill. Those in the main house are a little bigger, a couple have claw-foot-baths, three are dog friendly. Special indeed.

Rooms	11 doubles: £95-£135. 1 suite for 4: £150. Singles from £55. Sofabed £25.
Meals	Lunch & dinner £5-£30. Sunday lunch from £15.
Closed	Rarely.
Directions	Leave A5 south of Chirk for B4500. Llanarmon 11 miles on.

Jackie & Jonathan Greatorex
The Hand at Llanarmon
Llanarmon Dyffryn Ceiriog,
Llangollen, LL20 7LD

Tel	+44 (0)1691 600666
Email	reception@thehandhotel.co.uk
Web	www.thehandhotel.co.uk

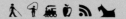

Plas Dinas Country House

The family home of Lord Snowdon dates to the 1600s and stands in 15 rural acres with an avenue of oak sweeping you up to the house. Princess Margaret often stayed and much of what fills the house belongs to the family: striking chandeliers, oils by the score, gilt-framed mirrors – an Aladdin's cave of beautiful things. There's a baby grand piano in the drawing room, where you find a roaring fire and an honesty bar, but potter about and find masses of memorabilia framed on the walls (make sure you visit the private dining room). Bedrooms – some with views across fields to the sea – mix a graceful past with modern design. You get four-posters, period colours, bold wallpapers, a sofa if there's room. A cute room in the eaves has mountain views, all have hot-water bottles, Apple TVs and excellent bathrooms, some with showers, others with free-standing baths. Good food waits in the restaurant, perhaps fishcakes with lime and ginger, lamb shank with a rosemary jus, chocolate tart with white chocolate ice-cream. Snowdon is close, as you'd expect, so bring walking boots and mountain bikes. *Minimum stay: 2 nights on bank holiday weekends.*

Rooms	3 doubles, 5 twin/doubles: £109-£169. 2 suites for 2: £159-£249. Extra beds £50.
Meals	Dinner, 3 courses, £25-£35.
Closed	23-27 December.
Directions	South from Caernarfon on A487. Through Bontnewydd and signed right after half a mile at brow of shallow hill.

Neil Baines & Marco Soares
Plas Dinas Country House
Bontnewydd,
Caernarfon, LL54 7YF

Tel +44 (0)1286 830214
Email info@plasdinas.co.uk
Web www.plasdinas.co.uk

Plas Bodegroes

A beautiful house, one of the loveliest places to stay in Wales. It may be far flung, but it's worth every second it takes to get here. Outside, six acres of mature gardens include a 200-year-old avenue of beech trees. Inside, a cool elegance roams freely: golden wallpapers, smouldering fires, a quirky bar that appears from thin air. French windows flood the house with light and open on to a veranda that comes wrapped in wisteria in summer. In good weather you take afternoon tea here while watching sheep graze in the fields; it's a little like being in a period drama. Bedrooms have chic fabrics, good beds, white linen, super bathrooms – it really doesn't matter which one you get. Some open onto a courtyard, a lovely spot for pre-dinner drinks in the evening. As for dinner, you eat in a dining room that doubles as an art gallery, a suitably theatrical spot for some very good food, perhaps braised pork cheek with crispy ham hock, wild sea bass with lemon and basil, cassis mousse with crème fraîche sorbet. The Llyn Peninsula waits: excellent walking, sandy beaches, towering cliffs. Pure heaven.

Rooms	4 doubles, 3 twin/doubles: £120–£170. 3 suites for 2: £160–£190. Dinner, B&B from £124 p.p. (min. 2 nights). Singles from £130.
Meals	Sunday lunch £24.50. Dinner £49.
Closed	Sunday nights & Mondays.
Directions	From Pwllheli A497 towards Nefyn. House on left after 1 mile, signed.

Holly Kotkowicz
Plas Bodegroes
Efailnewydd, Pwllheli, LL53 5TH

Tel	+44 (0)1758 612363
Email	info@bodegroes.co.uk
Web	www.bodegroes.co.uk

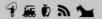

Llwyndû Farmhouse

The view here is fabulous – a clean sweep across Cardigan Bay to the Llyn Peninsula beyond. Below, a ten-mile beach runs north to Harlech Point; behind, the Rhinog mountains rise. As for the farmhouse, it sits high on the hill and dates to 1581. It's a small, homespun world – Peter and Paula do it all themselves – a simple retreat with delicious slow food at the end of the day. Inside, you find thick stone walls, comfy sofas and a wood-burner in the inglenook. Bedrooms are scattered about. Those in the main house have a cosy feel with warm colours, low ceilings, perhaps a four-poster. Those in the outbuildings tend to be a little bigger and have painted stone walls, then ceilings open to the rafters. By day you explore the wonders of Snowdonia – you can climb mountains, take to cycle tracks or merely walk in the hills. By night you return to feast on local delights under ancient beams, perhaps Rhydlewis smoked salmon, Welsh Black steak, apple tarte tatin; if you're still hungry after that, excellent Welsh cheeses wait. Don't miss Portmeirion, or links golf at Harlech and Aberdovey. *Minimum stay: 2 nights.*

Rooms	3 doubles, 2 four-posters: £104-£126. 1 family room for 4: £104-£146. Dinner, B&B from £82 p.p. Singles from £52.
Meals	Dinner £25-£30.
Closed	January.
Directions	A496, 2 miles north of Barmouth when street lights stop. Llwyndû signed on right.

Peter & Paula Thompson
Llwyndû Farmhouse
Llanaber, Barmouth, LL42 1RR

Tel +44 (0)1341 280144
Email intouch@llwyndu-farmhouse.co.uk
Web www.llwyndu-farmhouse.co.uk

Penmaenuchaf Hall

This grand old house sits high on the hill with fine views over the Mawddach estuary. It stands in 21 acres of woodlands and gardens, with daffodils, snowdrops and bluebells running riot in spring and a walled garden that bursts with colour in summer. The hall dates to 1865 and was home to a Bolton cotton merchant. Inside you find an open fire in the half-panelled hall, views of the estuary from the morning room, then a stunning drawing room, where mullioned windows frame views of water, mountain, sky. There's a tiny bar, a grand piano, sofas to sink into, country rugs on original wood floors. An airy restaurant opens onto a terrace, where you can eat in good weather, perhaps seared scallops, Welsh beef, apple tart and honey ice cream. Bedrooms have a homely country-house feel: comfy beds, warm colours, pretty fabrics, a wall of paper; some are huge, a couple have balconies. There's lots to do: 13 miles of river to fish, mountain bike trails, zip wires and cave tours. Cader Idris is close (and far less crowded that Snowdon), so scale it for stunning views. Starry skies on clear nights delight. *Children over 6 welcome.*

Rooms	7 doubles, 5 twin/doubles, 1 four-poster: £180-£300. 1 family room for 4: £260-£300. Singles £130-£195. Extra bed/sofabed £50-£60 p.p.p.n.
Meals	Lunch from £6. Dinner, 3 courses, £28.50-£46. Afternoon tea from £7.95.
Closed	Rarely.
Directions	From Dolgellau A493 west for about 1.5 miles. Entrance on left.

Mark Watson & Lorraine Fielding
Penmaenuchaf Hall
Penmaenpool,
Dolgellau, LL40 1YB

Tel +44 (0)1341 422129
Email relax@penhall.co.uk
Web www.penhall.co.uk

Y Meirionnydd

By day you explore the mighty wonders of Snowdonia, by night you return to this lovely small hotel and recover in style. It's one of those places that delivers just what you want; it's smart without being posh, the welcome is second to none, tasty food hits the spot, the bedrooms are excellent. You're in the middle of a small country town with a terrace at the front, so sit outside in summer and watch the world pass by. Inside, soft colours and warm lighting create a relaxed feel. There's a cute bar with armchairs and games, an airy breakfast room for the full Welsh works, then a smart restaurant cut into the rock, which was once the county jail; the food is somewhat better these days, perhaps game terrine with mustard piccalilli, rump of Welsh lamb with rosemary dumplings, Penderyn Welsh whisky and honey ice cream. Bedrooms upstairs fit the bill nicely. Some are bigger than others, but all have the same style: clean lines, cool colours, big beds, beautiful linen. You get the odd stone wall, an armchair if there's room, then super bathrooms. There's secure storage for bikes, too. *Minimum stay: 2 nights at weekends.*

Rooms	3 doubles, 2 twin/doubles: £89-£125. Singles £69-£79. Extra bed/sofabed available £20 p.p.p.n.
Meals	Dinner, 3 courses, £25. Not Mondays in low season.
Closed	One week at Christmas.
Directions	In centre of town on one-way system, off A470.

Marc Russell & Nick Banda
Y Meirionnydd
Smithfield Square,
Dolgellau, LL40 1ES

Tel +44 (0)1341 422554
Email info@themeirionnydd.com
Web www.themeirionnydd.com

The Whitebrook

You're in the Wye valley, on a spur that takes you into the middle of nowhere, with birdsong and a gurgling stream supplying the soundtrack. It's a fairytale setting, a small house on a hillside in a forest that has conquered the valley. Light sparkles in ancient trees, footpaths meander through woods, the terrace for drinks before dinner has delightful views. As for the Whitebrook, it's a restaurant with rooms, where Chris whisks up incredible food – this must be the healthiest Michelin star you're likely to eat. His ethos is simple: take the best local produce, cook it without excessive embellishment, then draw out the cleanest expression of its flavour. It's gobsmacking stuff, lots of it foraged, perhaps Wye Valley asparagus with hogweed and pine; Hereford snails with aromatic flowers; suckling pig with hop shoots and artichokes; honey mousse with caramel and lemon Verbena. Rooms are a treat. Expect comfy beds, crisp linen, warm colours, excellent bathrooms; those at the front have valley views. You can walk in the forest, kayak on the Wye or explore Tintern Abbey. Hard to beat.

Rooms	4 doubles, 4 twin/doubles: £223-£363. Price includes dinner for 2.
Meals	Lunch (Wed-Sun) £29-£47. Dinner included; non-residents, 3 courses, £59; tasting menu (obligatory Fri & Sat) £74.
Closed	Mondays. Two weeks in January.
Directions	M48, junction 2, then A446 north for 8 miles. Left before bridge, keeping the river on your right. In village, on left, after 1.5 miles

Chris & Kirsty Harrod
The Whitebrook
Whitebrook,
Monmouth, NP25 4TX

Tel	+44 (0)1600 860254
Email	info@thewhitebrook.co.uk
Web	www.thewhitebrook.co.uk

The Bell at Skenfrith

The position here is magical: an ancient stone bridge, a river snaking through the valley, glorious hills rising beyond, cows grazing in lush fields. It's a perfect spot, not least because providence blessed it with this chic little inn. Inside, you find a locals' bar for the odd game of rugby, sofas in front of a wood-burner in the sitting room, then an airy restaurant for some very good food. In summer, doors fly open and life spills onto a stone terrace with views of hill and wood – a fine spot for lunch in the sun. Elegant country-house bedrooms brim with light. Some are beamed, most are big, you'll find padded bedheads, Farrow & Ball colours, perhaps a walnut bed or a claw-foot bath in your room. Those at the front have river views, those at the back look onto the hills, some have sofas, all have robes in excellent bathrooms. Seven circular walks start at the front door with maps to show you the way. Delicious food awaits your return, perhaps Welsh rarebit with a poached egg, braised beef brisket with dauphinoise potatoes, apple doughnuts with toffee sauce and mulled cider. *Minimum stay: 2 nights at weekends*

Rooms	5 doubles, 3 twin/doubles, 3 four-posters: £150-£230. Singles £90. Dinner, B&B from £95 p.p. Extra bed/sofabed £10-£20 p.p.p.n.
Meals	Lunch from £5.95. Dinner, 3 courses, around £35. Sunday lunch from £12.95.
Closed	Rarely.
Directions	From Monmouth B4233 to Rockfield; B4347 north for 5 miles; right on B4521; Skenfrith 1 mile.

Richard Ireton & Sarah Hudson
The Bell at Skenfrith
Skenfrith,
Abergavenny, NP7 8UH

Tel +44 (0)1600 750235
Email enquiries@skenfrith.co.uk
Web www.skenfrith.co.uk

32 Townhouse

Narberth is lovely – quirky and colourful, lively and independent. It's wrapped up in Pembrokeshire's rolling hills with the coast and its path waiting ten miles south. As for this stylish restaurant with rooms, it sits on the high street, dates to 1820, and has a smart Georgian exterior with early Victorian bay windows. Inside, the style is hard to miss: Russian red in the bar with a picture of Gorbachev on the wall; then period green in the restaurant, where gilt-framed oils hang by the score. Potter about and find original tiles and ironwork, parquet floors and stained glass windows; the zinc-topped bar was made from a Methodist pulpit. There's a conservatory bistro that opens onto a pretty terrace for strong coffee, homemade quiche and posh burgers. Bedrooms above are soundproofed and come with smart beds, white linen, travertine bathrooms and attractive prices; some interconnect, others in the eaves have the odd beam. Delicious food waits downstairs, perhaps calamari with chorizo and fennel, chicken with braised shallots, toffee apple and blackberry crumble. A great little base.

Rooms	6 doubles, 2 twin/doubles: £98–£155.
Meals	Lunch from £4.95. Light bites from £7.45. Dinner, 3 courses, about £30.
Closed	Christmas Day.
Directions	M4 west, then A40 past St Clears. After 10 miles, south on A478 for Narberth. On High Street by clock tower.

Dominic Swingler
32 Townhouse
32 High Street,
Narberth, SA67 7AS

Tel	+44 (0)1834 218338
Email	info@32townhouse.com
Web	www.32townhouse.com

Penally Abbey

This beautifully refurbished country-house hotel sits high on the hill with long views over Carmarthen Bay. Outside, there's a small courtyard, then five acres of lawns and woodland, where bluebells run riot in spring. Inside, chic interiors come with cool colours, painted panelling, parquet flooring and the odd Doric column. There's an elegant bar in deep charcoal with fine art on the walls, then a big drawing room with an open fire and huge sea views. Big windows in the main house flood the rooms with light, while doors in the sunroom open onto a gravelled terrace, where you can read the papers, dig into afternoon tea, or fall asleep in the sun. Bedrooms have a stunning new look: off-white walls, beautiful beds, crisp white linen, elegant fabrics. Big rooms in the main house have vast windows to frame the view, all have sublime white marble bathrooms. You eat in style in the restaurant – period colours, grand chandelier – perhaps steamed clams with lemon and ginger, chicken with chestnuts and a pear tarte tatin, a dark chocolate torte with pistachio ice cream. There's fine coastal walking, too.

Rooms	3 doubles, 6 twin/doubles, 2 four-posters: £130-£260. Dinner, B&B from £90 p.p.
Meals	Lunch from £5. Dinner, 3 courses, £30-£35. Sunday lunch from £14.95.
Closed	January.
Directions	From Tenby A4139 for Pembroke. Right into Penally after 1.5 miles. Hotel signed above village green. Train station 5-mins walk.

Melanie & Lucas Boissevain
Penally Abbey
Penally,
Tenby, SA70 7PY

Tel	+44 (0)1834 843033
Email	info@penally-abbey.com
Web	www.penally-abbey.com

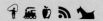

Stackpole Inn

This lovely inn sits in a pretty village that's marooned in beautiful country. It's a few miles back from the sea, with Barafundle Bay – one of the finest beaches in Britain – a short walk away. You can pick up the coastal path, too, and follow it round past Stackpole Quay and St Govan's Chapel to the cliffs at Linney Head, then the surfers at Freshwater West. It's pure heaven, one of those sleepy areas you drop into for a couple of days and hardly use your car. As for the Stackpole, it's a great little base – stylish and welcoming with tasty rustic food, perhaps deep-fried whitebait, rib of local beef, almond and hazelnut tart. Outside, the pub is drenched in honeysuckle and there's a small garden to the front for a drop of Welsh ale in summer. Inside, you find low wooden ceilings, exposed stone walls, a hard-working wood-burner and four hand pumps at the slate bar. Super bedrooms have comfy beds, stripped floors, seaside colours and excellent bathrooms. All have sofabeds, two have velux windows for star gazing. Dogs and children are very welcome.

Rooms	2 twin/doubles: £90. 2 family rooms for 4: £90-£120. Singles from £60.
Meals	Lunch from £5. Dinner, 3 courses, £25-£30. Sunday lunch, 3 courses, £18.95.
Closed	Rarely.
Directions	B4319 south from Pembroke for 3 miles, then left for Stackpole. Through Stackpole Cheriton, up hill, right at T-junction. On right.

Gary & Becky Evans
Stackpole Inn
Stackpole,
Pembroke, SA71 5DF

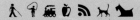

Tel +44 (0)1646 672324
Email info@stackpoleinn.co.uk
Web www.stackpoleinn.co.uk

Crug Glas

St Davids is one of the most magical places in Britain. It sits in Pembroke's national park, has an imperious 12th-century cathedral, and is surrounded by magnificent coastline that's dotted with cliffs and vast sandy beaches. As for Janet's wonderful retreat, it's part chic hotel, part farmhouse B&B, stylish yet personal, a great place to stay. The house dates from 1120 and sits in 600 acres of arable and grazing land (they rear cattle and grow cereals). Outside, you find lawns and a small copse sprinkled with bluebells, then field and sky, and that's about it. Inside, there's an honesty bar in the sitting room and a Welsh dresser in the dining room, where Janet serves delicious food: homemade soups, home-reared beef, chocolate mousse with clotted cream. Fancy bedrooms are the big surprise: a vast four-poster, the odd copper bath, old armoires, beautiful fabrics. All have robes in gorgeous bathrooms, bigger rooms come with sofas, one room occupies most of the top floor. Two rooms in an old barn have exposed timbers and underfloor heating. The coast is about five fields to the west.

Rooms	5 doubles, 2 twin/doubles: £150-£190. Singles from £95.
Meals	Lunch, 2 courses, from £18. Dinner, 3 courses, £25-£30. Sunday lunch £22.50. Afternoon tea from £12.50.
Closed	22-27 December.
Directions	South from Fishguard on A487. Through Croes-goch, then signed right after 2 miles.

Janet & Perkin Evans
Crug Glas
Solva,
Haverfordwest, SA62 6XX

Tel +44 (0)1348 831302
Email janet@crugglas.plus.com
Web www.crug-glas.co.uk

Sawday's British Hotel Awards 2018

National Treasure

The Manor Town House

Fishguard is quirky – arty and friendly with a folk festival in May and a jazz festival in August. You'll find great coastal walks, sandy beaches and magical St Davids a few miles south. In short, it's much more than an overnight stop on your way to Ireland and, with a happy vibe waiting at the Manor Town House, hard to resist. Chris and Helen escaped London and have taken to their new world like ducks to water. Inside, you're greeted by a couple of gorgeous sitting rooms – stripped floorboards, cool colours, local art, and crackling fires in winter. One has an honesty bar, you get fresh flowers, lots of books, and comfy sofas from which to plan your day. Homely bedrooms have lots of charm: bold colours, beautiful fabrics, the odd antique, super-comfy beds. Those at the back have sea views, perhaps a sofa or a padded window seat, while compact bathrooms do the trick. Breakfast is a treat, there's a garden for afternoon tea overlooking the harbour, and it's a one-minute stroll up the road to Bar 5 for cocktails and The Lounge at No.3 for the best food in town. Pembrokeshire awaits. Brilliant. *Minimum stay: 2 nights at weekends in summer.*

Rooms	2 doubles, 3 twin/doubles: £95-£125. 1 single: £75-£95. Extra bed/sofabed £20 p.p.p.n.
Meals	Local restaurants within 100m. Packed lunches £8.50.
Closed	23-27 December.
Directions	M4 west, A48 west, A40 north, then A487 into town. Right at roundabout and on left. Parking close by.

Chris & Helen Sheldon
The Manor Town House
11 Main Street,
Fishguard, SA65 9HG

Tel +44 (0)1348 873260
Email enquiries@manortownhouse.com
Web www.manortownhouse.com

Llys Meddyg

This beautiful small hotel has a little bit of everything: chic bedrooms that pack a punch, a cellar bar for cocktails before dinner, a stylish restaurant for delicious local food. In summer you decant into the garden, where a café/bistro opens up for coffee and cake or pizza from a wood-fired oven. There's a smokehouse out here, too, then a yurt tucked away around the corner that comes with a wood-burner and a hot tub. It's an intimate place, where staff stop to chat, where locals pop in for a coffee, where you can take home a jar of quince jelly made by Ed's mum. Food lies at the heart of the affair and you eat in a stylish restaurant with Welsh art on the walls, perhaps home-smoked salmon, slow-cook lamb, caramelised pear with blue-cheese ice-cream. Beautiful bedrooms are scattered about. Those in the main house have cool colours, vast beds and fancy bathrooms. Those in the mews have a rustic feel and garden views; all have fluffy bath robes. Pembrokeshire's coastal path waits for windswept cliffs and sandy beaches. Don't miss St Davids or the Preseli Hills. Dogs are very welcome. *Minimum stay: 2 nights at weekends.*

Rooms	8 doubles: £100-£180. 1 yurt for 2: £100-£120. Singles from £85.
Meals	Lunch from £7. Dinner from £14.
Closed	Rarely.
Directions	East from Fishguard on A487. On left in Newport towards eastern edge of town.

Louise & Edward Sykes
Llys Meddyg
East Street,
Newport, SA42 0SY

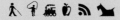

Tel +44 (0)1239 820008
Email info@llysmeddyg.com
Web www.llysmeddyg.com

Gliffaes Hotel

A charming country-house hotel that towers above the river Usk as it pours through the valley below. In summer, doors open onto a large terrace, where you can sit in the sun and soak up the view – red kites circle above, sheep graze beyond. You're in 35 peaceful acres of formal lawns and mature woodland. Inside, interiors pack a punch. Afternoon tea 'on the house' is served every day in the panelled sitting room – family portraits hang on the wall, logs crackle in the grandest fireplace. This is a well-known fishing hotel and fishermen often gather in the bar for a quick drink and a tall tale. Eventually, they spin into the restaurant and dig into lovely seasonal food (the hotel is part of the Slow Food Movement), perhaps goat's cheese soufflé, fillet of halibut, lemon tart with passion fruit sorbet. Country-house bedrooms wait above. Expect smart fabrics, warm colours, crisp linen, fresh flowers. Several have river views, a couple have small balconies, one has a claw-foot bath that overlooks the front lawn. Outside, beautiful gardens include a small arboretum of specimen trees. Wonderful. *Minimum stay: 2 nights at weekends.*

Rooms	19 twin/doubles: £112-£265. 4 singles: £100. Dinner, B&B from £90 p.p.
Meals	Light lunches from £5. Dinner, 3 courses, £42. Sunday lunch £22-£29.
Closed	January.
Directions	From Crickhowell, A40 west for 2.5 miles. Signed left and on left after 1 mile.

James & Susie Suter
Gliffaes Hotel
Gliffaes Road,
Crickhowell, NP8 1RH

Tel	+44 (0)1874 730371
Email	calls@gliffaeshotel.com
Web	www.gliffaeshotel.com

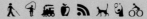

The Felin Fach Griffin

So what are the ingredients of one of the loveliest inns in the land? Well, it's quirky, homespun, and thrives on a mix of relaxed informality and colourful style. The bar resembles the sitting room of a hip country house, with timber frames, cool tunes and comfy sofas in front of the fire. Painted stone walls come in blocks of colour and you dine informally in the white-walled restaurant, with stock pots simmering on an Aga. The food is excellent, perhaps Portland crab, boeuf Bourguignon, chocolate mousse with mascarpone; much of what you eat comes from a half-acre kitchen garden, with meat and game from the hills around you. Pretty bedrooms have colour and style. Expect comfy beds and crisp linen, good bathrooms with fluffy towels, Roberts radios and a smattering of books (but no TV unless you ask). Breakfast is a leisurely treat: read the morning papers, make your own toast, scoff the full Welsh works. A road passes outside, but quietly at night, while lanes lead into the hills, so come to walk, ride, bike, canoe. Hay is close for books galore. Don't miss excellent off-season deals.

Rooms	7 doubles, 3 twin/doubles, 1 four-poster: £135-£175. 1 family room for 3: £175. Dinner, B&B £190-£230 (based on double occupancy).
Meals	Lunch from £7. Dinner, 3 courses, about £30. Sunday lunch from £20.
Closed	Christmas Eve & Day (evening). 4 days in Jan.
Directions	From Brecon A470 north to Felin Fach (4.5 miles). On left.

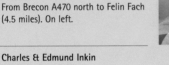

Charles & Edmund Inkin
The Felin Fach Griffin
Felin Fach,
Brecon, LD3 0UB

Tel +44 (0)1874 620111
Email enquiries@felinfachgriffin.co.uk
Web www.felinfachgriffin.co.uk

Lake Country House & Spa

An elegant country-house hotel lost in beautiful hills with deep peace all around. Fifty acres of lawns, lakes and ancient woodland wrap around you, there's a spa with treatment rooms, an indoor pool and a tennis court by the lake. You can sit in a hot tub and watch guests fish for their supper, try your luck on the nine-hole golf course, saddle up nearby and take to the hills. Come home to afternoon tea in the old-school drawing room, where an archipelago of rugs warms a brightly polished wood floor and chandeliers hang from the ceiling. The hotel opened over a hundred years ago; leather-bound fishing logs date to 1894. A feel of the 1920s lingers. Fires come to life in front of your eyes, grand pianos and grandfather clocks sing their songs, snooker balls knock about in the distance. Dinner is a treat, perhaps crab with wasabi ice cream, duck with fennel and honey, blood orange cheesecake with chocolate sorbet. Lovely rooms wait. Most are suites: those in the house are warmly traditional, those in the lodge softly contemporary. The London train takes four hours and stops in the village.

Rooms	6 twin/doubles: £195. 24 suites for 2: £240-£260. Singles from £145. Dinner, B&B (min. 2 nights) from £122.50 p.p.
Meals	Lunch, 3 courses, £22.50. Dinner, 4 courses, £38.50.
Closed	Never.
Directions	From Builth Wells A483 west for 7 miles to Garth. Signed from village.

Jean-Pierre Mifsud
Lake Country House & Spa
Llangammarch Wells, LD4 4BS

Tel +44 (0)1591 620202
Email info@lakecountryhouse.co.uk
Web www.lakecountryhouse.co.uk

Milebrook House Hotel

An old-school, country-house hotel with three acres of gardens that run down to the river Teme. You'll find Wales on one side and England on the other, so bring your wellies and wade across; the walking is magnificent. The house was once home to writer Wilfred Thesiger; his friend, Haile Selassie, visited in the 1920s. These days it's informally run by three generations of the Marsden family with Beryl and Rodney leading the way. Step inside and enter a world that's rooted in a delightful past: clocks tick, cats snooze, fires crackle, the odd champagne cork escapes its bondage. Beautiful art hangs on the walls, the sitting room is stuffed with books, the bar comes in country-house style, and there's food to reckon with in the dining room, perhaps local pigeon with caramelised apple, slow-roasted shoulder of Welsh lamb, apple crumble and butterscotch sundae. A kitchen garden supplies much for the table. You can fish, spot deer in the woods, play croquet on the lawn. Red kite, moorhens, kingfishers and herons live in the valley. Homely bedrooms wait. Presteigne and Ludlow are close.

Rooms	5 doubles, 5 twins: £144. 1 family room for 3: £172. Singles from £87.50. Dinner, B&B from £102.50 p.p.
Meals	Lunch, 2 courses, £14.95 (not Mon). Dinner, 3 courses, £30-£35. Sunday lunch from £17.
Closed	Rarely.
Directions	From Ludlow A49 north, then left at Bromfield on A4113 towards Knighton for 10 miles. Hotel on right.

Rodney, Beryl & Joanne Marsden
Milebrook House Hotel
Stanage, Knighton, LD7 1LT
Tel +44 (0)1547 528632
Email hotel@milebrookhouse.co.uk
Web www.milebrookhouse.co.uk

Photo: The Zetter Townhouse, entry 122

Wheelchair-accessible

At least one bedroom and bathroom accessible for wheelchair users. Phone for details.

England

Bath & N.E. Somerset 1
Berkshire 8
Cornwall 16 • 17 • 18 • 19 • 26 • 27 • 30 • 31
Cumbria 34 • 35 • 37 • 40 • 45
Devon 52 • 53 • 54 • 57 • 58 • 61 • 63
Dorset 75 • 79
Durham 81 • 82
Essex 83 • 86
Gloucestershire 90
Hampshire 94 • 96
Herefordshire 98 • 99
Isle of Wight 102
Kent 107 • 108
Lancashire 110
London 122
Norfolk 128 • 129 • 130 • 132
Northumberland 137 • 138
Nottinghamshire 139 • 140
Oxfordshire 141 • 142 • 144 • 146
Rutland 150 • 151
Somerset 161
Suffolk 168 • 169 • 171 • 176 • 178
Sussex 179 • 183
Warwickshire 192
Wiltshire 197
Yorkshire 201 • 203 • 205 • 206 • 207 • 211

Scotland

Argyll & Bute 219 • 220
Highland 236
Isle of Skye 240
Perth & Kinross 244 • 248
Scottish Borders 251

Wales

Ceredigion 260
Denbighshire 263
Gwynedd 264
Pembrokeshire 272
Powys 277 • 279 • 280

Children of all ages welcome

These owners have told us that they welcome children of all ages. Please note cots and highchairs may not necessarily be available.

England

Bath & N.E. Somerset 1 • 2 • 3 • 4 • 5 • 6
Berkshire 7 • 8
Brighton & Hove 11
Bristol 12 • 13
Cambridgeshire 14 • 15 •
Cornwall 16 • 17 • 19 • 22 • 23 • 24 • 25 • 26 • 28 • 29 • 30 • 31 • 33
Cumbria 34 • 35 • 36 • 37 • 40 • 42 • 45 • 46 • 47 • 48 • 49
Derbyshire 50
Devon 52 • 54 • 55 • 56 • 57 • 58 • 60 • 63 • 64 • 65 • 67
Dorset 68 • 69 • 71 • 72 • 74 • 75 • 76 • 77 • 78 • 79 • 80
Durham 81 • 82
Essex 83 • 84 • 85 • 86
Gloucestershire 87 • 88 • 89 • 90 • 91
Hampshire 92 • 93 • 95 • 96
Herefordshire 97 • 98 • 99 • 101

Kent 103 • 104 • 105 • 106 • 107 • 108
Lancashire 110 • 111
Lincolnshire 112 • 113
London 114 • 115 • 117 • 119 • 120 • 121
London 122 • 123 • 124 • 125
Norfolk 126 • 127 • 128 • 129 • 130 • 131 • 132 • 133 • 134 • 135 • 136
Northumberland 137 • 138
Nottinghamshire 139 • 140
Oxfordshire 141 • 142 • 143 • 144 • 145 • 146 • 147 • 148
Rutland 150 • 151
Shropshire 153 • 154 • 155 • 157
Somerset 158 • 159 • 160 • 162 • 164 • 166
Suffolk 168 • 169 • 171 • 172 • 173 • 174 • 176 • 177 • 178
Sussex 179 • 180 • 181 • 182 • 183 • 187 • 188
Warwickshire 191 • 192
Wiltshire 193 • 194 • 195 • 197 • 198 • 199
Worcestershire 200
Yorkshire 201 • 203 • 204 • 205 • 206 • 207 • 208 • 211

Channel Islands

Alderney 212
Guernsey 213
Jersey 215

Scotland

Argyll & Bute 216 • 218 • 219 • 220 • 221
Dumfries & Galloway 223 • 224 • 225
East Lothian 226
Edinburgh 227 • 228 • 230 • 231
Fife 232
Glasgow 233
Highland 234 • 236 • 237
Isle of Skye 240
Perth & Kinross 242 • 243 • 244 • 245 • 246 • 250
Scottish Borders 251 • 253
Western Isles 254

Wales

Carmarthenshire 255 • 257
Ceredigion 259 • 260
Denbighshire 263
Gwynedd 265 • 266
Monmouthshire 270
Pembrokeshire 272 • 273 • 275 • 276
Powys 277 • 278 • 279

Pets

Pets welcome; please let the owner know if you want to bring pets.

England

Bath & N.E. Somerset 1 • 2 • 3
Berkshire 7
Bristol 12
Cambridgeshire 15
Cornwall 16 • 17 • 18 • 19 • 22 • 23 • 24 • 25 • 26 • 28 • 31
Cumbria 35 • 36 • 37 • 38 • 40 • 45 • 47 • 48 • 49
Derbyshire 51
Devon 52 • 54 • 55 • 56 • 57 • 58 • 60 • 62 • 63 • 64 • 65 • 67
Dorset 68 • 70 • 71 • 72 • 75 • 77 • 79
Durham 81
Essex 83 • 85 • 86
Gloucestershire 87 • 88 • 91
Hampshire 92 • 95
Herefordshire 97 • 99 • 100 •

101
Kent 107
Lancashire 111
Lincolnshire 112 • 113
London 115 • 124
Norfolk 126 • 127 • 128 • 129 • 130 • 131 • 132 • 133 • 135 • 136
Northumberland 138
Nottinghamshire 139 • 140
Oxfordshire 142 • 144 • 146
Rutland 150 • 151
Shropshire 152 • 153 • 154 • 157
Somerset 160 • 163 • 166 • 167
Suffolk 168 • 169 • 170 • 171 • 173 • 178
Sussex 179 • 187 • 189 • 190
Wiltshire 193 • 197 • 199
Worcestershire 200
Yorkshire 203 • 204 • 205 • 206 • 207 • 211

Channel Islands
Guernsey 213 • 214

Scotland
Argyll & Bute 216 • 217 • 218 • 219 • 220 • 221
Dumfries & Galloway 223 • 224 • 225
Fife 232
Highland 234 • 235 • 236 • 238
Isle of Skye 240
Perth & Kinross 243 • 244 • 245 • 247 • 250
Scottish Borders 251 • 252
Western Isles 254

Wales
Carmarthenshire 256 • 257
Ceredigion 259 • 260
Denbighshire 263
Gwynedd 264 • 265 • 267
Monmouthshire 270
Pembrokeshire 272 • 274 • 276
Powys 278 • 279

Pool
Swimming pool on the premises; use may be by arrangement.

England
Bath & N.E. Somerset 6
Berkshire 7
Bristol 12 • 13
Cornwall 17 • 18 • 19 • 26 • 30
Cumbria 36 • 37 • 44
Devon 67
Essex 83
Hampshire 96
Herefordshire 99
Norfolk 128 • 132
Rutland 151
Sussex 179
Wiltshire 193

Channel Islands
Guernsey 213

Wales
Powys 279

Bike
Bikes on the premises to hire or borrow.

England
Cornwall 16 • 24
Cumbria 34 • 35 • 39 • 42
Devon 61 • 63
Dorset 73 • 77
Essex 84
Gloucestershire 91

Hampshire 93 • 96
Isle of Wight 102
London 122
Norfolk 136
Oxfordshire 141 • 142
Rutland 151
Shropshire 154
Somerset 163 • 166
Suffolk 171 • 174
Sussex 179 • 190
Yorkshire 201 • 206 • 208

Scotland
Argyll & Bute 218 • 219 • 220 • 221
Dumfries & Galloway 223 • 225
Edinburgh 228
Highland 236 • 238
Perth & Kinross 245

Wales
Ceredigion 260 •
Powys 277 •

Tennis

Tennis court on the premises; use may be by arrangement.

England
Bath & N.E. Somerset 6
Berkshire 7
Cornwall 17 • 26
Cumbria 34 • 35
Devon 61
Dorset 79
Essex 83
Hampshire 96
Isle of Wight 102
Kent 103
Norfolk 128
Rutland 151
Sussex 179
Worcestershire 200
Yorkshire 208

Channel Islands
Guernsey 213

Scotland
Argyll & Bute 221

Wales
Powys 277 • 279

Public transport

These places are within 10 miles of a bus/train station and owner can arrange collection, with notice.

England
Bath & N.E. Somerset 1 • 2 • 3 • 5 • 6
Berkshire 7 • 8
Brighton & Hove 9 • 10 • 11
Bristol 12
Cambridgeshire 14 • 15
Cornwall 16 • 18 • 19 • 20 • 21 • 24 • 25 • 27 • 28 • 31 • 32 • 33
Cumbria 34 • 35 • 36 • 37 • 39 • 40 • 42 • 43 • 44 • 45 • 46 • 49
Derbyshire 50 • 51
Devon 54 • 55 • 58 • 60 • 63 • 64 • 65 • 66
Dorset 68 • 69 • 71 • 72 • 73 • 74 • 75 • 76 • 78 • 79 • 80
Durham 81 • 82
Essex 83 • 84 • 85 • 86
Gloucestershire 87 • 88 • 89 • 91
Hampshire 92 • 93 • 94 • 95 • 96

Herefordshire 97 • 98 • 99
Isle of Wight 102
Kent 103 • 104 • 105 • 106 • 107 • 108 • 109
Lancashire 110 • 111
Lincolnshire 112 • 113
London 114 • 115 • 117 • 118 • 119 • 120 • 121 • 122 • 123 • 124 • 125
Norfolk 126 • 127 • 128 • 129 • 131 • 133 • 134 • 136
Northumberland 137 • 138
Nottinghamshire 139 • 140
Oxfordshire 141 • 142 • 143 • 144 • 145 • 146 • 148 • 149
Rutland 151
Shropshire 152 • 153 • 154 • 155
Somerset 159 • 160 • 161 • 163 • 166 • 167
Suffolk 168 • 169 • 170 • 171 • 172 • 173 • 174 • 176 • 177 • 178
Sussex 179 • 181 • 182 • 183 • 184 • 186 • 187 • 188 • 189 • 190
Warwickshire 191
Wiltshire 194 • 195 • 196 • 197 • 198
Yorkshire 201 • 202 • 203 • 204 • 206 • 208 • 210 • 211

Channel Islands

Guernsey 214
Jersey 215

Scotland

Argyll & Bute 217 • 219 • 221
Dumfries & Galloway 224 • 225
East Lothian 226
Edinburgh 227 • 228 • 229 • 230 • 231
Glasgow 233
Highland 234 • 236 • 237 • 238
Isle of Skye 240
Moray 241
Perth & Kinross 242 • 245 • 246 • 247 • 248 • 249 • 250
Scottish Borders 252 • 253

Wales

Carmarthenshire 257
Ceredigion 259 • 260
Conwy 261 • 262
Denbighshire 263
Gwynedd 264 • 265 • 266 • 267 • 268
Monmouthshire 270
Pembrokeshire 272 • 273 • 275 • 276
Powys 277 • 279 • 280

Sawday's
Discover our inspected and selected pubs – great gardens, cosy firesides, pints of real ale and pies worth writing home about
sawdays.co.uk/eatdrink
SWYNNERTON
STOUT

Alastair Sawday has been publishing books for over 20 years, finding Special Places to Stay in Britain and abroad. All our properties are inspected by us and are chosen for their charm and individuality. And there are many more to explore on our perennially popular website: www.sawdays.co.uk. You can buy any of our books at a reader discount of 25%* on the RRP.

List of titles:	RRP	Discount price
British Bed & Breakfast	£15.99	£11.99
British Hotels and Inns	£15.99	£11.99
Pubs & Inns of England & Wales	£15.99	£11.99
Dog-friendly Breaks in Britain	£14.99	£11.24
French Bed & Breakfast	£15.99	£11.99
French Châteaux & Hotels	£15.99	£11.99
Italy	£15.99	£11.99

*postage and packaging is added to each order

How to order:

You can order online at: www.sawdays.co.uk/bookshop/
or call: +44 (0)117 204 7810

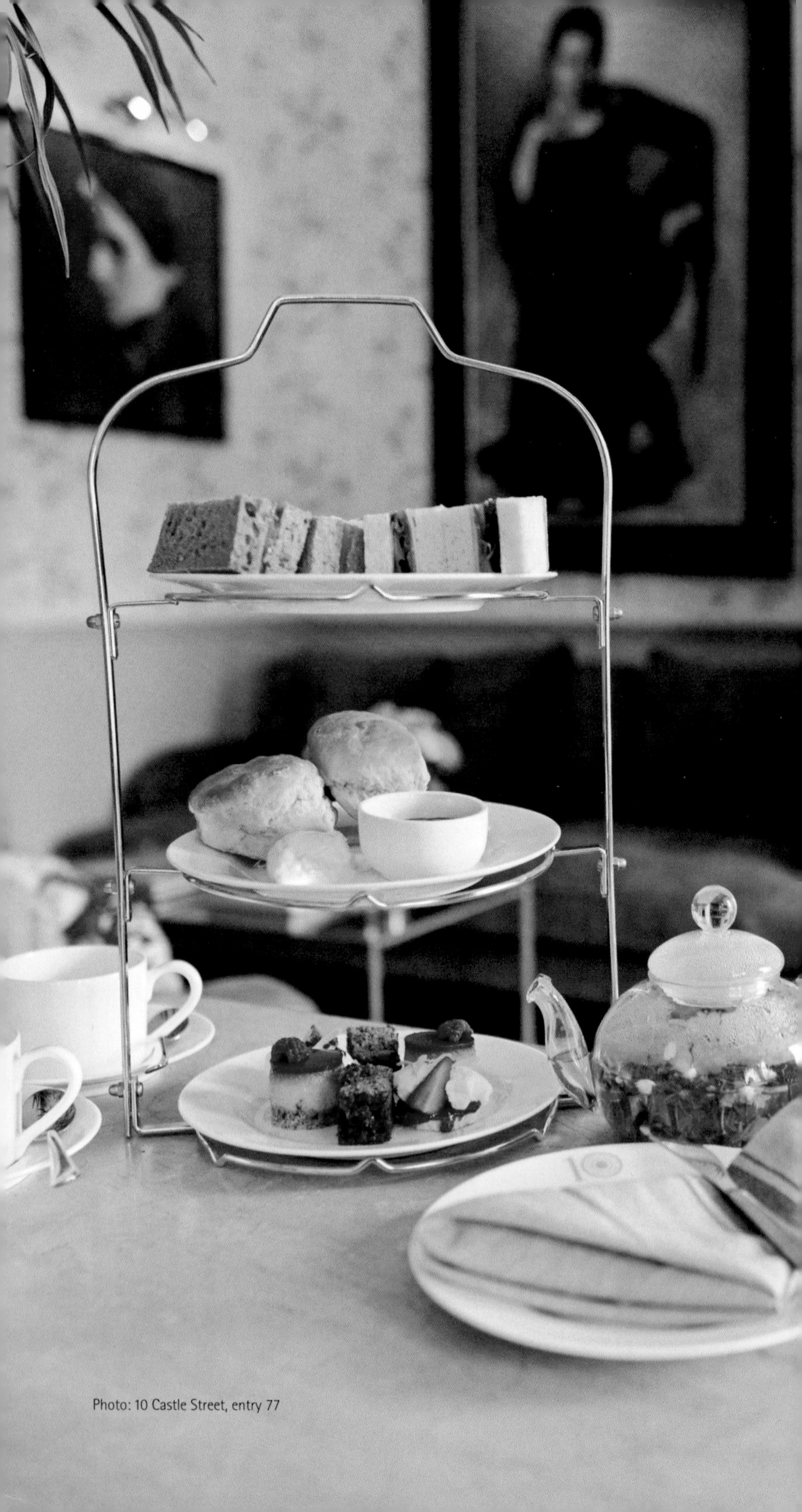

Photo: 10 Castle Street, entry 77

10 Castle Street	77
15 Glasgow	233
21212	229
23 Mayfield	227
32 Townhouse	271
94DR	228
Abbey Hotel	1
Albion House	107
Alexandra Hotel & Restaurant	68
Another Place – The Lake	37
Ardeonaig Hotel	245
Artist Residence Brighton	9
Artist Residence London	118
Artist Residence Oxfordshire	145
Artist Residence Penzance	25
Askham Hall	36
Augill Castle	34
Aynsome Manor Hotel	48
Backwell House	13
Barley Bree	242
Bath Paradise House Hotel	5
Bay Hotel	27
Bayards Cove Inn	64
Bedruthan Hotel & Spa	17
Belle Tout Lighthouse	185
Blue Hayes Private Hotel	20
Borrowdale Gates	40
Bridge House Hotel	71
brightonwave	10
Bristol Harbour Hotel	12
Brocco on the Park	201
Brooks Country House	99
Broom House at Egton Bridge	210
Burgh Island Hotel	61
Captain's Club Hotel and Spa	75
Castle House	98
Castleman Hotel & Restaurant	78
Cavendish Hotel	50
Cavens	223
Cedar Manor Hotel	42
Chalk & Cheese	127
Chapel House	24
Chewton Glen	96
Cley Windmill	133
Cliveden House	7
Combe Grove Hotel	6
Congham Hall	128
Coruisk House	239
Craigatin House & Courtyard	248
Cringletie House	251
Cross Lane House	167
Crug Glas	274
Culdearn House	241
Daisybank Cottage Boutique B&B	94
Doune Knoydart	237
Drakes	11
Driftwood Hotel	29
Dunalastair Hotel Suites	246
Escape Boutique B&B	261
Estbek House	209
Europa House	114
Gilpin Hotel	43
Gilpin Lake House & Spa	44
Glazebrook House Hotel	59

Glenisle Hotel 222
Gliffaes Hotel 277
Halfway Bridge Inn 180
Hambleton Hall Hotel & Restaurant 151
Hart's Nottingham 139
Hell Bay 26
Hever Castle Luxury Bed & Breakfast 103
Hillside 102
Hotel Ziggurat 214
Houndgate Townhouse 82
Howard's House 199
Howtown Hotel 38
Hurley House Hotel 8
Jeake's House 189
Kesgrave Hall 171
Kilcamb Lodge Hotel & Restaurant 238
Killiecrankie House Hotel 250
Knockendarroch Hotel & Restaurant 249
Knockinaam Lodge 224
Lake Country House & Spa 279
Langar Hall 140
Letham House 226
Lewtrenchard Manor 57
Lime Tree Hotel 119
Linthwaite House 45
Little Barwick House 163
Littleton Lodge 196
Llwyndû Farmhouse 266
Llys Meddyg 276
Lord Poulett Arms 164
Loyton Lodge 52
Luttrell Arms 166
Mackay's Rooms 234
Maison Talbooth 83
Meeson Hall 156
Mhor 84 243
Milebrook House Hotel 280
Mill End 56
Monachyle Mhor 244
Nanteos Mansion 260
No. 131 89
No. 15 Great Pulteney 2
No. 38 The Park 88
Northcote Manor 54
Old Bank Hotel 141
Old Downton Lodge 152
Old Parsonage Hotel 142
Osborne House 262
Park House Hotel & Spa 179
Pen-y-Dyffryn Country Hotel 154
Penally Abbey 272
Penbontbren 259
Penmaenuchaf Hall 267
Plantation House 60
Plas Bodegroes 265
Plas Dinas Country House 264
Plumber Manor 79
Read's Restaurant with Rooms 109
Rose & Crown 81
Sands Hotel Margate 108
Saracens Head 135
Scarista House 254
Scourie Hotel 235
Sebastian's 155

Sidmouth Harbour Hotel 67
Six Brunton Place 230
South Sands Hotel 63
Southernhay House 66
Stackpole Inn 273
Strand House 187
Strattons 126
Swain House 165
Talland Bay Hotel 33
Temple Lodge Club 116
The Airds Hotel & Restaurant 219
The Allanton Inn 253
The Anchor 168
The Angel Inn 205
The Barrow House 105
The Beckford Arms 198
The Bell Alderminster 191
The Bell at Skenfrith 270
The Bildeston Crown 175
The Black Swan 35
The Blakeney Hotel 132
The Bridge House 100
The Bridge Inn at Ratho 231
The Bull 182
The Bull Hotel 69
The Burgoyne Hotel 207
The Cartford Inn 110
The Cary Arms at Babbacombe Bay 65
The Castle Hotel 153
The Coach House at Middleton Lodge 208
The Collingwood Arms Hotel 137
The Colonsay 221
The Cors 258
The Cottage in the Wood 39
The Crab & Lobster 181
The Creggans Inn 216
The Crown 176
The Crown & Castle 170
The Crown at Woodbridge 172
The Crown Inn 14
The Devonshire Arms 162
The Dolaucothi Arms 255
The Eltermere Inn 41
The Feathered Nest Country Inn 149
The Feathers Hotel 144
The Felin Fach Griffin 278
The Fish Hotel 200
The Fritton Arms 136
The Gallivant 190
The George in Rye 188
The Georgian House, Alderney 212
The Georgian House, London 117
The Globe Inn at Wells-next-the-Sea 131
The Great House 174
The Greyhound 72
The Griffin Inn 183
The Gurnard's Head 22
The Hand at Llanarmon 263
The Haughmond 157
The Henley Hotel 62
The Horn of Plenty 58
The Hoste 129
The Howard Arms 192
The Inn at Loch Tummel 247

The Inn at Whitewell 111
The Kings 76
The Kings Head 134
The Kings Head Inn 148
The Lamb at Hindon 197
The Lamb Inn 55
The Levin Hotel 120
The Manor at Sway 95
The Manor House 217
The Manor Town House 275
The Masons Arms 47
The Master Builder's House Hotel 92
The Methuen Arms 194
The Milk House 104
The Mistley Thorn 85
The Montagu Arms 93
The Northgate 177
The Old Bridge Hotel 15
The Old Coastguard 23
The Old Court House 215
The Old Quay House Hotel 32
The Old Rectory 186
The Old Rectory Hotel Exmoor 53
The Old Stocks Inn 87
The Olive Branch 150
The One Tun Pub & Rooms 121
The Packhorse Inn 178
The Parisi Hotel 202
The Peacock at Rowsley 51
The Pheasant Inn 138
The Pier at Harwich 86
The Pierhouse 218
The Pilgrims Restaurant with Rooms 161
The Portobello Hotel 115
The Priory Hotel 73
The Punch Bowl Inn 46
The Queensberry Hotel 4
The Rectory Hotel 193
The Relish 106
The Rosevine 30
The Scarlet 18
The Seafood Restaurant 16
The Seaside Boarding House 70
The Shaven Crown 146
The Ship Inn 232
The St Mawes Hotel 28
The Stapleton Arms 80
The Sun Inn, Carnforth 49
The Sun Inn, Colchester 84
The Swan at Lavenham Hotel & Spa 173
The Swan, Burford 147
The Swan, Wedmore 159
The Talbot Hotel 211
The Talbot Inn at Mells 158
The Tommyfield 123
The Torridon 236
The Traddock 206
The Verzon 97
The Victoria Inn 124
The White Bear Hotel 204
The White Hart 160
The White Horse 130
The Whitebrook 269
The William Cecil 113

The Zetter Townhouse 122
Three Choirs Vineyards 90
Timbrell's Yard 195
Tiroran House 220
Trevalsa Court Hotel 31
Trevose Harbour House 21
Trigony House Hotel 225
Tudor Farmhouse Hotel 91
Tulse Hill Hotel 125
Turl Street Kitchen
& Tower House Rooms 143
Ty Mawr Country Hotel 256
Urban Beach Hotel 74
Viewfield House Hotel 240
Villa at Henrietta Park 3
Washingborough Hall 112
Watergate Bay Hotel 19
Wentworth Hotel 169
West Park Hotel 203
White House Hotel 213
Wilton Court Restaurant with Rooms 101
Windlestraw 252
Wingrove House 184
Wright's Food Emporium 257
Y Meirionnydd 268

Photo: Littleton Lodge, entry 196

Photo: Another Place – The Lake, entry 37

Abergavenny	270
Aberystwyth	260
Acharacle	238
Aldeburgh	169
Alderney	212
Ambleside	41
Appin	218, 219
Askham	36
Bakewell	50
Barmouth	266
Barnard Castle	81
Barnstable	53
Bath	1-6
Beachy Head	185
Beaminster	71
Bildeston	175
Bishops Castle	153
Blanford Forum	78
Bournemouth	74
Bradford-on-Avon	195
Brancaster Staithe	130
Brechfa	256
Brecon	278
Bridport	69
Brighton	9-11
Bristol	12, 13
Broadway	200
Brockenhurst	92-94
Burford	147
Burton Bradstock	70
Bury St Edmunds	177
By Achnasheen	236
By Duns	253
Caernarfon	264
Cairndow	216
Carnforth	49
Castle Cary	161
Cheltenham	88, 89
Chichester	181
Chipping Norton	148, 149
Christchurch	75, 76
Clearwell	91
Clitheroe	111
Cornhill-on-Tweed	137
Corsham	194
Cranborne	77
Cranbrook	104
Crediton	55
Crickhowell	277
Darlington	82
Dartmouth	64
Dedham	83, 84,
Devizes	196
Dolgellau	267, 288
Dorchester	72
Dumfries	223
Dunster	166
Edenbridge	103
Edinburgh	227-230
Egerton	105
Elgol	239
Elie	232
Exeter	66
Faversham	109
Fishguard	275
Folkestone	106
Fowey	32
Frome	158
Gillingham	80
Glasgow	233

Grange-over-Sands 47, 48
Grantown on Spey 241
Great Yarmouth 136
Haddington 226
Harrogate 203
Harwich 86
Hassocks 182
Hastings 186
Haverfordwest 274
Helston 27
Hereford 98
Herm Island 213
Hexham 138
Hinton St George 164
Holt 132-134
Huntingdon 15
Hurley 8
Ilmington 192
Ipswich 171
Isle of Arran 222
Isle of Colonsay 221
Isle of Harris 254
Isle of Mull 220
Isles of Scilly 26
Ivybridge 60
Kendal 46
Kennington 123
Keswick 39, 40
King's Lynn 127-129
Kingsbridge 61, 62
Kinloch Rannoch 246
Kirkby Stephen 34, 35
Knighton 280
Lairg 234, 235
Langport 162
Laugharne 258
Lavenham 173, 174
Ledbury 97
Llanarthne 257
Llandudno 261, 262
Llandysul 259
Llangammarch Wells 279
Llangollen 263
Llanwrda 255
Lochearnhead 243, 244
London – Belgravia 119
London – Clerkenwell 122
London – Fitzrovia 121
London – Hammersmith 116
London – Knightsbridge 120
London – Maida Vale 114
London – Notting Hill Gate 115
London – Pimlico 117, 118
London – Tulse Hill 125
Looe 33
Ludlow 152
Lyme Regis 68
Lymington 95
Mallaig 237
Malmesbury 193
Malton 211
Manningtree 85
Margate 108
Matlock 51
Mawgan Porth 18
Meeson 156
Midhurst 179
Minehead 167
Monmouth 269
Muthill 242

Narberth 271
Near Killin 245
New Milton 96
Newent 90
Newmarket 178
Newport 276
Newquay 17
Newton Abbot 56
Norwich 135
Nottingham 139, 140
Oakham 150, 151
Oban 217
Okehampton 57
Oswestry 154, 155
Oxford 141-143
Padstow 16
Peckham 124
Peebles 251
Pembroke 273
Penrith 37, 38
Penzance 23-25
Peterborough 14
Petworth 180
Pitlochry 248-250
Polegate 184
Portree 240
Preston 110
Pwllheli 265
Ramsgate 107
Ratho 231
Richmond 207, 208
Ripon 204
Ross-on-Wye 99-101
Rye 187-190
Salcombe 63
Salisbury 197-199
Settle 206
Sheffield 201
Shipton under Wychwood 146
Shrewsbury 157
Sidmouth 67
Skipton 205
Somerton 160
South Brent 59
Southwold 168
St Austell 31
St Brélade 215
St Ives 20-22
St Mawes 28
St Peter Port 214
Stamford 113
Stoke-by-Nayland 176
Stow-on-the-Wold 87
Stranraer 224
Stratford-upon-Avon 191
Strathtummel 247
Sturminster Newton 79
Swaffham 126
Taplow 7
Tavistock 58
Tenby 272
Thornhill 225
Tiverton 52
Torquay 65
Truro 29, 30
Uckfield 183
Umberleigh 54
Ventnor 102
Walkerburn 252
Wareham 73

Washingborough	112
Watchet	165
Watergate Bay	19
Wedmore	159
Wells-Next-The-Sea	131
Whitby	209, 210
Windermere	42-45
Witney	145
Woodbridge	170, 172
Woodstock	144
Yeovil	163
York	202

Photo: The Northgate, entry 177

BREAD
PETERS
& SONS.
83 QUEENS PARK
BRIGHTON.

INSPECTED & SELECTED
Sawday's
CANOPY & STARS
SPECIAL PLACES
A beautiful collection of treehouses, cabins, yurts, Gypsy caravans, wagons and more – across the UK, France, Italy, Spain and Portugal...
Everything you love about Sawday's, but outdoors.
+44 (0)117 204 7830
www.canopyandstars.co.uk